THE SOVIET HOME FRONT, 1941–1945

The Soviet Home Front, 1941–1945:

a social and economic history of the USSR in World War II

JOHN BARBER and MARK HARRISON

Longman
London and New York

LONGMAN GROUP UK LIMITED,
Longman House, Burnt Mill, Harlow,
Essex CM20 2JE, England
and Associated Companies throughout the world.

Published in the United States of America
by Longman Inc., New York

© Longman Group UK Limited 1991

First published 1991

British Library Cataloguing in Publication Data
Harrison, Mark
  The Soviet home front, 1941–1945.
  I. Title   II. Barber, John
  947.084

  ISBN 0–582–00964–2
  ISBN 0–582–00965–0 pbk

Library of Congress Cataloging in Publication Data
Barber, John, 1944–
    The Soviet home front, 1941–1945: a social and economic history
  of the USSR in World War II / John Barber and Mark Harrison
        p.   cm.
    Includes bibliographical references and index.
    ISBN 0–582–00964–2 (cased). -- ISBN 0–582–00965–0 (paper)
    1. Soviet Union--History--1939–1945. 2. World War, 1939–1945
  --Soviet Union. I. Harrison, Mark, 1949– . II. Title.
DK273.B27 1991   91–2406
947.084'2--dc20   CIP

Set in Bembo

Produced by Longman Singapore Publishers (Pte) Ltd.
Printed in Singapore

Contents

List of tables and maps   viii
Preface   ix
Acknowledgements   xi
Abbreviations and technical terms   xii

PART ONE: On the Eve   1

1. Building Socialism   3
   'Socialism in a single country'   3
   The economy – strength and weakness   5
   Society in flux   8
   The Stalin regime   10
   The threat of war   13
   Soviet war preparations   15

2. The Great Patriotic War   19
   The Molotov–Ribbentrop pact   19
   Deception, miscalculation, surprise   21
   The retreat to Leningrad and Moscow   26
   From Moscow to Stalingrad   30
   The grand alliance   33
   From Stalingrad to Berlin – and Manchuria   36
   The costs of victory   39

3. The State in Wartime   45
   'All that Lenin created we have lost forever'   45
   The structure of wartime government   46
   Central–local relations   48

The high command   50
The security organs   51
Stalin and the Soviet leadership   53

PART TWO: Soviet Society at War   57

4. **Mobilisation**   59
    'All for the front!'   59
    Discipline   63
    Propaganda   68
    The people's militia   73

5. **Subsistence and Survival**   77
    Supplying the population   77
    Rationing   79
    Local resources   82
    Hunger   86
    The family   90

6. **The Social Order**   94
    Workers   94
    Peasants   99
    Intellectuals   104
    Officials   108
    Nationalities   112
    Prisoners   116

PART THREE: The Productive Effort   121

7. **Fortresses of the Rear**   123
    The needs of war   123
    Invasion and evacuation   127
    Conversion to war production   133
    Capital construction in wartime   137

8. **Labour: The 'Ultimate Bottleneck'**   143
    The degree of labour shortage   143
    Wartime losses and mobilisation needs   145
    The mobilisation process   147
    The centralisation of work-force controls   152

9. **'In Labour as in Combat'**   158
   Productivity in prewar perspective   158
   Work discipline (I) – public sector employees   163
   Work discipline (II) – collective farmers   168
   Work discipline (III) – forced labour   169
   Economic incentives   171
   Morale and national feeling   174
   Wartime productivity – success and failure   177

10. **Production: The Power of Victory**   180
    Demand and supply   180
    Production for war   183
    Civilian industry and transport   184
    Food and agriculture   187
    Mutual aid   189
    The overall burden of the war   190

11. **Planning: 'The Military–Economic Staff'**   194
    Planning in prewar perspective   194
    The emergency regime, 1941–2   197
    The revival of formal planning   200
    Limits to centralisation   203

Epilogue   206

Tables   213
Important Dates   223
References   231
Maps   241
Index   246

List of Tables and Maps

TABLES

1. Consumer products available, per head of population, 1942–3   213
2. Official rations in 1944: some examples   214
3. The composition of the Soviet working population, 1940–5   215
4. The Soviet industrial work-force, 1940 and 1942–5   216
5. Women's share in employment, 1940–5   216
6. The Soviet kolkhoz work-force, 1941–5   217
7. The Gulag work-force, 1940–5   217
8. The Soviet war economy, 1941–5: official indices   218
9. Soviet employment, by branch of output, 1940–5   219
10. Net output per worker, 1940 and 1942–4   220
11. Net national product by branch of origin, 1940 and 1942–4   220
12. The burden of Soviet defence outlays, 1940 and 1942–4   221

MAPS

1. The republics, major cities and other towns of the USSR, 1941–45   242
2. The Soviet–German front, 1941–2   244
3. The Soviet–German front, 1942–4   245

Preface

The events which are the subject of this book, although now nearly fifty years away, remain among the most tragic of the twentieth century. In eastern Europe, World War II was bloody to a degree far exceeding the experience of western Europe, or of the Mediterranean or Pacific theatres. By the war's end, for every dead Briton or American (including both soldiers and civilians), some seven Japanese, twenty Germans and eighty-five Soviet citizens had died. Of all nations, it was the Soviet Union which paid by far the highest price for victory.

How did Soviet society respond to the threat, then the reality of war with Germany? How did the USSR's political and economic system stand up to the colossal strain of an invasion which penetrated deep into Soviet territory, and to the immense burden of total war? How did the wartime experience change the USSR's social and economic order, and influence its political future? These are the questions which this book seeks to answer.

The book is divided into four parts. Part I reviews the background to Soviet involvement in World War II and outlines the main military and political developments. Chapter 1 describes the condition of Soviet society, the economy and political system on the eve of war, and Soviet military preparedness. An overview of the war itself, its main phases and turning points, and its effects on the Soviet state, follow in Chapters 2 and 3.

Part II deals with the mobilisation of Soviet society and the impact of the war on the population. Chapter 4 considers the means employed to rally people behind the war effort. Chapter 5 describes the effect of the war on living standards, while Chapter 6 examines the contributions and conditions of the main social groups.

Part III assesses the wartime productive effort. Chapter 7 deals with the Soviet capital stock and its restructuring for war through evacuation, conversion and new investment. The subject of Chapters 8 and 9 is the work-force – its mobilisation, motivation and productivity. Chapter 10 evaluates Soviet wartime production, the development of the main branches of productive activity (war industry, civilian industry and transport, food and agriculture), the vexed problem of the contribution of American aid, and the overall economic burden of the war. Finally Chapter 11 recounts the role of wartime economic planning and management in the productive effort.

The book concludes with a short Epilogue about the wartime experience and its implications for postwar Soviet history.

Responsibility for writing was divided between the authors as follows: Mark Harrison wrote Chapters 1, 2 and 7–11, and compiled the tables, maps and chronological outline. John Barber wrote Chapters 3–6. Both authors contributed to the Epilogue. They are 'jointly and severally' responsible for the book as a whole, including all remaining errors of fact and interpretation.

Acknowledgements

The authors wish to acknowledge their considerable debt to the following people, for helpful discussions, and for valuable criticism and advice:

Richard Bidlack
Włodzimerz Brus
Sir Alec Cairncross
Julian Cooper
Viktor Petrovich Danilov
Robert W Davies
Peter Gatrell
Christine Harrison
Katherine Hodgson
Jacqueline Johnson
Georgii Aleksandrovich Kumanev
Catherine Merridale
William Moskoff
Lewis Siegelbaum
Peter J D Wiles
Eugène Zaleski
Margarita Stefanovna Zinich

The authors are also grateful to their respective Universities of Cambridge and Warwick for periods of study leave during which this book was prepared.

Abbreviations and Technical Terms

All-Union Communist Party (Bolsheviks) – the name of the only legal political party in the USSR (q v); from 1952, the Communist Party of the Soviet Union.

Central Committee – the governing body of the All-Union Communist Party (Bolsheviks) (q v), elected by the party congress.

Commissar – the rank accorded to political oficers of the Soviet Armed Forces.

GKO or **GOKO** (*Gosudarstvennyi komitet oborony*) – State Defence Committee, the name for Stalin's war cabinet.

Gosplan (*Gosudarstvennaya Planovaya Kommissiya*) – the economic planning office of the Sovnarkom (q v).

Gulag (*Glavnoe upravlenie trudovo-ispravitel'nykh lagerei*) – Chief Administration of Corrective Labour Camps of the NKVD (q v).

kolkhoz (*kollektivnoe khozyaistvo*) – collective farm, taking the form of a producer cooperative.

Komsomol (*Vsesoyuznyi Leninskii Kommunisticheskii soyuz molodezhi*) – the All-Union Leninist Communist League of Youth, the youth wing of the All-Union Communist Party (q v).

MTS (*mashinno-traktornaya stantsiya*) – vehicle and tractor station, under state ownership, supplying machinery services to local kolkhozy (q v) in return for a share of the harvested crop.

narodnoe opolchenie (people's militia) – home defence units established from the civil populations of the main towns and cities of the front-line regions after the outbreak of war in 1941.

NKVD (*Narodnyi kommissariat vnutrennykh del*) – People's Commissariat of Internal Affairs, with responsibility for internal and frontier security and the administration of prisons and labour camps and colonies.

nomenklatura – the schedule of posts in Soviet government, the economy, and other occupations of 'state significance', reserved for party appointees; also used to refer collectively to government, economic and cultural officials as a social group.

Peoples' Commissar – the title by which Soviet government ministers were known from the October 1917 Revolution until 1946, not to be confused with commissars (q v) of the Soviet Armed Forces.

plenipotentiary (*upol'nomochennyi*) – a trouble-shooting personal agent from Moscow, e g from the GKO, Sovnarkom, or Central Committee (q v), armed with full powers of the body concerned.

Politburo (Political Bureau) – the executive core of the party Central Committee (q v), chaired by Stalin as the party's General Secretary.

RSFSR or **Russian Federation** (Russian Soviet Federative Socialist Republic) – the largest of the Soviet Socialist Republics comprising the USSR (q v).

soviet (council) – the basic organ of representative government in the USSR (q v).

sovkhoz (*sovetskoe khozyaistvo*) – state farm, a nationalised enterprise owned by the state.

Sovnarkom (*Sovet narodnykh komissarov***)** – Council of Peoples' Commissars (q v), the government of the USSR, chaired by the Prime Minister.

Stavka VGK (*Stavka Verkhovnogo Glavnokomandovaniya*) – Supreme HQ, the wartime headquarters of Stalin as Supreme Commander-in-Chief of the Soviet Armed Forces.

USSR or **Soviet Union** (Union of Soviet Socialist Republics) – constituted in 1922 by the Russian Federation (q v) and the Ukrainian, Belorussian and Transcaucasian Soviet Socialist Republics (SSRs), joined in 1925 by the Central Asian SSRs; in 1940 Estonia, Latvia and Lithuania were also annexed to the USSR as SSRs.

workpoint (*trudoden'*) – the unit of payment on the kolkhoz (q v); each workpoint was supposed to correspond to a day's labour of average skill and intensity, and each farm worker's accumulated annual total would determine their share in the farm's net income.

For Cathy, Jamie, and Sam

PART ONE
On the Eve

CHAPTER ONE
Building Socialism[1]

'SOCIALISM IN A SINGLE COUNTRY'

The first German troops and planes crossed the Soviet border at 4.00 a.m. (Moscow time) on Sunday, 22 June 1941. Soon there was gunfire along a continuous front which stretched more than a thousand kilometres across the entire width of continental Europe, from the Baltic Sea in the north-west to the Black Sea in the south-east. Hitler had launched his armies on the greatest land war in history. He expected to attain victory quickly and easily.

This is what Stalin had told the Soviet Union's new generation of industrial managers just ten years earlier, in February 1931:

> One feature of the history of old Russia was the continual beatings she suffered for falling behind, for her backwardness. She was beaten by the Mongol Khans. She was beaten by the Turkish beys. She was beaten by the Swedish feudal lords. She was beaten by the Polish and Lithuanian gentry. She was beaten by the British and French capitalists. She was beaten by the Japanese barons. All beat her – for her backwardness: for military backwardness, for cultural backwardness, for political backwardness, for industrial backwardness, for agricultural backwardness. She was beaten because to do so was profitable and could be done with impunity. . . .

---

1 On Soviet history in the 1920s a classic overview is that of Carr 1979. Stalin's rise and the Stalin phenomenon have been analysed in standard works by Deutscher 1966, McNeal 1988, and Medvedev 1989. The social history of the interwar years is challengingly analysed by Lewin 1985, while economic developments are surveyed in depth by Nove 1982. New thinking in Soviet historical and literary accounts of the Stalin period is summarised by Davies 1989. On prewar military-economic trends and war preparations, see Erickson 1962, and Harrison 1985: chs 1, 2.

That is why we must no longer lag behind.

We are fifty or a hundred years behind the advanced countries. We must make good this distance in ten years. Either we do it, or they crush us.[2]

The events which began just ten years later gave this speech the status of a magically accurate prophecy. In reality, of course, Stalin could have had no precise idea of the time remaining. In Germany, Hitler had not yet come to power; the aggressors which Stalin feared were, in the Far East, Japan, and, in Europe, Poland, France and Great Britain. The 'ten years' of which Stalin spoke were just a round number, not an exact forecast, and his accuracy was coincidental.

To Stalin's credit, however, was the perception that industrial modernisation was a key to Soviet security. The Soviet system of government and social ownership meant nothing if it could not compete with the advanced technical, commercial and military standards set by the capitalist industrial powers, and if it could not be defended against attack.

In interwar Soviet policy, therefore, there was no dividing line between apparently distinct objectives. Building up new industries under public ownership, building new fuel, energy and transport complexes and new cities, building up the defence industries and military–economic power, building the armed forces themselves and their combat stocks – all these things are fused together in what they called 'building socialism in a single country'.

Building socialism meant a process of astonishing contradictions and paradoxes. In the decade before World War II, the Soviet Union went through a whirlwind transformation. The backward, largely agrarian economy was forced through years of fundamental reconstruction, downgrading agriculture and rapidly throwing up new factories, power stations, railways and residential blocks. All the productive wealth that had not been brought into public ownership in the years of revolution and civil war (1917–21) was now either nationalised or placed in the hands of *kolkhozy* (cooperative farms); the main methods of transferring assets and jobs from private to public or cooperative ownership were political campaigns and forced confiscations.

In the 1930s, tens of millions of peasants became workers; hundreds of thousands of workers and peasants were promoted into the official strata administering the first centrally planned economy. Of the expanded resources available to the nation, the greater part was allocated to additional investment funds, then to military expenditures. Raising living standards came last as an economic objective; in the early 1930s,

2 Stalin 1940: 365–6.

labour incomes fell sharply in both country and town, and even by the end of the decade many were no better off than they had been in the 1920s.

In the years before the war, Soviet politics shared the general flavour of paradox. Stalin had become the undisputed leader of a great power. His personality dominated the decisions of both the Communist Party and the Soviet system of government. In spite of the poor conditions under which many lived, internal criticism of his policies and personal position had been silenced. None the less the regime seemed more insecure than ever, beset with criminal conspiracies and seditious plots; according to the 'evidence' of police investigation and show trials, the counter-revolutionary underground seemed to have strengthened its grip among the roots of Soviet society. Externally, a traditional enemy (Japan) had embarked on a more dangerous, militarist course of territorial expansion in the Far East, while a friend of the 1920s (Germany) was similarly committed in Europe.

In 1936, Stalin declared that the USSR's socialist foundations had been successfully completed.[3] 'Socialism in a single country' was now a reality. The basis of this claim was the far-reaching expansion of public sector industries, the comprehensive collectivisation of small-scale peasant farming, and virtual elimination of private capital. After World War II, Stalin would claim that these prewar policies had also laid the basis for wartime supply of what was necessary to beat Germany.[4] What, in reality, was the nature of the prewar economic achievement?

THE ECONOMY – STRENGTH AND WEAKNESS

From the vantage point of 1941, most obvious of prewar economic achievements was the dramatic rise of Soviet industries under public ownership. According to authoritative western estimates, between 1928 and 1940 the output of civilian industries multiplied 2.6 times (and munitions output grew seventy-fold). In these twelve years industry, construction and transport expanded their contribution to the na-

3 Stalin 1940: 564.
4 *Pravda*, 10 February 1946.

tional income from little more than one-quarter to not far short of one-half.[5]

But a big price tag had been attached to this radical change in the economic structure. The Stalinist drive to industrialise the country at 'Bolshevik tempos' tried to do too much too fast. Economic plans were overambitious, reflecting the triumph of political decrees over economic appraisal. Factories were driven to raise immediate output regardless of cost, quality or returns to society. Deadly campaigns of purging and arrests were waged in order to attain impossible objectives.

The industrialisation drive had been accompanied by wholesale reorganisation in agriculture. At the end of the 1920s the market relationship with the peasantry was suspended. From then on, the state removed much of the food surplus from the countryside by official levies. This was accompanied by 'comprehensive collectivisation'. Within a few years, 25 million peasant farms were amalgamated into a quarter of a million *kolkhozy* (collective farms), many of them in a few weeks in the winter of 1929–30.

In the process, decisive damage was done to the rural economy. Much of it was done at the very outset by the new procurements system. Villages were stripped of food and fodder. Unable to feed their animals, peasants slaughtered them; then there was a shortage of animals to pull carts and ploughs. Unable to plough and harvest on time, peasants saw their grain yields plummet. By 1932 famine conditions prevailed. Recovery took many years; meanwhile, the base for industrial accumulation was narrowed, rather than enlarged.

The Stalinist economic transformation therefore contained negative results as well as positive achievements. Public ownership was not sufficient to make everything go according to plan. New resources were created, but at the same time existing resources were destroyed, and all resources were used with less efficiency than before. Reduced efficiency was reflected in underutilised capacity, lost output and wasted investments. Lost resources were counted in the damage to agriculture (which resulted in turn in loss of food supplies), and in excessive mortality of the population; the latter included those losses attributable to famines and deportations, and the destruction of skilled personnel resulting from purges.[6] Less ambitious plans and less forcing of the pace

5 Calculated from Moorsteen, Powell 1966: 622–3. All estimates are measured in rouble prices of 1937. This traditional western estimate is roughly consistent with more recent Soviet unofficial reassessments, e g Selyunin, Khanin 1987, and Sovetskii Soyuz 1988.

6 For example, Hunter 1983: 196.

could have given industrial growth perhaps equal to (but more likely less than) that actually achieved, together with fewer social and economic tensions and higher morale of the population.

The expansion of public sector industries under Stalinist policies was rapid and violent. It was also discontinuous; there were waves of forward motion, which came periodically to a halt in a state of exhaustion. In the dozen years before the war there were two complete cycles and perhaps the beginning of a third. The first involved a great upsurge under the first Five Year Plan (1928–32), culminating in industrial crisis and famine. Recovery was followed by another great mobilisation in the middle years of the second Five Year Plan (1933–7). By 1937, however, the economy was once again in deep trouble. Years of determined effort were required before the expansion process was at last resumed, already half way through the third Five Year Plan (1938–42), and with only months of peace remaining.

Why did the economic growth process regularly grind to a halt? On each occasion, there was a fatal combination of internal and external circumstances. The economy's leaders pushed it too hard. At first there would be tremendous achievements and great leaps into the future. Meanwhile, however, tensions would accumulate. Too many big capital projects meant too many unfinished building sites which used up the economy's stocks of investment goods and then demanded more than could be made available from current production. Until they were finished, production could not be increased further. Too much investment meant too much pressure on farmers for food and raw materials, and on workers for industrial goods, and it meant tightened belts all round. At the same time, planners incorporated overoptimistic assumptions in their plans about productivity and food yields, and about the prospects for world peace and international trade.

When harvests withered, when war threatened and external markets failed, Stalinist politicians who had grown used to having everything their own way demanded fulfilment of the plan at all costs; rather than lower their sights and accept retrenchment, they preferred to launch new campaigns of mass mobilisation, and new purges against the 'enemies' responsible for alleged sabotage of the economy. Disintegration and demoralisation would ripple through the economy, halting expansion.

The fact that by 1932, or 1937, the economy was in a mess was not, of course, the end of the story. Countervailing forces were also at work which would eventually restore sanity and enable growth to be resumed. When the strains became intolerable, and when pushing and shouting had clearly failed to improve matters, more expert advice would prevail. Big expensive projects far from completion would be quietly mothballed. Investment budgets would be cut back and bureaucratic austerity decreed. Available resources would be concentrated on projects near completion, allowing production to increase again. The spotlight would be turned back to improving information, morale and consumer supplies.

Restoring economic balance, and the basis for its continued expansion, were never easy. The crisis of the late 1930s involved a destabilising combination of a great investment mobilisation, huge unplanned increases in defence spending, and deadly repressions which swept through both the civil and military bureaucracies. There were three years of stagnation, just when Soviet leaders most wanted additional resources. The crisis was further prolonged in 1939–40 by the further demands of military operations in eastern Poland and the Baltic region and the 'winter war' with Finland. However, by the beginning of 1941 economic growth was being resumed.

SOCIETY IN FLUX

Industrialisation and collectivisation together had meant restructuring of the social order at a colossal rate. Transformations which had taken a century or more to secure in western Europe would be achieved within a single generation.

The quantitative change had many dimensions. The motor of change was forced industrialisation, which had created 22 million jobs in the public sector and trebled its size in the twelve years, 1928–40. The bulk of new employment was concentrated in the basic industries, in factories, on railways and building sites. At least half of the new workers were of rural origin. While millions of new recruits flooded into the factories and towns, hundreds of thousands of others were promoted upward from the field and factory floor to positions of managerial and ministerial responsibility; they staffed the burgeoning party and ministerial apparatus.

Many had gained, but for many others life had not improved. Those who benefited were the millions who participated most directly in the restructuring: peasants who became workers, workers who upgraded their skills or became foremen and managers, workers who became officials and party organisers, officials promoted upward through the expanding hierarchies of government. The losers were those left behind or trodden down by the process of change: peasants who remained in the hungry village, manual and staff workers unable to reconcile themselves to the changing demands of work, and millions who were victimised by the security organs because of their opinions, associations or background, or just by accident.

The haste of the transformation had many unintended consequences. Among them was the extent to which socialist modernisation unexpectedly reproduced prerevolutionary traditions in twentieth-century forms. Remodelling society in a hurry, faced with countless urgent problems, 'practical' yet inexperienced men and women reached for ready-made solutions which as often as not were the traditional resorts of the prerevolutionary past.

These could be found in every branch of life. The Russian Empire was succeeded by a new Soviet brotherhood of Russians and minority nations. A new Stalinist bureaucracy replaced the old Imperial system of domination over society. The economy was modernised and industrialised, but modern factories were operated at low productivity by a migratory work-force. Serfdom was long gone, but the peasantry was once more reduced to second-class status, tied to the land and compelled to labour. Women were invited to participate in social labour on equal terms with men, yet were expected to bear reinforced burdens of family, fertility and male authority. The old religion was suppressed, but a new secular religion of Marxism-Leninism took its place.

Most visible of all was the revival of autocracy, with Stalin, general secretary of the Central Committee of the All-Union Communist Party of Bolsheviks, as the autocrat. Like a Tsar, a 'little father of all the Russias', his personal rule aspired to an absolute and arbitrary character, unrestrained by laws, made tolerable only by a contract of personal loyalty with his subordinates and subjects. Like the Tsars, Stalin and the 'little Stalins' under him also found that they could not govern society entirely without legality, constitutionalism and recognition of the rights of others.

The social basis of the Stalin regime was at first perilously narrow. At its core was a minority of a minority – those officials and industrial workers who were typically young, of urban working-class origin, politically militant, impatient to get the job done. They saw 'the job' in terms which were in one sense sweeping and revolutionary, in another sense blinkered. A planned economy directed consciously, not by the blind forces of the market; a society in which political consciousness and experience of working life would count for more than education and manners; a culture of material abundance and women's economic independence combined with conventional family life. The effort to achieve these things trampled on many people, including many of its most ardent supporters. Possibly, however, as the new working class stabilised and officialdom broadened its membership, its social foundations also grew wider for a time.

THE STALIN REGIME

There was no precedent in modern history for the growth and powers of the Soviet state before the war. How real was the new authority of the party and government, and of their leader Stalin? How sturdy was the towering edifice of state? Was it built on firm rock or on shifting sands?

The turn to rapid industrialisation at the end of the 1920s had brought a colossal increase in the role, and hence the size and authority, of the state. Whole areas of Soviet life previously independent of the state now came under its direct control. To discharge its greatly enlarged functions, the size of its apparatus increased hugely. 'State building' proceeded apace. The ambitions of the new Leviathan, however, exceeded its capacities. The fantastic scale of the tasks set by the leadership and the hectic speed of change it demanded, the inexperience of officials thrust into positions of authority, the bewilderment, alienation and hostility of many ordinary people whose lives were abruptly altered, the sheer size of the country and remoteness of many of its regions from central government – all these worked against the fulfilment of the rulers' plans. That great changes were none the less accomplished reflects their determination to succeed.

In the process, the political system created under Lenin was transformed. First and foremost, the role of the Communist Party changed substantially. From being a forum for debate and the making of policy at both higher and lower levels, it became primarily an instrument for implementing policies determined on high. Party congresses and conferences, convened with diminishing frequency, became occasions not for the exchange of opinions but for the display of unanimity. Increasingly, decisions were taken by informal groups of top leaders rather than by formal party bodies. While party officials wielded great and growing authority, the significance of rank-and-file party membership in terms of political influence declined.

Meanwhile the importance of the state apparatus, especially the commissariats (ministries) and agencies in charge of the economy, grew rapidly. So also did the role of the secret police. The political leadership, insecure and impatient, looked increasingly to the OGPU (from 1936, NKVD) to cut through red tape, widen bottlenecks, deal with opponents. The secret police became responsible for much more than intelligence gathering, state security and the repression of opponents. Key projects of economic and military significance were put under its jurisdiction. Its heads – Yagoda, Ezhov, then Beriya – were leading members of the ruling group. (Membership of the ruling group did not carry security of tenure for anyone except Stalin himself, as Yagoda and Ezhov would find, each being arrested and executed in turn in the late 1930s.)

Along with the strengthening of the state went ever greater centralisation. Having defeated their opponents and removed them from the leadership by 1930, the group around Stalin ruled without any open dissent or challenge to its policies. Stalin himself increasingly concentrated power in his hands. His personal secretariat occupied the key position in the apparatus while, as general secretary of the party central committee, his views were decisive in policy-making. Clearly he did not personally decide everything. He may often have acted as arbiter between different groups in the leadership. But he was able to intervene in any debate and, when he did, the effect could be devastating. His 'cult of personality' which blossomed from his fiftieth birthday in December 1929 onwards, although contrived and exaggerated in style, was a true reflection of his enormous authority.

At the same time, the power of the Soviet leadership was limited by several factors. First, the ruling group was less monolithic than it appeared. Behind the scenes there were continual differences over economic, political and diplomatic issues. In the early 1930s these sometimes resulted in challenges to Stalin. There is evidence that at the seventeenth party congress (February 1934), many delegates wanted to replace Stalin with Kirov.

Second, the party and state apparatus on which the ruling group relied was far from being an efficient, dependable machine for implementing policy. In the provinces, especially, it was often disorganised, understaffed, overworked, corrupt, and unresponsive to Moscow's demands.

Third, the population, although deprived of open channels for expressing its views about official policies, displayed remarkable inventiveness in evading and undermining directives from above. Workers, collective farmers, managers, officials, even local representatives of the police and prosecution service, were – to Moscow's frustration – frequently engaged in evading regulations and distorting information in order to mitigate the effects of unworkable or unpopular policies.

The response of Soviet leaders was often to resort to coercion. Peasants who resisted, or might potentially have resisted farm collectivisation, were branded 'kulaks' (peasant capitalists exploiting the poor) and deported from their villages. Between 1930 and 1932 some 5 million were exiled, imprisoned or sent to labour camps, many perishing in the process. 'Bourgeois specialists', professionals of prerevolutionary origin in government or academic work, were periodically purged, as were former oppositionists. And in a series of purges from 1933 onwards, 'harmful' elements were removed from the party on a variety of pretexts.

In the spring of 1937 there was a quantum leap in state-directed repression. What precise combination of circumstances precipitated the Great Purge is impossible at present to say. Fears of a coup, a desire to pre-empt any potential for a 'fifth column' in the event of war, a genuine belief that the system was riddled with traitors and 'enemies of the people', may all have played their part. Stalin's distrust of those who, behind the scenes, had tried to limit his powers in the early 1930s may also have been at work. And there may also have been a more widespread desire to raise a new generation of officials and experts, educated and promoted under Stalin and owing everything to him, into the shoes of the older generation.

The fact is that Stalin unleashed the NKVD in an orgy of repression. No part of the population was immune, though workers and peasants suffered least in proportion. The main targets were party and state officials, the armed forces, and the intelligentsia. The number of victims can only be guessed at. By the end of 1938, after the machinery of the purge had been brought back under control, hundreds of thousands had died; nearly 2 million were reportedly held in NKVD labour camps and colonies, half a million of them condemned as 'counter-revolutionaries'.[7] This was an immense trauma, and its effects would be long lasting.

For all this, it would be inaccurate to see terror as the main basis of the Stalin regime. Stalin and his colleagues enjoyed considerable support from the population. Despite its savage treatment, the stratum of officials, composed overwhelmingly of promoted ex-workers and ex-peasants, gave loyal and active service. Many workers, who had benefited from the regime's economic and social policies, had faith in Stalin and identified with government goals. Like other dictatorships

7 Dugin 1990.

12

before and since, the Stalinist political system rested on a combination of coercion and mass support.

THE THREAT OF WAR

Two countries threatened the peaceful development of the Soviet Union in the 1930s – Japan and Germany. Japan was Russia's traditional enemy, but in many ways Germany was traditionally her friend. As it turned out, the threat from Japan never materialised, and it was Germany which embroiled the USSR in a deadly war.

As far as Japan was concerned, there had been many years of historic rivalry with Imperial Russia and the Soviet Union over territory in the Far East, mainly in Manchuria (now China's north-eastern provinces). In the late 1920s the Manchurian issue arose again, being resolved in 1931 by Japanese military occupation. The turn to a more aggressive foreign policy signalled social and political changes in Japan itself. Militarism and colonial expansionism were becoming more and more influential in Japanese government, with momentous results.

At several points in the 1930s a new war of Japan against the USSR must have seemed more likely than hostilities between Japan and the United States or Great Britain. To the Soviet advantage, however, were two factors. First, the Japanese secretly defined their sphere of strategic interest in the territories to the south – in China, and in the British, French and Dutch possessions of east Asia and the Pacific. There were no Japanese designs on Soviet territory. The Japanese attitude to the Soviets resulted from this, and was simply one of enforcing a 'Keep out' notice.

Second, in 1938 and 1939, the Soviets actually fought two small and undeclared border wars with Japan. At Lake Khasan (Changkufeng) and then at Khalkin-Gol (Nomonhan) Soviet troops held off Japanese incursions into disputed territory. As a result, the military forces of the two sides learnt mutual respect. The Soviet and Japanese governments concluded a pact of non-agression in April 1941. However, the Soviets continued to fear war with Japan, maintained significant military and economic reserves in the Far East, and could not realistically assess the reliability of the Japanese treaty until well into the war with Germany.

When militarist Japan is compared with Nazi Germany, there can be no question that Germany was the more dangerous opponent. Yet, for much of the interwar period, at least at an official level, Soviet–

German relations were closer and more friendly than relations with Japan – or indeed with any other country.

Soviet complacency, fear and wishful thinking all came to play a certain part in this paradox. Initially, however, the good interwar relations between Germany and the USSR were based simply in mutual interest. Once the dust of World War I had settled in Europe, these two countries found themselves both, for different reasons, cast out of the international diplomatic and trading community. The Germans, having begun the war, had lost it; the Russians, having joined the war against Germany, had then diverted their efforts into revolutionary upheaval, had reneged on treaty commitments to their British and French allies and had confiscated their assets in Russia.

After the war, this shared isolation was expressed in the German–Soviet treaty of Rapallo (April 1922). While Britain and France made some progress in subsequently weaning the new German republic away from its Soviet links, the two countries retained unusually close links of diplomatic, commercial and military cooperation until the late 1920s.

At the end of the 1920s, a number of developments conspired to upset this pragmatic friendship. The Wall Street crash and the slump in world markets destabilised the German economy, society and political system. Hitler and the National Socialists gathered support for a radical alternative of the right to the existing structures of liberal capitalism and parliamentary democracy. The German left found itself in a blind alley of infighting and paralysis. (And Moscow carried a share of the blame for this, for misreading Hitler's significance.) Mass unemployment, falling living standards and farm closures drove Germany's citizens not towards socialist revolution, but in the direction of militarisation and colonial annexations. Hitler became the German Chancellor in January 1933, and soon assumed dictatorial powers.

Although at first Hitler often sought to present a diplomatic and statesmanlike face to the world, the Nazi regime was bent on overturning the balance of power in Europe by means of aggressive warfare. Hitler believed that the survival of the German race and nation state depended upon colonial annexations to give 'living space' for Germans in eastern Europe. Reinforcing eastward expansionism was Nazi hatred of Bolshevism, which Hitler regarded as an alien creed, undermining German racial purity and national supremacy.

In Nazi perspectives on the future, Germany was to become the industrial centre of a European trading area, exchanging her manufactured products against the foodstuffs and raw materials to be made available from eastern and south-eastern Europe. Germans would be the master race, tolerating coexistence with Europeans of Anglo-Saxon, Latin and Baltic ancestry, exploiting the Slavic races and rooting out the Jews. Hitler's aim was to use military means to make Germany the chief continental power, accepting for the time being Britain's role as the chief maritime power. But beyond this lay more hazily defined vistas of world domination, and the conquest of Anglo-American resources.

What all European nations feared was another Great War, on the model of 1914–18, which would bleed them white for a second time in a generation. The Nazi strategy, which played upon this fear, depended upon the assumption that such a war could be averted. Instead, rearming as far as possible by stealth, Germany must use limited resources of military manpower and equipment to launch a series of lightning wars against her neighbours in central and eastern Europe, picking them off one by one in brief campaigns before their powerful allies in the west could come together and mobilise their forces. In this way, Germany could secure her strategic objectives without ever becoming involved in another Great War.

At first, Stalin and his advisers understood nothing of this. In the mid-1930s, however, a Soviet reassessment took place. In Soviet military calculations Germany began to replace Japan as the most dangerous enemy. In the Soviet approach to European politics, the mistaken belief that the socialists were worse than Hitler gave way to concerted bids to build anti-fascist coalitions of communists, socialists and other like-minded people called 'Popular Fronts'. In formal diplomacy, moves were set afoot to build an anti-German alliance of nations for 'collective security'.

But the response of other world leaders was cool. The British and French continued to believe they could live with Hitler. The Poles and Czechs trusted in their western allies; the Poles distrusted the Russians as much as they feared Germany. And, after 1937, with the exposure of 'traitors' and 'enemies' in the highest reaches of Soviet government, and the arrest of the greater part of the Soviet officer corps, none of them was disposed to treat with the Soviet Union as a serious candidate for a military alliance.

SOVIET WAR PREPARATIONS

High military spending and continual preparation for war were already ingrained in Soviet military-economic policy in the 1930s. This was in sharp contrast to the background of low military spending in most other European countries where, after World War I, it was believed that Great Wars had become prohibitively costly.

The only country to rearm on a scale approaching Germany's was the Soviet Union. The Soviet readiness to maintain high military spending in peacetime went back to the first years of the revolution, when Bolshevik leaders had learnt the readiness of powerful imperialist adversaries to take advantage of any moment of weakness, and to intervene against the Russian revolution by force. They had learnt then to put more trust in guns and shells, ships, tanks and aircraft than in paper treaties or diplomacy.

Soviet policy prepared continually for war. At the same time, this was not preparation for any particular war, forecast or planned for any specific time and place, but insurance against the possibility of war in general. Soviet military and economic planners did not set their sights on some particular operation to be launched on a set date, but instead aimed to build up an all-round, generalised military power ready for war at some point in the indefinite future.

This pattern of rearmament suffered from two main drawbacks. First, it was enormously costly. It required diversion from the civilian economy both of millions of young men who would otherwise have been available for work, and also of just those industrial commodities in which the Soviet Union was poorest: refined fuels, rare metals and high-quality alloys, precision engineering, scientific knowledge and technical expertise. All this was at the expense of the civilian economy. With less military spending, living standards would have been higher, the deprivations and tensions of rapid industrialisation would have been mitigated, workers and farmers would have been better rewarded for their efforts, and morale would have been higher throughout Soviet society.

The other drawback lay in the possibility of miscalculation. Because the Soviet rearmament pattern aimed at some future war, it was never ready for war in the present. Changing forecasts and expectations meant that military plans were always under revision. The armed forces were always in the midst of re-equipment and reorganisation. Military products already in mass production were always on the verge of obsolescence; defence industries were always half way through retraining and retooling.

German leaders recognised this possibility and, in part, relied upon it. They planned their campaigns to overwhelm countries with a major potential for military power in the long run, like France or the USSR, using concentrated force with lightning speed to overrun the adversary immediately, well before its long-run potential for resistance could be marshalled and brought to bear.

At the same time, compared to Germany's rearmament, the Soviet pattern carried important advantages. Germany's strategy was a gamble, staking everything on the possibility of immediate victory. If Soviet resistance could deny victory to the aggressor in the short run, and turn the lightning war which the aggressor expected to win into a protracted struggle, if the Soviets could finally bring to bear their entire national resources upon the struggle, then the aggressor would have lost the advantage. In Germany's case, she would have entered the war with limited military stocks and low rates of defence output, expecting to win without major loss or need of replacement of weapons on any significant scale. If this expectation were frustrated, Germany's position would be relatively weak; it would be Germany's turn to mobilise frantically, to be forced to sacrifice the civilian economy to the needs of the Army. Conscious of the fragility of the Nazi regime, Hitler was determined to avoid this outcome.

Soviet rearmament proceeded in the 1930s in two main waves. The first wave accompanied the first Five Year Plan. By the end of it Soviet defence output had already reached a high plateau, considerably exceeding the level of output of any other European power. Here it remained until 1937 when growth was resumed. But by then, Soviet rearmament had lost its head start, in terms of both quantity of forces and quality of weapons produced. In the Spanish civil war, Soviet advisers found that Soviet-produced munitions had already fallen behind new technical standards embodied in German supplies to the fascists. Now Soviet defence output and force levels began to multiply again. Technical modernisation and re-equipment were accelerated. And on 1 September 1939, on the occasion of the German–Soviet non-aggression pact, a new conscription law was introduced.

The Soviet rearmament of the last years before the war was impressive in its volume and scope. It meant the further doubling and trebling of defence output and Red Army force levels. By June 1941 there were 5.4 million Soviet citizens in uniform (6 per cent of the working population); every month, Soviet industry was producing 230 tanks, 700 military aircraft, 4,000 guns and mortars, more than 100,000 rifles and more than 1 million shells.

At the same time, all this activity won far less immediate military security for the Soviet Union than might have been expected. One reason is that the Soviet concept of combining massive expansion with modernisation resulted in wide differences of quality. Of the millions of soldiers, few were properly trained, or experienced in combat. Most

17

were operating large numbers of obsolete weapons according to out-moded tactical guidelines; a minority was just learning to operate new ones in relatively restricted quantities, using new military doctrines which were only poorly absorbed.

Then there were further reasons for poor results, which stemmed from domestic politics. In the Great Purge of 1937–8 the Red Army command had been decimated. The experienced core of general and field officers had been replaced by a relatively immature, ill-educated cohort whose members were typically either drilled in Stalinist dog-mas, or cowed by Stalinist threats. Those who had advocated a flexible response to external aggression, including the inevitability of giving ground to the invader and the need to plan for defence in the interior of the country, had been accused of conspiring with Nazi leaders to hand over territory, and executed or imprisoned.

In military doctrine, the concept of the operation in depth was replaced by a rigid insistence on frontier defence: invading forces must be met on the Soviet border and repulsed by an immediate Soviet counteroffensive; then the war must be carried on to enemy territory. Thus Stalin, like Hitler, was preparing his country for a short war, and an offensive one. By massing Soviet forces on Soviet frontiers and giving the appearance of an offensive deployment, Stalin hoped to deter German aggression. In practice, the bluff worked badly; it calmed Soviet fears and stimulated Stalin's own complacency, while German observers were not impressed.

The atmosphere of repression inevitably influenced the content of military-economic plans drawn up in the prewar years. There were plans for boosting ammunition production in the event of war, but no realistic assessment of combat needs because it was assumed that the war would end quickly in a victorious offensive. In factories and cities contingency plans were drawn up for war production in the event of war, but some of the most obvious preparations for a defensive cam-paign were neglected. Specialised defence factories were concentrated in the vulnerable territories to the south and west. There was talk of dispersing capacity into the interior regions, but nothing was done; it was always cheaper to expand output where production was already concentrated. Nothing was done to prepare vital industrial assets for defence against air attack, or for possible evacuation, since the idea that territory might be yielded to an invader had itself become treasonous.

Everyone in positions of responsibility believed that there would always be time to make good any oversights.

CHAPTER TWO
The Great Patriotic War[1]

THE MOLOTOV–RIBBENTROP PACT

On 23 August 1939, the Soviet and German foreign ministers signed a
'pact of non-aggression', which committed each country to settle differences through negotiation, and to neutrality with respect to each
other, should the other become involved in war. The effect of the
treaty was to give Germany a free hand in Poland, where a German
invasion followed on 1 September. On 3 September came the British
and French declarations of war; World War II had begun.

Behind the scenes, Stalin had abandoned his search for collective
security and an anti-German coalition with Poland, France and Britain.
Appeasement of Hitler, even collaboration, seemed the only remaining
alternative to war. But Stalin did not now abandon all his defences. In
addition to the pact, which was published, there was also a further
protocol, which remained secret, but which had infamous consequences. This dealt with the entire territory between existing Soviet and
German borders. It gave western Poland to Germany, but assigned

1 There already exist two Soviet official histories of the war, and a third is now in
preparation. First was the six-volume IVOVSS 1961–5, a product of the Khrushchev
era of post-Stalin reformism. A highly readable but now rather dated western account
based partly on the latter, partly on the author's personal experiences as a war corre-
spondent, is Werth 1964. Bialer 1970 represents a useful synthesis of Soviet memoirs
and western analysis from the same period. Next comes the Brezhnev era's twelve-vol-
ume IVMV 1973–82. For a detailed and authoritative western military history, also
dating from the 1970s, see Erickson 1975, 1982. A third ten-volume official Soviet
history is currently being written, intended (like all the others in *their* day) to tell the
real truth about the war. Davies 1989 recounts current Soviet controversies over wartime history.

eastern Poland to the Soviet Union. In the north it allotted Finland, Estonia and Latvia (later Lithuania was added, in exchange for the Polish district of Lublin) to a Soviet sphere of influence. To the south-east it recognised a Soviet interest in Bessarabia, which was part of Romania.

During the next year, Stalin called in all these commitments. Polish resistance to Germany collapsed speedily, and during the second half of September eastern Poland was absorbed into the Soviet Ukraine and Belorussia. At the same time, under new treaties of 'mutual aid', Soviet military garrisons were sent to Estonia, Latvia and Lithuania. Next came Soviet demands on Finland for greater coordination of military policy, and to grant strategic bases for the defence of Leningrad. A Finnish refusal was answered by war, which broke out on 30 November 1939. The 'winter war' was short, but terribly costly to both sides. Finnish forces resisted bitterly. The Soviet attackers, neither trained nor equipped for guerrilla fighting in sub-Arctic conditions, were unable to win a decisive victory without huge reinforcement. In four months of fighting, 25,000 Finnish soldiers and perhaps 200,000 Soviet troops lost their lives. At the end, Finland conceded territory around Leningrad but her orbit now moved closer to Germany. Meanwhile the Soviet Union had suffered international condemnation and was more isolated than ever.

In the summer of 1940, as the German military machine rolled over France and poised itself on the English channel, the Soviet Union cashed its last cheques under the Molotov–Ribbentrop pact's secret protocol. In June, high-ranking Soviet emissaries, acting together with Soviet military garrisons, overthrew the governments of the Baltic states and established new, pro-Soviet regimes. They were absorbed into the USSR as new Union Republics, and the annexations were legitimised by rigged 'plebiscites'. At the same time the USSR annexed Bessarabia, which became Soviet Moldavia. In all of these new territories, the ownership system was quickly refashioned on Soviet lines so that industry and trade were nationalised and farms collectivised; many were arrested and imprisoned or deported.

By these means, Soviet frontiers were moved 200–350 kilometres westward, further away from important centres of population and industry. The Soviet fleet acquired important new naval bases. On the map, Soviet security had been greatly enhanced. But in reality, the lines on the map were deceptive. The new territories could not be fully integrated into defensive plans and fortifications in time. Instead of adding to Soviet security, they proved a trap, a deadly quagmire of popular hostility and national resentment where invading German divisions would be greeted as liberators and Soviet defenders would flounder and sink.

DECEPTION, MISCALCULATION, SURPRISE

The German decision to attack the Soviet Union in the summer of 1941 had two main motives. One was to realise the longstanding Nazi ambition of eastward colonial expansion; this would make room for German farming settlers, and would also give the German economy access to the raw materials and food produce of the Ukraine and southern Russia. Poland, the Ukraine and the Caucasus would become vassal states; the Baltic republics would eventually be absorbed into Greater Germany. European Russia itself would be parcelled up into colonies of the Reich. Russian industries would be dismantled; the population of the industrial north would be driven to Siberia, or suffer death by starvation. This would make possible the transfer of living space to ethnic Germans, and at the same time create a food surplus for transfer to Germany.

In such a brutal enterprise, ideological and economic calculations were evenly mixed. The whole thing was inconceivable without an initial presumption that the Russians were subhumans (*Untermenschen*), whose needs and aspirations could be trampled on without regard. Also significant was the Nazi view of Bolshevism as a Jewish–Slavic conspiracy against the German race. There was a complete rejection of the idea that Germany had any civilising mission in the east. The Russians and the other Slavs were not just barbarians, they were un-worthy of civilisation, and the greatest service they could perform was to die to make room for the Reich. In the months of preparation for what Hitler had called a 'war of extermination', Wehrmacht orders threw out the traditional rules of war. The civilian population of the east, acting in resistance to the occupying forces, was to be subject to summary shootings and collective punishments. Crimes committed by German soldiers against civilians were to go unpunished. Captured Soviet officials and Army commissars (political officers) were to be executed at the front line.[2]

Hitler's decision to invade Russia was also stimulated by events and circumstances nearer at hand. In September 1939, German aggression against Poland had resulted in a war with Britain and France which

2 Dallin A 1957: chs II, III.

Hitler had not intended – for then, at least. Hostilities with France had been resolved by a successful invasion and the French surrender of June 1940. Expecting the British now to come to terms, Hitler's thoughts turned immediately to the next stage, an attack on the USSR in the spring of 1941. Soon Hitler became convinced that Churchill's refusal to negotiate was based on the Soviet presence in Germany's rear. Stalin was encouraging Churchill to hold out; only with the defeat of Russia would the British sue for peace, guaranteeing German domination of Europe from the Channel to the Urals.

Hitler's determination to knock the Soviet Union out of the balance of forces in Europe was only strengthened by the Luftwaffe's failure in the Battle of Britain (August–October 1940); Britain's air defences had not broken, and there was now no immediate prospect either of a British surrender or of a successful invasion across the Channel. More than ever, Germany's key to victory in the west was seen to lie in the east.

In December 1940, Hitler issued his Directive No 21, 'Case Barbarossa'. This ordered the preparation, by mid-May 1941, of a massive invasion of Soviet territory. Its aims would be the rapid destruction of the Soviet armed forces; the securing of territory up to a line running from Arkhangel'sk on the White Sea to the Volga River from its upper reaches north and east of Moscow down through Stalingrad to the Caspian Sea; and the subsequent elimination of Soviet industries remaining to the east of this line by aerial bombing. The main weight of the attack would be delivered in the north, penetrating first to Leningrad, then turning to Moscow and beyond; in the south, the immediate objective would be occupation of the coal-metallurgical region of the Donets River basin (the Donbass). The invasion would be reinforced by Finnish and Romanian troops.[3]

Preparations for this colossal operation were now pursued intensively. They were delayed for a few weeks in the spring of 1941 by a crisis in the Balkans and the temporary diversion of German forces to the occupation of Yugoslavia and Greece. By June 1941, however, the Wehrmacht had assembled a huge force on Soviet frontiers. It included 2,800 tanks, 5,000 aircraft, 47,000 artillery pieces and 5.5 million troops.[4] The first troops and aircraft crossed the Soviet border at 4.00 a.m. Moscow time (3.00 a.m. German summer time) on Sunday, 22 June. German field guns began shelling Soviet frontier positions and lines of command and communication. Armoured and infantry

3 Trevor-Roper 1966: 93–8.
4 Soviet estimates cited in Harrison 1985: 111.

units moved across the border in strength. The main Luftwaffe assault began at 4.15 a.m.; bombers raided towns, troop encampments and airfields in the border area.

This was a moment of triumph for German arms. The Wehrmacht had undertaken the biggest ground operation in history, securing for it conditions of virtually complete surprise of the adversary. Surprise of the Soviet forces was both tactical and strategic. Tactical surprise meant that Soviet units were caught unawares. For most of them, the first and only warning of attack was a directive of the People's Commissariat of Defence dispatched by telegraph at 11.45 p.m. on the eve of the invasion, warning of the likelihood of an attack in the next two days, but requiring troops not to respond to provocations 'liable to create serious complications'.[5] For many field units, this ambiguous warning arrived after the invasion had actually begun. But the Soviets were surprised not only tactically. Strategic surprise meant that the Soviet general staff was caught unprepared for the timing of the German assault, for its conditions, scale and character, and for the whole nature of the resulting campaign. They did not expect the Germans to invade; in the event of a German attack, they expected a period of heightened tensions, border incidents, negotiations and provocations to precede any large-scale fighting; in the event of outright war, they expected the main blow to fall on the Ukraine; they planned to throw off the invading forces and proceed immediately to a counteroffensive which would carry the war on to German soil.

Given the necessary scale and duration of German preparations for 'Barbarossa', how could Soviet leaders have been surprised? The conditions for Soviet surprise were created partly in Berlin, partly in Moscow.

The Germans themselves considered surprise to be essential to success in mounting a speedy knockout blow against the Soviet Union. Only by surprise could the adversary be prevented from mobilising beforehand to frustrate German plans and inflict unacceptable losses on invading forces. Hitler and his generals therefore mounted a campaign of deception, surrounding the preparation of 'Barbarossa' with a deliberate fog of unreality; this was just as much a part of preparing the invasion of Russia as concentrating troops and tanks on the eastern frontier. The mist of deception was to be dense, and each successive attempt to penetrate it was to be confronted with enveloping layers of illusion.

In the first stages, German preparations were disguised as part of a

5 Great Patriotic War 1974: 50.

build-up for 'Sea lion', the cross-Channel invasion of the British Isles. Then, as the eastward orientation of preparations for 'Barbarossa' became unmistakable, they were portrayed as a back-up operation auxiliary to 'Sea lion', a deception against the British, to lull them into a false sense of security. Once the idea of 'Sea lion' had itself lost reality, and German preparations for war with the Soviet Union could no longer be disguised as anything else, the idea was spread about that these were defensive preparations against the threat of Soviet aggression. Lastly, as the threat of German aggression became unmistakable, preparations for invasion were disguised as a psychological pressure on Stalin and a back-up for possible German demands on Soviet territory and resources in the Ukraine, perhaps even an ultimatum, which could be followed by negotiation rather than inevitable hostilities.[6]

In spite of German security surrounding 'Barbarossa', Soviet authorities received many accurate warnings of the coming attack. These came through diplomatic, military and intelligence channels, from Soviet field agents (notably Richard Sorge in Tokyo), from the British and United States governments including directly from Churchill and Roosevelt, from German deserters and even from the German ambassador to Moscow. All correctly predicted the main directions and even the date of the onslaught.

The result of German deception, however, was that, while Stalin and other Soviet authorities received many indications of an impending German attack, they also received very many contra-indications. Even direct and detailed forecasts of invasion need not be interpreted at face value, since they could always be understood as German disinformation designed to attract attention away from German plans in the west, or as British provocation designed to draw the Soviet Union into an unnecessary war with Germany, or as German disinformation designed to provoke the Soviet Union into a war in which the Soviets would be branded the aggressors, or as German psychological pressure designed to influence Soviet behaviour in negotiations. Only with hindsight would it be possible to discriminate with complete certainty between truths, half-truths and outright lies.

At the same time, the situation in Moscow guaranteed the success of the German campaign to deceive. Here the political atmosphere was very important. Everyone understood the damage which war would inflict upon plans for peaceful economic development, for raising living standards and the quality of life after a decade of economic struggle and deprivation; the desire to avoid war was very strong. If

6 Whaley 1973: 172–5.

war could not be averted altogether, then at least it must be postponed for a few years so that military preparations could be completed without undue additional sacrifice. This atmosphere itself acted as a filter, tending to enhance the apparent value of signals suggesting that war was not really inevitable or intended by Germany, and to discredit those which reflected German intentions faithfully.

When it came to evaluating German intentions, the politicians were to blame. It was Stalin's views which dominated to the exclusion of all others, but in this Stalin was keenly supported by Politburo members such as Zhdanov, Malenkov, and Beriya as head of security. They distrusted Hitler, but they distrusted Churchill and Roosevelt more; they still hoped to appease Germany, to avert Soviet involvement in the war and to remain spectators while Europe burned. They completely underestimated the seriousness of the German determination to dismember the Soviet Union and incorporate its European part into a greater German empire.

To make matters worse, the possibility of a realistic professional assessment of German intentions and appropriate Soviet responses had been all but destroyed in the Red Army purge of 1937–8. There was no one in the general staff capable of standing up to the wishful thinking of the politicians, and delivering a sober, worst-case evaluation of available intelligence, without fear of being branded a traitor or provocateur. As a result, the German surprise attack was not only a military shock but also a devastating political and psychological blow.

Stalin and his closest colleagues were primarily responsible for this state of affairs. But they accepted no blame for it. On the contrary, in the first weeks of fighting Stalin made scapegoats out of the military commanders responsible for frontier defence; a number of them were charged with cowardice or treason and were shot. Only after victory would Stalin half-humorously refer to the mistakes of the early period, knowing that no one would ask him to settle the account.

It is also true that, even if Stalin had made no mistakes, if Hitler had not secured any advantage of strategic surprise or political or psychological shock, the German forces would still have had the capacity to inflict huge losses of men and territory on the Soviet defenders. On the other hand, without the advantage ceded to them by Stalin's mistakes, they might not have reached Stalingrad and the Caucasus.

THE RETREAT TO LENINGRAD AND MOSCOW

Germany was now to fight the USSR for four years along a front which, at its widest, stretched 2,000 kilometres across Europe from the Baltic Sea to the Caucasus mountains and, at its furthest, 2,000 kilometres from Berlin. It was fought with tens of millions of soldiers, and hundreds of thousands of aircraft, tanks and guns on each side. It was the greatest land war of all time.

From a military point of view, the war on the eastern front can be divided into four stages. In the first (June–December 1941), the Germans had nearly everything their own way, but still did not win a knockout blow. For the Soviets, with German troops at the gates of Moscow, survival itself was at stake. The end of this first phase was marked by the regeneration of Soviet resistance.

At first the Soviets fought alone, but before the end of 1941 they had been joined by two great allies, the British and the Americans (Japan's bombing of the United States naval base at Pearl Harbor in December 1941 was immediately followed by a German declaration of war). For the time being, Allied aid to Russia remained largely diplomatic and symbolic, but it grew in importance in the second phase, which lasted the whole of 1942. Throughout this second phase the eastern front was characterised by a strategic stalemate, with both sides struggling for advantage, with great new offensives, counteroffensives and manoeuvres; Soviet military determination nearly broke a second time, but in the end proved the stronger.

The stalemate was ended by decisive Soviet victories at Stalingrad at the beginning of 1943, and later in the same year at Kursk-Orel. The balance was moving more and more against Germany, both because of the rising Soviet war effort and because Allied military and food aid to the Soviets at last became significant in amount. Now German defeat in the Soviet Union became certain, although its speed, significance and cost to the Soviets remained to be seen. The third phase lasted until the summer of 1944. In this period, Soviet forces chased the Germans out of Soviet territory.

In June 1944, as Soviet troops were entering eastern Europe, the western Allies finally joined the war on land in western Europe, opening a second front in France. From now the Germans were retreating from both directions. The final phase culminated in Berlin in May 1945 with Soviet capture of Germany's capital and Germany's unconditional surrender to the Allies.

The rest of this section is devoted to the first six months – the

Soviet struggle for military survival. To begin with, 'Barbarossa' went well for Germany. In the first hours and days, Soviet frontier defences were pulverised and Soviet borders were deeply penetrated. The Luftwaffe quickly secured supremacy in the air; just in the first eight hours, the Red Army lost one in seven of its front-line combat aircraft, most of them on the ground.[7] Within weeks, Wehrmacht divisions had swept through the Baltic region. German troops entered Belorussia and the Ukraine.

German successes continued to mount in August and September. Lightning advances and great wheeling manoeuvres outflanked Soviet defences, seizing cities and trapping huge armies. In early September Leningrad was cut off by land, its remaining link with Soviet forces lying across Lake Ladoga. But the Germans failed to storm the city as the shattered Soviet divisions, retreating more slowly, finally dug their heels in. Instead, they laid siege to the city, which Hitler intended to 'wipe from the face of the earth', its population to be destroyed by starvation, shelling and shooting. To the south, the Ukraine was deeply penetrated; its capital, Kiev, was captured and the main coal and metallurgical region of the Donbass became a theatre of war. A million Red Army soldiers were lost in two great encirclements, at Kiev in September and farther north at Vyaz'ma in the following month.

At the end of September the Germans launched the first stage of Operation 'Typhoon', a knockout blow against Moscow itself. This was to be the first battle of Moscow, and it lasted a month until the German offensive ran out of momentum. Moscow itself was almost captured; at the point of nearest advance, the German tank commander could see the golden cupolas of the Kremlin glinting in the sunshine through his field glasses. In mid-October the civilian ministries and foreign embassies were ordered out of Moscow and dispersed to cities in the interior. It was rumoured that Stalin himself had fled, and there was momentary panic among the city's remaining civilian population.

But within a few days of this the German advance had exhausted itself. There were many reasons for this. One reason was that the implementation of 'Barbarossa' had proceeded too far and too fast, across a front 600 kilometres deep and 1,500 kilometres wide. As lines of supply lengthened and multiplied, more and more of the

7 By midday on 22 June the Soviet air force had lost 1,200 aircraft, 900 of them on the ground, according to Bialer 1970: 205. An official figure of 1,540 front-line combat aircraft on 22 June is available from VO voina 1970: 579, but this excludes numerous 'obsolete' types. According to Tupper 1982: 200, new types amounted to 19 per cent of front-line strength, giving a total of 8,105 front-line aircraft.

Wehrmacht's capacities were pre-empted by the need to bring up food, fuel and munitions from the rear, less and less being left available for fighting the defender. Tanks ran out of fuel and parts, guns ran out of shells, troops became exhausted, had to dig in and could not maintain their initial momentum.

A factor of decisive significance in the exhaustion of the German advance was the growing resistance of Soviet civilians and soldiers. Military resistance was both weaker and stronger than German expectations. The sheer panic and disorder of the Soviet retreat meant that the German advance proceeded at times much more rapidly than expected. This contributed to German supply problems partly because German combat forces became more easily separated from the German rear; partly because they took many more Soviet prisoners than was anticipated, and these prisoners had to be funnelled back to the rear, at the same time as combat stores were being brought forward.

Soviet military resistance was also stronger than expected. Although panicked, often cut off and leaderless, not all Soviet units gave up; instead many fought on desparately, without orders or supplies, to the last bullet and the last ration, even preferring death to surrender. Under fire Soviet commanders, too, began to learn generalship in holding together shattered units, slowing their retreat, turning them around with speeches, with orders and threats of shooting, with examples of personal leadership, throwing them back into combat no matter how weakened or short of equipment, smashing back at the invading troops, counterattacking ceaselessly. Stalin's Order No 270 of mid-August 1941 also no doubt played a role. This decreed that Soviet deserters' families were liable to arrest; it also declared that soldiers falling alive into German captivity had betrayed the motherland, and deprived their families of soldiers' pensions.

Because of the unexpectedly bitter and unyielding character of the Soviet forces in the midst of this great catastrophe, the triumphant invader suffered casualties on a far greater scale than hitherto. In 1940, in the whole of the western campaign the Wehrmacht had lost some 156,000 men, including 30,000 dead. By December 1941, the Russians had cost them three-quarters of a million, the German dead totalling nearly 200,000.[8] Although far exceeded by Soviet losses, these were a price which Germany had not expected to pay.

Civilian resistance, too, eventually slowed the German advance. At first, in the Baltic republics and in much of the Ukraine, civil resistance was negligible. The local population, if not pro-Nazi, was at least

---

8 German military sources, cited by Werth 1964: 259.

not anti-German. But as the German forces advanced the position soon changed. Home guard militias were recruited in the front-line districts, helping the regular troops of the Red Army by digging ditches and shelters, building anti-tank defences, assisting evacuation and eventually fighting the enemy hand to hand. A policy of 'scorched earth' was in force on the Soviet side, denying the Wehrmacht the means to recoup its supply shortages at the expense of captured stocks of food and fuel. As people fled, they took with them what they could; what they left, they destroyed. Those who stayed behind soon learnt the reality of German occupation policy and this, too, would eventually contribute to resistance.

In November, the mud turned to frost. The German supply situation became still more critical. Hitler had not intended a winter campaign. Winter equipment, available in the rear, could not be brought forward because Wehrmacht transport troops were already fully employed on bringing up munitions and fuel. Now German soldiers and their weapons began to freeze into immobility. The second stage of 'Typhoon' was launched on 16 November, but the renewed German offensive against Moscow lasted a bare three weeks. On all fronts, the German momentum was entirely lost, while Soviet resistance was consolidated under Zhukov. On the southern front German troops gave ground for the first time anywhere in Europe since Hitler had begun to implement his plans of aggression when, at the end of the month, the Soviets recaptured Rostov-on-Don.

On 5 December the Red Army launched a counteroffensive outside Moscow. This was a critical moment, because it confirmed German loss of the strategic initiative in the World War as a whole. Soon the enemy was pushed back 150–200 kilometres. With the recapture of significant territory, Soviet troops saw for the first time on a large scale the consequences of occupation for people the Nazis regarded as *Untermenschen* – burnt-out huts, the disappearance of able-bodied men to the German rear, corpses hanging from telegraph poles, the first mass graves.

In this first phase of the war, decisive steps were taken to the rallying of national unity. The unification of the Soviet people behind their war effort was a process, not a single moment, and the process was not completed until the end of 1942. At the end of 1941, national survival still hung in the balance. Soviet troops were fighting with increasing effectiveness, for the time being; Soviet workers and industries were supplying them with the means of combat, for the moment. The outlook, however, remained utterly grim. Up to the end of the year the Red Army had lost more than 3 million taken prisoner, and at least half that number dead from all causes. Although temporarily stalemated, the enemy was deep inside Soviet territory and, as 1942 would show, retained the capacity to inflict further huge damage. The civilian economy was in ruins. The ability, and willingness, of Soviet people to fight and to labour on for years of struggle hung in the balance. Soviet leaders, and Stalin himself, helped ensure they would do so by deferring to Russian national feeling and national and military traditions. The prewar themes of internal division and 'intensified' class struggle against the enemy within gave way to national unification in order to drive out the foreign invader.

FROM MOSCOW TO STALINGRAD

The year 1942 was the one in which things got still worse before they got better. The German forces scored further outstanding successes over the Soviet defenders; in spite of rising force levels and accelerating war production, Soviet morale and the Soviet economy teetered on a knife-edge.

Success in the second battle of Moscow emboldened Stalin. In early January 1942 he ordered a general counteroffensive with ambitious objectives: to lift the siege of Leningrad, to smash the three main Wehrmacht army groups (North, Centre and South), and to clear German troops out of the Donbass and Crimea. The counteroffensive continued through the early spring to April, by which time it had petered out on all fronts. Ill supplied, with insufficient reserves and too thinly deployed, the Soviet Army achieved none of its main objectives. One main failure was to lift the siege of Leningrad; however, the German stranglehold was eased, and with the opening of the ice road (the 'road of life') across Lake Ladoga in January the Leningraders could again be supplied, and many of them evacuated by the returning transports. In general, the Soviet Army was able to push back German lines some 100–350 kilometres.

The Wehrmacht, however, did not only lose territory. Fifty German divisions lost more than half their troops and armament, and total military losses exceeded 400,000 men. A crisis resulted which was both military and political. The military crisis was reflected in Hitler's immediate removal of his commander-in-chief of ground forces (Hitler himself assumed personal command) and of all army group commanders. But a long crisis of German policy was also beginning because the strategy of *Blitzkrieg* was finished. Germany's lightning war against the USSR had failed, and a still more bloody war of attrition had begun, in which each nation's full human, material and moral resources would be thrown into the balance. Germany now had to adjust herself to the prospect of a war of long duration and unremitting national effort.

Frustrated outside Moscow, now Hitler planned another decisive offensive. Again the ground was prepared by a campaign of deception, to make Stalin think that the Wehrmacht intended to repeat the previous autumn's frontal assault in the northern and central sectors, against Leningrad and Moscow. Again Stalin was taken in, and ordered strengthening of Soviet deployments away from the southern sector. The German operation, launched in May, was to send army group South back through the Crimea and across the Ukraine to the Don and lower Volga rivers and to the oil-rich Caucasus; then there was the option of turning to join with the central and northern army groups to encircle and take Moscow. At first everything went well. In May, on the southern flank of the advance, the Wehrmacht pushed the Soviet Army out of the Crimea with heavy losses, though it still took the Germans two months to conclude the long siege of Sevastopol', where they took 90,000 prisoners. By the time the Germans reached Rostov-on-Don at the end of July the Soviet defenders were in a panic, and soldiers fled in large numbers.

Meanwhile, on the northern line of advance, German troops lunged across the Ukrainian steppe; a Soviet counteroffensive to retake Khar'kov ended disastrously in late May with the encirclement and capture of two more Soviet armies – 200,000 men. The Germans reoccupied the Donbass, and prepared an assault on Voronezh, which was necessary in order to secure the northern flank of the advance and threaten Stalingrad's defences from the rear. At Voronezh, however, the German advance was held. For six weeks the front line ran through this sleepy provincial market town, which was almost completely destroyed.

Temporarily frustrated, Hitler shifted his priorities away to Stalingrad and the Caucasus. Meanwhile, in the southern sector Red Army discipline was tightened. Part of this story was Stalin's Order No 227 of 28 July, four days after the Rostov panic; it accused the troops of giving up the southern cities without resistance and against orders, out of cowardice, and ordered: 'Not a step back.' Military police were deployed behind the lines, authorised to arrest stragglers and shoot those retreating without orders. Officers who failed to hold their units together would be sent to the front to die in penal battalions. To many of the troops to whom it was read, this harsh message resonated with a ring of necessity. To others, however, it was recalled afterwards as no more than an encouragement to further pointless expenditures of human life.[9]

At the same time, Army reforms were set in motion. The professional status of Army officers was raised, and political commissars subordinated to military commanders. New (or rather old, that is prerevolutionary) insignia and privileges of rank were introduced. Old national and military traditions were once again thrown into the balance.

There would be no more panics. However, in the south the German forces continued to advance. At the end of August they reached the Volga, entering Stalingrad itself in mid-September (at the same time German forces were rapidly occupying the Caucasus). Beyond Stalingrad there was nowhere left for the Soviet defenders, under Chuikov and Voronov, to retreat; Stalin refused to authorise the city's evacuation. Now weeks of house-to-house fighting began, every inch of every street being bitterly contested. On both sides the attrition of forces was appalling.

Then, in the latter part of November, Soviet forces under Zhukov and Vasilevskii struck an unexpected and decisive blow in the German rear, closing a ring around a third of a million German troops. In the next two months most of them would die because of disease, hunger and cold as well as in the fighting, because they could not break out, and because Hitler would not let them capitulate. When the surrender came only 90,000 were still alive. In the whole operation the Wehrmacht had lost 800,000 troops, as well as thousands of guns, tanks and aircraft.

At their farthest reach, the Germans had engaged on a front which stretched 2,000 kilometres from Finland in the north-west to Turkey in the south. When they reached Mozdok in the Caucasus they were 2,000 kilometres from Berlin. This was the exact measure of the retreat which now faced them. With disaster at Stalingrad, the German forces in the Caucasus were hopelessly exposed and fell back as rapidly as they had advanced. From now on the Soviet Army would advance continuously, although still at great cost, to Berlin.

9 Davies 1989: 105–6.

THE GRAND ALLIANCE

The Great Patriotic War of the Soviet Union was a part (arguably, the decisive part) of World War II. The Soviet Union fought in alliance with Britain and the United States. This, like any alliance, suffered from clashes of interest and opinion, resentment at the distribution of costs and benefits, suspicion of each other's motives and intentions; and it did not long survive the end of the war. Despite these strains, the alliance provided the indispensable basis for victory. It did so for two main reasons: awareness that fascism posed a deadly threat to both western democracy and Soviet communism, and recognition that no one partner in the alliance could achieve victory alone.

This common interest was reflected in the speed with which the alliance took shape. On the very day of the invasion, Churchill publicly offered to 'give whatever help we can to Russia and the Russian people.' Three weeks later a mutual assistance pact was signed. At the end of July 1941, Roosevelt's special envoy, Harry Hopkins, arrived in Moscow to discuss the supply of American military and economic aid, already being provided in huge quantities to Britain under the Lend-Lease Act. In September, Lend-Lease was extended to include the USSR. Goods supplied under it were neither lent nor leased, but amounted to a conditional gift in recognition of the American national interest in preventing a German victory. With American entry into the war in December 1941, American–Soviet cooperation became a full alliance.

From the earliest days of the war to its end, therefore, there was continuous contact between the Soviet Union and its western allies – through diplomatic and military missions, visits of special envoys and foreign ministers, frequent communications between heads of government, and summit meetings. Churchill, Roosevelt and Stalin met at Tehran in November 1943 and at Yalta in February 1945; in addition, Churchill and Stalin met in Moscow in August 1942 and October 1944.

In the dire conditions after the German attack, Soviet hopes of western assistance, reflected in official statements, ran very high. In his first letter to Churchill, four weeks after the invasion, Stalin asked Britain to open a front in northern France and to join with the USSR in opening another front in Norway and Finland. When he met Hopkins at the end of July, besides asking for weapons and industrial goods, Stalin said American troops would be welcome anywhere on the Soviet front. At the beginning of September, with the military situation rapidly worsening, he told Churchill that without help the Soviet Union would either suffer defeat or be weakened to such an extent that it would be unable to assist its allies for a long period. Specifically, a second front was needed that year in either the Balkans or France to relieve pressure on the Soviet Union. When Churchill declared this impossible, Stalin proposed that Britain send 25 or 30 divisions to Arkhangel'sk or, via Iran, to the southern regions of the USSR.

In the event, the western Allies were more forthcoming with material aid than with strategic support. During 1942, the trickle increased. Most of it took the form of munitions and military vehicles, but there was an increasing element of industrial equipment and foodstuffs. Almost all of it was American, although the British and Canadians also made a small contribution. In 1943 it became a steady flow; American shipments, which had averaged $100 million per month in 1942, now rose to $250 million monthly and remained at that level through 1944. This was a significant addition to Soviet strength.

Behind it lay a pooling of Allied resources on an unprecedented scale. There was nothing to compare with it in relations between the Axis powers. At the same time, officially speaking, the main American motive was self-interest, not generosity, because Roosevelt had calculated that the United States would lose only from a German victory on the eastern front. But other factors included wider public sympathy for the Soviet Union, and admiration too, particularly after the Stalingrad victory. There was also a sense of guilt at the relatively low level of British and American engagement with Germany; as late as the end of 1942, the Red Army faced 266 Axis divisions, 193 of them German, while Anglo-American forces in Africa faced 15 Axis divisions, only 4 of them German.

Soviet people were undoubtedly grateful for Allied aid, but in one aspect it grated on their sensibilities. The American strategy of arming the Russians to fight Germany in the east (and Britain to fight Germany in the air, and in the Mediterranean) cost America dollars and resources, but the cost to the USSR was measured in blood and lives. British and American soldiers and sailors were dying in the Mediterranean; RAF and USAF aircrews were dying over Germany, and the bombing of German cities and industries diverted the Luftwaffe from the eastern front to home defence. Still, the British and Americans died in relatively small numbers. Soviet citizens could not help but reflect that if British and American leaders had been as ready to spend lives as the Russians, then they would have gone to war against Germany on land in Europe long before June 1944. There was an agonising gap between Soviet demands for the western Allies to open up a 'Second Front' in France as early as possible, and the Anglo-American determination to wait until absolutely overwhelming force had been accumulated.

Timing the opening of a second front became one of the thorniest problems. In May 1942, Roosevelt and Churchill committed themselves, albeit in vague terms, to 'a second front in Europe in 1942'. Its postponement in favour of a landing in North Africa, which Churchill announced to Stalin in August 1942, provoked a contemptuous attack on British cowardice and fear of the Germans. In February 1943 at Casablanca the western Allies discussed an invasion of France in August or September that year. In June, however, they informed the Soviet Union that they would land in Sicily instead. Bitterly, Stalin reproached his partners for 'withholding from our army, which has sacrificed so much, the anticipated substantial support of the Anglo-American armies'. It was hardly coincidental that the following month he used the term 'Great Patriotic War' for the first time. Not until the Tehran conference in November 1943 did Churchill and Roosevelt give a firm commitment to open the second front in the spring of 1944.

The Normandy landings of 6 June 1944 created a temporary mood of euphoria in Moscow. Not least in military circles, Soviet hopes of a rapid German collapse ran high. They were disappointed by strong German resistance. And although Germany now transferred substantial forces to the west, two-thirds of its army remained in the east. It would take eleven more months' heavy fighting before victory in Europe was won.

If strategic issues were a continual source of friction, ideological differences had minimal visible effect on relations between the allies. In marked contrast with past (and future) practice, each country's propaganda concentrated heavily on its partners' merits. To allay western fears of communist subversion, the Communist International was dissolved in April 1943, although the underlying power relations of Soviet dominance over foreign communist parties remained intact. Far more divisive were questions concerning the postwar fate of eastern Europe and Germany. As the situation on the eastern front evolved to the Soviet advantage, and its determination and capacity to build a strong barrier against any future attack from the west became clear, disagreements grew sharper. Spheres of influence, postwar borders and governments (especially of Poland), the exaction of German reparations and Germany's partition increasingly occupied the Allies.

Meanwhile, there were ever-present fears, fed by rumour and press speculation, that one partner or another would renege on the commitment to fight until Germany's unconditional surrender to all the Allies, and conclude a separate peace. Given the prewar background of western appeasement and the Molotov–Ribbentrop pact, such fears were hardly groundless. And tentative contacts were made: between Soviet and Bulgarian representatives in October 1941, between Soviet and German representatives in Sweden in June 1943, and between the American and German sides in Switzerland in March 1945.

Despite these tensions, the forces holding the Allies together proved stronger than those dividing them. Recognising this, Roosevelt wrote to Churchill only hours before his death in April 1945: 'I would minimize the general Soviet problem as much as possible because these problems, in one form or another, seem to arise every day, and most of them straighten out.' The alliance held. Substantial military and economic cooperation was achieved. Germany was defeated.

FROM STALINGRAD TO BERLIN – AND MANCHURIA

The remainder of the war on the eastern front is the story of how the Soviet Army pursued the enemy back to Berlin. There was only one more significant setback in March 1943 when Soviet forces on the south-western front, advancing too rapidly, were caught by surprise in a German counteroffensive; Khar'kov was occupied again, and the German line stabilised. This prepared the ground for Hitler's last throw in Russia.

In Operation 'Citadel', Hitler planned to entrap Soviet forces massing around Kursk for a summer offensive. The German offensive was launched on 5 July 1943, and lasted for ten days. It failed to achieve an encirclement, and was answered by a huge Soviet countermove which developed into a five-week running battle. At the end of it, the Germans had been pushed back 150 kilometres. This was the biggest tank engagement of World War II, with 6,000 tanks on either side as well as thousands of aircraft and hundreds of thousands of troops. It was also the last German offensive on the eastern front; after it, the Wehrmacht could no longer do anything to stop the Soviet advance, and could only seek to slow it down.

Essential to the Soviet Army's firepower, supply and movement after 1942 was the emergence of what Stalin called 'an efficient and rapidly expanding war economy'. Having overcome the early crises, the economy was now geared up for a protracted war. Soviet factories were pouring out guns, bullets, tanks and shells on an unprecedented scale. The cost of this economic effort was no longer the shambles which had prevailed in every other sector of activity in 1941–2, since the civilian economy had been roughly stabilised and would now expand again (although it remained far below peacetime levels, and life in the rear remained extremely tough). The Soviet effort was also boosted by the fact that American supplies were now beginning to arrive in quantity; these would add substantially to Soviet Army resources, especially to food rations, means of communications and mobility in pursuit of the retreating Wehrmacht.

Between August and December 1943, the Soviet Army liberated most of central Russia and the Ukraine. In the north foundations were laid for the final relief of Leningrad. To the south, 200,000 German and Romanian troops were trapped in the Crimea. By the end of the year the Nazis had lost two-thirds of the territory they had occupied since June 1941. With the recovery of occupied territory came a sharpening of many issues – the rehabilitation of populations decimated by undernourishment, homelessness, deportations, reprisals and policies of extermination; the reabsorption of burnt-out villages, farmland stripped of stock and poisoned by explosives and metal fragments, factories and transportation systems broken and stripped of machinery and power sources; attitudes to the German nation whose military forces had brought these things about; the character and objectives of postwar recovery.

The year 1944 was to be known as the year of Stalin's 'ten great victories'. These comprised

  1 the relief of Leningrad (January)
  2 the encirclement of German troops in the south-west Ukraine and entry into Romania (February–March)
  3 the destruction of German forces in the Crimea (May)
  4 the defeat of Finnish forces and re-establishment of the 1940 frontier (June)
  5 the liberation of Belorussia, including the destruction of twenty-five German divisions (June)
  6 the entry of Soviet forces into Poland against fierce resistance (July)
  7 the occupation of Romania and Bulgaria (August)
  8 the liberation of Latvia and Estonia (September)
  9 the liberation of Belgrade (October)
  10 the expulsion of German troops from northern Finland and Norway (October).

The other decisive development of 1944 was, of course, the Allied invasion of Normandy which began on 6 June 1944, and which at last brought substantial diversion of Germany's ground forces from east to west.

Missing from the list of Soviet victories in 1944 was the liberation of Warsaw. Soviet forces under Rokossovskii reached the Vistula river across from the city at the end of July 1944, where the advance was halted. The next day the leaders of Warsaw's underground resistance made a call to insurrection. They fought until October, without assistance; in the course of the uprising, 300,000 Poles lost their lives. Soviet troops did not actually enter Warsaw until mid-January 1945.

A few days later, Soviet forces crossed the border into Germany. Against desperate resistance they fought their way to Berlin, linking up with the United States Army on the Elbe river. Right up to the end, the eastern front retained its bitterly contested character, the Red Army suffering more than 300,000 casualties just in the final, two-week Battle of Berlin. With Soviet official attitudes at their most harshly anti-German, Soviet Army troops not only secured the defeat of the military adversary but also carried out acts of revenge upon the civilian population. Hitler killed himself on 30 April, and the Berlin garrison surrendered to Zhukov on 2 May; the German capitulation followed with surrenders to the Anglo-American command on 7 May and to the Soviet command on 8 May. The European war was over.

The final blow remained to be struck against Japan. At Yalta, in February 1945, Roosevelt had secured Stalin's promise that the Soviet Union would enter the war against Japan three months after victory in Europe; this was at a time when the military defeat of Japan, although ultimately certain, seemed still far in the future. Stalin now prepared to fulfil this promise.

But Roosevelt had died on 12 April, and Truman had a secret. This was the atomic bomb, first exploded experimentally on 16 July. The Americans now hastened to use the bomb, to force a Japanese surrender before Soviet forces could enter the war, take part in the occupation of the Japanese islands and claim a share in the postwar settlement in the Pacific. On 6 August, two days before expiry of the deadline for a Soviet declaration of war on Japan, the United States Air Force bombed Hiroshima, destroying the city and causing 75,000 immediate deaths. The destruction of Nagasaki, with 40,000 immediate deaths, followed on 9 August. On 14 August the Japanese government broadcast its intention to surrender.

Meanwhile, the Soviet Union had declared war on Japan. On 9 August Soviet forces under Vasilevskii invaded Manchuria and began the rout of Japan's occupying forces. By the time their surrender began on 19 August, the Japanese had lost 80,000 dead and 600,000 prisoners. But the truth was that the Japanese war machine was already knocked out. The Manchurian victory simply confirmed the fact.

The real significance of Hiroshima and Nagasaki now became apparent. The United States had demonstrated its new weapon not only in order to shatter further the broken will of Japanese resistance, but also in order to send a message to Moscow. A Soviet invasion of the Japanese islands was forestalled. With the atom bomb, the western Allies had lost the need and the incentive to secure Soviet cooperation in the government of world affairs. Thus, the dead of Hiroshima and Nagasaki were both the last casualties of World War II, and the first casualties of the Cold War.

THE COSTS OF VICTORY

This was the most costly war in history. What made it so was its essential character. For the war had several features which, in combination, distinguished it from all wars before and afterwards.

First, for Germany it was a 'war of extermination'. Germany's fundamental aims were living space for German settlers and German financial interests; grain for German workers, oil for German industry. With this were associated plans for reduction of the Russian population by tens of millions by expulsion and starvation. On the Soviet side, this made it a war of national survival – a war for the fatherland, a patriotic war like the war of 1812 against Napoleon's invasion; soon it became known as the Great Patriotic War.

Second, for both sides it was, or else it soon became, a war of production – although Hitler did not intend it so. Germany sought a quick victory before the Soviets could mobilise their war industries, and before Germany would need to do the same. German failure to achieve this made a protracted war inevitable, in which the decisive weight would be exercised by war production. The war as a whole would be won or lost by the side that could bring to bear the greatest volume of resources.

Third, it became a war of unique scale and intensity, and the eastern front became its decisive theatre. From the moment of its inception until the western Allies opened the Second Front in Normandy, the Soviet forces faced never less than 90 per cent of Germany's front-line fighting strength on land.[10] The eastern front saw the biggest single land operation ('Barbarossa'), the biggest artillery battle (Stalingrad), the biggest tank battle (Kursk). On the western front there was nothing to compare until D-Day, except the costly and militarily ineffective thousand-bomber raids on German cities. In the winter of 1942, decisive Allied victories were won at Stalingrad in the east and at El Alamein in North Africa. The entire battle of Egypt cost Germany 75,000 troops, 500 tanks and 1,000 artillery pieces.[11] In the battle of Stalingrad Germany lost 800,000 men (of whom only 90,000 remained alive at the moment of surrender), 2,000 tanks and 10,000 guns.[12] As for civilians, in the winter of 1941–2, more Leningraders starved to death every month than the total of British civilians killed by German bombs in the entire war; the 1 million premature deaths in this one city greatly exceeded the combined military and civilian casualties of the British Empire and dominions and of the United States.

The overall costs arising directly from this war can be counted up in both human and financial terms. As for the human losses, the war would directly cause the premature deaths of 50 million to 60 million people throughout the world.[13] Up to half of these were Soviet citizens.

In Stalin's lifetime only 7 million Soviet war deaths were admitted, in an attempt to conceal the country's weakened state from new postwar adversaries abroad. Later this number was raised by Khrushchev to 20 million, and by Brezhnev to 'more than 20 million'. Forty-five years would pass before a higher total, now set at 27 million to 28 million, would be officially acknowledged.[14] This figure means that

10 VO voina 1984: 502.

11 War seen from Britain 1945: 20.

12 VO voina 1984: 200.

13 The leading Soviet demographer, Urlanis 1971: 294, gave a detailed analysis of world-wide premature deaths totalling 50 million, on the basis of a Soviet figure of 20 million.

14 Soviet war losses are difficult to calculate because there were no population censuses between 1939 and 1959, and neither the prewar nor the postwar population is known for sure. After adjusting for altered Soviet frontiers, census data for 1939 can be projected forward to 1946, and those for 1959 can be run backward to the same point, suggesting an overall Soviet population deficit in 1946 of not more than 50 million. From this figure an estimate of the birth deficit resulting from the war must be deducted in order to estimate the excess of mortality from all causes in the war years. The figure of 27 million to 28 million excess deaths was cited authoritatively by the Soviet Commander-in-Chief of the Warsaw Pact forces in a VE Day anniversary speech in 1990 (*Guardian*, 8 May 1990); this was apparently based on an emerging consensus among Soviet demographers, summarised by Rybakovskii 1989. However, a maximum scholarly estimate of up to 40 million (one-fifth of the prewar Soviet population), supplied by Kozlov V I 1989, cannot be excluded.

the war carried off no fewer than one in seven of the prewar Soviet population.

Who were the main elements in this number? Clearly, among the military, men were in the great majority (women also served in uniform, but in far fewer numbers). But in the civilian population both women and men perished in millions. Overall, the excess of women over men in the Soviet population (there were already more women than men before the war) rose by perhaps 13 million.[15] If so, the total number of male deaths attributable to the war may be put at 20 million to 20.5 million, and female deaths at 7 million to 7.5 million.

What were the proportions between soldiers and civilians? In 1988–9, for the first time, the Soviet general staff carried out an official count of reports of military losses from front-line and supporting units of the Armed Forces which, after checking against the wartime count kept by the general staff itself, gave a figure for overall fatalities among the regular forces of 8,668,400 killed, died of wounds, illness and accidents, missing, and captured and not returned. The Soviet account also established a total of 18 million soldiers wounded (some more than once), frostbitten or sick.[16]

The figure of 8.7 million military fatalities may still involve understatement, however, given our knowledge of the scale of mortality in German prisoner of war camps. The Soviet general staff has estimated 1.5 million killed up to the end of 1941. But according to German sources 3.35 million Soviet soldiers had fallen into German hands by the end of 1941, of whom more than 2 million had died already by February 1942.[17] Taking the war as a whole, 5,754,000 Soviet prisoners of war fell into German hands. The number of deaths among them (from shooting, hunger, cold, illness, and excessive labour) had already reached 3,222,000 by 1 May 1944,[18] and may ultimately have reached up to 4.7 million.[19] This would leave the number of Soviet military fatalities in combat and in the rear as a residual of no more than 4

15 Calculated from the 1959 census by Urlanis 1971: 286.
16 Moiseev 1990: 14.
17 Schulte 1989: 203.
18 Dallin A 1957: 427.
19 Berghahn 1982: 165. By comparison, deaths totalled 3.5 per cent among western Allied prisoners in German hands, and 31.5 per cent among German prisoners in Soviet hands (Schulte 1989: 181).

millions. Yet it seems unlikely that fewer Soviet soldiers fell in battle than died in captivity.[20]

If the total of premature deaths stands at 27 million to 28 million, and losses of regular forces are taken as up to 9 million, then some 19 million civilians made up the majority of Soviet war dead, caught in military crossfire, killed by bombing, by blockade and hunger, dying as partisans, hostages and slaves. But we have only fragmentary information about the composition of this huge number – 1 million Leningraders, 1 million or more Jews.[21]

As for financial costs of the war, a Soviet government commission reported in September 1945 that the war had destroyed Soviet property costed at 679 billion prewar roubles, or roughly 30 per cent of the prewar capital stock. In the occupied territories (most of the destruction had been wrought on the territory of the Russian Federation, the Ukraine and Belorussia), two-thirds of the prewar capital stock had been destroyed.[22] In official words,

> The German-fascist invaders completely or partially destroyed and burnt 1,710 towns and settlements and more than 70,000 villages and hamlets; burnt and destroyed more than 6 million buildings and rendered homeless about 25 million people; destroyed 31,580 industrial enterprises, decommissioned metal works in which before the war was smelted about 60 per cent of the steel, and mines yielding more than 60 per cent of the coal in the country; destroyed 65 thousand kilometres of railway lines and 4,100 stations, 36 thousand post and telegraph installations, telephone exchanges and other communications enterprises; destroyed and looted tens of thousands of collective and state farms, slaughtered, seized or drove back to Germany 7 million horses, 17 million cattle and oxen, 20 million pigs, 27 million sheep and goats. In addition they destroyed and looted 40 thousand hospitals and other medical establishments, 84 thousand schools, colleges, universities and research institutes, and 43 thousand public libraries.[23]

Nor do these costs include the years of wartime deprivation of the

20 Thus Kozlov VI 1989: 138 put Army losses at no fewer than 11 million to 13 million.

21 Officially 632,000 Leningraders died of hunger and cold; adding in hunger deaths in the Leningrad suburbs, and deaths from other war-related causes, yields the higher (but unofficial) figure of 1 million or more. See Pavlov 1965: xiv (introduction by H E Salisbury); Salisbury 1971: 610–12. German sources (Michalka vol 2 1985: 401) suggest losses from the Jewish population of the occupied territories of the USSR of between 700,000 and 1 million, but Kozlov VI 1989: 137 has again proposed a higher figure of 'more than 2.5 millions'.

22 Tamarchenko 1967: 134.

23 Narkhoz 1987: 46.

population, the huge resources diverted from civilian uses to defence. The same official commission calculated wartime spending on the up-keep of the Armed Forces at 551 billion prewar roubles (to which was to be added a further 50 billion roubles paid in war pensions and state support of servicemen's families). These, together with further expenditures on wartime defence and economic conversion, and lost national income, made up a grand total of 1,890 billion roubles.[24] The whole sum would represent some seven years' earnings of the prewar population.[25]

At the end of the day, however, all this destruction was just so much collateral damage. At the core of what was going on lay killing and deaths in millions.

That so many died suggests a last feature of the war's character. In the broad sweep of history, witnessed by intellectuals and commentators and government leaders, the war had meaning. It was a war against aggression and colonial annexations, and it was waged to rid the world of fascism. It was called a 'just' war, the people's war, the war of the democracies. Most Soviet people would remember World War II as a 'patriotic war'. Their husbands, sons and brothers had gone to fight for the fatherland, not for the sake of some 'faraway country of which we know so little',[26] and they did not go to die in 'some corner of a foreign field'.[27] But when it came to dying these meanings often disappeared. Ordinary people died, not in dozens or even hundreds but in millions, not furthering a cause, but senselessly. They died sometimes of neglect, because they were simply not important enough to be taken into account, they were killed often by miscalculation, because of big mistakes and little blunders, they were killed sometimes by their own side, out of fear or cowardice, and they died in many episodes of pointless savagery. No one had a monopoly of humane consideration, or scientific foresight, or rational calculation – not Hitler, not Churchill, not Roosevelt, and certainly not Stalin.

Even the deliberate sacrifices, the intended deaths and destruction, had almost been for nothing. There had been no guarantee of final success. On more than one occasion, the Soviet Union had stood on

24 Tamarchenko 1967: 135.

25 Millar, Linz 1978: 959. These authors' own, more conservative estimate suggests a total war cost of 3.9 years' prewar earnings by excluding servicemen's and dependants' consumption, and the costs of wartime evacuation and conversion.

26 These words of September 1938 expressed the disbelief of the British Prime Minister, Chamberlain, that Britain could have reached the point of war with Germany because of the crisis over Czechoslovakia. Cited by Calder 1969: 29.

27 Brooke 1926: 15

the brink of catastrophe. In fact, of all the countries of Europe, the Soviet Union was the only nation state to survive a deep invasion of its territory by Hitler's Wehrmacht. How had Soviet people pulled their country together? How had they adapted their society and institutions for war? How had they mobilised their economy? And with what consequences for their country's long-range development? These questions form the subject of our book.

CHAPTER THREE
The State in Wartime[1]

'ALL THAT LENIN CREATED WE HAVE LOST FOREVER'

The German invasion threw the Soviet leadership into confusion. To the shock of the collapse of its foreign and defence policy, and the numbing impact of surprise attack, was added the chaos caused by the virtual breakdown of communications between Moscow and the front line. It was some days before Stalin could even grasp the full magnitude of the disaster, and over a week passed before he assumed full command of the country's war effort.

The initial orders to the front-line forces reflected the prewar assumption that an attack was likely to be merely a provocation, and that in any case the Red Army would have no difficulty in repulsing any aggressor. The first order, issued less than four hours before war began, though received by front-line forces, if at all, only after hostilities had started, warned of a possible attack and put troops on combat readiness, but it also prohibited 'provocative actions of any kind.' The second, issued three hours after Operation 'Barbarossa' had been launched, ordered Soviet troops (by now retreating under heavy fire) to counterattack, and called on the airforce (most of which had already been destroyed on the ground) to bomb German airfields. The third, issued late in the evening of 22 June, summoned all Soviet front-line forces to take the offensive and 'annihilate' the enemy.[2]

A vacuum rapidly developed at the highest level. On the first day

---

1 The best analysis of the Soviet system of government in wartime is in Lieberman 1985. See also Kumanev 1988, Mitrofanova 1989 and Harrison 1985.
2 Erickson 1975: 106 ff.

of war, Stalin refused to make any public statement, and it was left to Molotov, Commissar of Foreign Affairs and Deputy Chairman of Sovnarkom, to broadcast the news of the German attack to the population. Although Stalin had long meetings with many leading political and military figures in the first week,[3] he signed no published documents and made no public appearances. His initial confidence that Hitler had made a major error, for which the Red Army would make him pay dearly within a few weeks, was soon shattered by events at the front. The fall of Minsk on 28 June threw him into despair. 'All that Lenin created we have lost forever,' he is said to have declared.[4] In deep depression, he appears to have withdrawn from affairs of state for a day or two. But his collapse was shortlived. On 3 July he addressed the nation by radio, and in so doing identified himself as leader of the Soviet people at war.

THE STRUCTURE OF WARTIME GOVERNMENT

Meanwhile the machinery of government was adjusting to the demands of war. Though based on the system of extreme centralisation, bureaucratic control and personalised power created in the 1930s, it had to meet the urgent need to streamline decision-making and cut through red tape. Accordingly, new institutions and practices were superimposed on the existing structure of the Party, people's commissariats and soviets.

The most important innovation was the establishment of the State Defence Committee (GKO). To leading Politburo members it rapidly became clear that a powerful war cabinet was needed. A deputation headed by Molotov proposed its creation to Stalin. Perhaps expecting to be forced out of office, he seemed surprised to be asked to head it.[5] The GKO was established on 30 June, to deal, as Stalin said in his broadcast three days later, 'with the rapid mobilization of all forces of the peoples of the USSR'.[6] No Soviet political institution before or since had such powers as the GKO exercised during World War II. Its decisions had the force of law; they were binding on all Party, Komsomol, soviet, government and military organisations, as well as on all

3 For a detailed record of the times of the meetings and of those present, see *Nachalo voiny* 1990: 216–20.
4 McNeal 1988: 239.
5 *Politicheskoe obrazovanie* (9) 1988: 75.
6 Stalin 1945: 16.

individual citizens. Its activities ranged from strategy and the administration of the armed forces to economic production and the supply of
labour, materials and energy, from state security and public order to
propaganda, ideology and foreign policy. As Stalin said, 'all the power
and authority of the State' were vested in it.

Initially comprising five men (Stalin, Beriya, Malenkov, Molotov
and Voroshilov), the GKO was essentially a war cabinet of civilian
politicians. Voroshilov was its only military member, and his influence
declined sharply after his failure as commander of the Leningrad front
in summer 1941. For a Soviet institution, the GKO was unusually
informal in its methods of working. Meetings were held frequently,
often at the shortest notice, and without written agendas or minutes.
Besides GKO members, participants included other Politburo and
Central Committee members, regional Party secretaries, people's commissars and specialists in the areas under discussion. Much of its power
was delegated to plenipotentiaries, while the detailed elaboration of its
policies tended to be left to to individuals. In the first year of the war
in particular, its members (as well as other Politburo members not in
the GKO) took direct individual responsibility for key sectors of industry: Malenkov for aircraft and tank production, Beriya for armament and munitions, for example. GKO plenipotentiaries were
frequently sent to investigate and resolve crises in the organisation of
the war effort. From the outset, business was also conducted through
committees (such as the Council for Evacuation and the Transport
Committee) whose role became ever more important as time went on.
In addition, local defence committees, similarly endowed with sweeping powers, were formed in more than seventy cities close to the front
line, though the GKO itself retained direct responsibility for the
defence of Moscow and Leningrad.

A crucial part of the GKO's role was coordinating the work of
different parts of the administrative structure. Important throughout
the war, this became crucial with the exodus of much of the central
Party and government apparatus from the capital in October 1941. As
the Germans drew close to Moscow, most personnel were evacuated
to destinations far in the rear: the Central Committee apparatus, Gosplan, and the Commissariat of Foreign Affairs to Kuibyshev, Finance
to Kazan, Iron and Steel to Gor'kii, Coal to Sverdlovsk, and so on.[7]
Some returned to the capital at the end of December 1941, but most
remained scattered for considerably longer, not returning to Moscow
until summer 1943.

7 Kumanev 1988: 105.

The GKO had only a small staff; its decisions were largely implemented through the government and Party apparatuses. With the subordination of both to the GKO, the distinction between their functions, which had always overlapped but had been kept formally distinct, diminished still further during the war. In the process, the significance of two of the main parts of the Soviet political system, the Communist Party and the elected soviets, declined. The Party's central bodies ceased to have any important decision-making function. The Politburo met irregularly, and the Central Committee only once, in January 1944, while there were no Party conferences or congresses for the duration of the war. The Secretariat of the Central Committee continued to be a key link in the political system, but only in an administrative capacity. The national legislature, the Supreme Soviet, and its Presidium, were reduced, even more than before the war, to rubber-stamping decisions taken elsewhere. The importance of government bodies – Sovnarkom, the people's commissariats, Gosplan – on the other hand was enhanced, since they had much of the practical responsibility for implementing GKO decisions.

Whether streamlining the decision-making process resulted in more efficient government during the war, however, is doubtful. The GKO system provided an indisputable source of authority as well as coordination between different administrative heirarchies. But it did not eliminate the conflict of departmental interests, the arbitrary and often damaging interference of powerful individuals, or the delays resulting from bureaucrats' notorious unwillingness to take decisions. Plenipotentiaries were not an administrative panacea, since those of the GKO could clash with those of Sovnarkom or of individual commissariats or of regional Party committees. Effective in dealing with crises and in concentrating the country's resources on the task of achieving victory, the wartime system of government may have been; efficient in the use of human and material resources it was not.

CENTRAL–LOCAL RELATIONS

Even before the war, relations between central and local authorities were often difficult. Despite the purges and the use of terror against recalcitrant local officials, the centre's orders were frequently only partly fulfilled or simply ignored altogether. War greatly exacerbated the problems of translating Moscow's will into action at the local level.

The immense administrative tasks of extracting vast quantities of materials and manpower from the economy and the population, coping with major dislocations to the transport and communications network and the supply system, organising a massive evacuation of plant and population, and later restoring order in the devastated liberated areas, had to be carried out by a diminished and weakened body of officials. Mass mobilisation of Communists for military or political service in the armed forces, including the departure of large numbers of Party and state cadres for the front, produced a chronic shortage of qualified personnel in local government. Many primary Party organisations ceased to exist, while it was often impossible to fill the executive committees (*ispolkomy*) of local soviets, as the law required, from the ranks of elected deputies.

Campaigns were launched to recruit new members to the Party and promote new people into the local apparatus, but standards of recruitment inevitably had to be lowered. The result is described in a recent Soviet history of wartime administration.

> Lack of experience of work, the difficulty and variety of the tasks which cadres of the soviets had to solve, poor knowledge of legislation, and at times inadequate political and general educational standards, created additional difficulties in the work of local organs of state power, and were some of the reasons for the large turnover of leading cadres.[8]

The centre responded to this situation by strengthening its own authority and power, particularly through the creation of the GKO. It made wide use of plenipotentiaries to implement its policies in the localities and to provide itself with reliable information. But there were limits to its capacity to direct local affairs, especially far in the rear, and it was obliged to devolve substantial responsibilities to local cadres. The evacuation of industrial plant and personnel between July and December 1941 is a case in point. While in theory all important decisions had to be taken by the Council for Evacuation or its plenipotentiaries, such was the extreme urgency of the operation that in practice many were taken on the spot by local authorities without reference to the centre.[9] In industry, managers had much more control over the running of their enterprises than before the war. And in the organisation of food supply, central government transferred much of the responsibility for feeding the civilian population to the local authorities.[10]

8 Mitrofanova 1989: 247.
9 Harrison 1985: 72, 79.
10 See p. 83.

Relations between central and local government during the war were therefore characterised by a combination of central control and local autonomy. The balance varied according to a region's distance from the centre, and its economic or strategic importance. It also changed over time, with a marked centralising trend towards the end of the war. But its main significance lay in the ability of the Soviet system to adapt to critical circumstances. Flexibility rather than extreme centralisation was the key to the successful organisation of the Soviet war effort.

THE HIGH COMMAND

The outbreak of war produced a rapid reorganisation of the military command structure. Its inadequacy had been immediately revealed by the German attack. One reason why the invasion was not met by a coordinated Soviet response, why Moscow at first had virtually no control over Soviet front-line forces, why for many days Soviet resistance consisted of centres of fierce fighting rather than a solid front, was the absence of any effective command organisation at the centre. Nothing had been done to provide strategic leadership in the event of war. While a Chief Military Council under the Commissariat of Defence determined general military policy, and a General Staff planned operations, there was no single body to formulate strategy and direct operations.

A high command was hurriedly improvised. On 23 June 1941, a 'General Headquarters (*Stavka*) of the High Command' was established. Headed by the Commissar of Defence, Marshal Timoshenko, its members included Stalin, the Chief of the General Staff, the marshals of the USSR, and the heads of naval and air forces. With Timoshenko immediately departing for the front, and Stalin preoccupied with other matters, more time went by before an effective organisation emerged. Eventually on 10 July the Stavka was renamed 'Stavka of the Supreme Command', with Stalin as Chairman. Commissar of Defence from 19 July, he became Supreme Commander on 8 August, and as such Chairman of 'the Stavka of the Supreme Commander of the Soviet Armed Forces'.[11]

11 Erickson 1975: 136 ff. On the functioning of the command structure during the war, see also Erickson 1982, Bialer 1970 and Shtemenko 1970.

The State in Wartime

The Stavka functioned as the highest organ of strategic and military command. While the work of detailed planning, intelligence gathering and assessment, and briefing the Supreme Commander was carried out by the General Staff, all important decisions about the preparation and conduct of operations were taken by the Stavka. A continuous stream of orders flowed from Stalin's office, the centre of its activity. Although its members, with the exception of Stalin and Molotov, were senior military personnel, the principle of political control over the armed forces, which had been laid down by Lenin at the start of the Civil War, was applied from beginning to end of World War II. Stalin's chairmanship of the GKO and Stavka, the presence of GKO members at Stavka meetings, the vesting of authority at the front in Military Soviets, headed by marshals but also including Politburo members – all were designed to ensure a unified and politically obedient high command. And to reinforce government control at all levels of the military heirarchy, political commissars were reintroduced into the armed forces in July 1941.

The military commanders were not, however, merely the executors of the political leadership's will. As the war turned in the Soviet Union's favour, their prestige and confidence grew. With millions of civilians and servicemen, as well as large areas of liberated territory, under their control, with first claim on economic resources and production, and with direct involvement in both industry and agriculture, they were in a position to exert substantial influence on the political leadership. The abolition of political commissars in October 1942, together with the reintroduction of ranks and the creation of new military orders for officers in 1942–3, clearly reflected their enhanced status. The battle of Stalingrad, moreover, marked a turning point in Stalin's willingness to listen to expert military opinion. Increasingly, senior military figures such as Antonov, Shaposhnikov, Vasilevskii and Zhukov made Stavka a collective organ of strategic leadership. For all this, ultimate authority in military affairs remained with the political leadership right up to the end of the war. Despite the objections of some in the high command, Berlin was taken by storm with heavy losses, Stalin successfully exploiting in the process Konev's and Zhukov's rivalry to be the first to reach the German capital.

THE SECURITY ORGANS

Although the war years saw no repetition of the mass terror of the late

1930s, the secret police remained as important an institution, and repression as basic an instrument of government, as before.[12] Given the problems of maintaining social order against the background of the traumatic defeats in the first year of the war and the hardships inflicted on the population, this was not surprising. The war created new threats, real or imaginary, to state security. From the outset, the NKVD was engaged in arresting all those suspected of disloyalty or indiscipline, at the front or in the rear. It was also the agent of retribution for failure. While for most of the war the Party and state apparatus was not subjected to widespread purging, the threat of punishment was ever-present: 'repression, unjustified expulsion from the Party and punishment for not fulfilling various, sometimes impossible tasks, continued.'[13] And in the latter stages of the war, several people's commissariats were purged, notably the Commissariat of Communications in March 1944.[14]

As time went on, the NKVD's activity increasingly focused on Soviet citizens who had been in German hands and were suspected of treason. Civilians who had lived in the occupied territories, prisoners of war who returned, even soldiers who had been temporarily cut off from their units, were automatically investigated and in many cases arrested. The largest category of repressions consisted of the national minorities deported to Central Asia or Siberia, supposedly to prevent or punish collaboration with the enemy: Soviet Germans at the beginning of the war, and from 1943 onwards, Crimean Tartars and small nationalities from the Caucasus. Among others who attracted considerable attention from the security organs were the foreign nationals trapped in the USSR by the war, particularly the Poles.

Coercion, repression and control, however, were not the only important functions of the NKVD. It also played a key role in the economy, supplying huge quantities of forced labour to industry and agriculture, and managing high-priority and high-security branches of industry; it had a major part in operations such as the evacuation of industry; and it was involved in many aspects of military organisation, including the partisans, the people's volunteers, and the penal battalions.

---

12 While the NKVD (People's Commissariat of Internal Affairs) headed by Beriya was the prime organ of political repression throughout the war, in the first month and from April 1943 onwards, some of its functions were shared with the NKGB (People's Commissariat of State Security) under Merkulov.

13 Mitrofanova 1989: 231.

14 Medvedev 1989: 778.

Altogether the NKVD's role in government, far from declining, may well have been enhanced by the war. It was not accidental that, although only a non-voting member of the Politburo, Beriya was on the GKO from the beginning. Nor is it surprising that the bulk of Stalin's time during the war, according to his Soviet biographer, was devoted to NKVD and military affairs, or that reports from Beriya and other security chiefs and memoranda to them comprised the largest part of his correspondence.[15]

STALIN AND THE SOVIET LEADERSHIP

In the first few days of the war, Stalin's position as Soviet leader was potentially highly vulnerable. His foreign policy had collapsed, and the disastrous consequences of the Soviet Union's lack of military preparedness were clearly visible. Such was his authority, however, that even now there was no challenge from the other members of the Politburo. From the moment he resumed active leadership, Stalin exercised greater control over his country's war effort than any other national leader in World War II, including Hitler. He occupied all the key posts in the civilian and military command structure: Chairman of the GKO and the Stavka, Commissar of Defence and Supreme Commander, General Secretary of the Communist Party and Prime Minister (Chairman of Sovnarkom). All lines of information and command ran directly to him. His involvement in the detailed planning, monitoring and direction of military operations, as well as in the running of the economy and the conduct of diplomacy, was continuous and decisive.

As war leader, Stalin displayed to the full the determination to achieve his objectives at all costs which had marked his policies and his consolidation of power in the 1920s and 1930s. His expenditure of military and civilian lives in pursuit of victory was, from beginning to end, profligate, and was one of the main reasons for the enormous Soviet losses. His treatment of failure was brutal. The execution in July 1941 of General Pavlov and others blamed for the initial disasters showed senior Soviet officers what they could expect in defeat; while his refusal to countenance surrender under any circumstances or to allow the International Red Cross to make contact with Soviet prison-

15 Volkogonov vol 2(ii) 1989: 130.

ers of war left the latter without any defence against their savage treatment in German camps.

Stalin repeatedly used his position as head of the GKO and Stavka to impose his own views regardless of the opinions of colleagues and advisers, General Staff or commanders in the field, although his judgement on military matters was far from infallible. He had been involved in major campaigns during the Civil War as a Politburo representative at the front, but he was essentially an amateur in strategic and operational matters—though one whose intervention could have dire consequences. Besides the catastrophic results of his miscalculation of Hitler's intentions in the months preceding the invasion, there was also the huge cost of his mistakes after the outbreak of war – his obsession with counterattacking at the earliest opportunity, his slowness in adopting a strategy of defence in depth, his extreme reluctance to allow Soviet troops to retreat, however hopeless their position, his support for military formations of highly questionable value, such as light cavalry divisions, as well as his constant interference in the detail of military operations. The Soviet Union's defeats cannot, of course, be blamed simply on its leader's errors. In Germany, it faced a highly efficient and ruthless enemy. For all this, Stalin's decisions, often made against the best military advice, were directly responsible for some of the worst disasters of 1941–2: including the loss of huge numbers of troops at Kiev in September 1941 and in the Vyazma region in October, the encirclement of Leningrad and the near capture of Moscow, the failure of the Soviet counteroffensive in early summer 1942 (resulting in the loss of Khar'kov, the Kerch peninsular and Rostov-on-Don), and the German advance to the Volga and almost to the Caspian. But for Stalin, it may well be argued, the Germans would never have reached Moscow or Leningrad, the Caucasus or Stalingrad.

While he frequently accused others of cowardice or treason, Stalin himself, according to recent accounts by Soviet historians, may well have attempted to take the ultimate step of capitulation to the enemy. In October 1941, he is said to have offered Germany the Baltic republics, Moldavia and a significant part of Belorussia and the Ukraine in exchange for peace. Hitler, confident of total victory, supposedly showed no interest in the proposal. It may, in any case, only have been a manoeuvre to buy time (as suggested by Molotov's description of it as a 'second Brest', recalling Lenin's decision to make peace with

Germany on humiliating terms in March 1918).[16] But at the very least, this episode indicates that behind Stalin's image of implacable hostility to the invaders and iron determination to defend the Soviet motherland lay more complicated motives and intentions.

Yet some credit for the Soviet Union's ultimate victory undoubtedly belongs to Stalin. He learnt from his mistakes, particularly after the disasters of 1942. He demoted, if belatedly, incompetent cronies from the Civil War period like Marshals Budennyi and Voroshilov, as well as ruthless political appointees in the Red Army such as Kulik and Mekhlis. He gradually mastered complex areas of strategy and logistics. (After meeting him in October 1944 General Sir Alan Brooke, the ablest British strategist of World War II, came away 'more than ever impressed by the dictator's military ability.')[17] At critical moments, the speeches, proclamations, orders of the day – such as the broadcast of 3 July 1941, the speech in Red Square on 7 November 1941 and the Order No 227 ('Not a step back') of 28 July 1942 to the Red Army – inspired millions of Soviet combatants and civilians to fight on. Whatever the means employed, he ensured the unity of the Soviet government and its total commitment to defeating Nazism. Stalin's contribution to Soviet victory may have been less than his propagandists claimed, but it was substantial none the less.

At the same time, others in the Soviet leadership also played major roles. Molotov, Deputy Chairman of the GKO and Commissar of Foreign Affairs, was primarily responsible for the conduct of diplomacy. Voznesenskii was effectively in charge of economic planning throughout the war, from December 1942 as head of Gosplan; he was also, as head of Sovnarkom in Kuibyshev, responsible for much of the government apparatus following its evacuation in October 1941. Zhdanov and Khrushchev, as the senior political figures on the Military Soviets of the northern and south-western fronts respectively, were heavily involved in the conduct of the war. With much of Stalin's time devoted to GKO and Stavka business, supervision of governmental administration was largely left to the Deputy Chairmen of

16 Pavlenko 1989: 9. Volkogonov vol 2(i) 1989: 172–3 also describes Stalin, Molotov and Beriya making the Soviet peace offer, but improbably gives its date as the end of the first week of the war. The main evidence that Stalin in effect proposed surrender comes from Beriya's interrogation after his arrest in June 1953, or rather from the recollections of one of his interrogators. This is obviously not the most reliable of sources. On the other hand, it would not be surprising if the Soviet government had explored the possibility of making peace with Nazi Germany in October 1941. In similarly dire circumstances following the collapse of France in May 1940, the British cabinet discussed coming to an agreement with Hitler.

17 Seaton 1975: 232–3.

Sovnarkom, particularly Andreev, Kosygin, Mikoyan and Voznesenskii. Mikoyan played a key role in organising the supply of food, goods and raw materials, as did Kaganovich in transport administration. The Central Committee Secretariat, the linchpin of the Party apparatus, was run by Malenkov, and the ubiquitous NKVD by Beriya.[18]

One effect of the war was to accelerate change in the leadership's composition. The GKO's initial membership was notable for the fact that, besides Stalin and two of his oldest allies, Molotov and Voroshilov, it included two younger, recently appointed candidate members of the Politburo, Malenkov and Beriya, who were promoted over several full members. Although two of the latter, Kaganovich and Mikoyan, were coopted in February 1942, so also was Voznesenskii, another younger candidate member, while in 1944 Voroshilov was replaced by Bulganin, not a Politburo member at all.

None of this diminished Stalin's influence, however; on the contrary, his accumulation of major responsibilities, together with the enormous prestige which the Red Army's victories in time brought him, made his predominance even greater during the war than before it.

18 Accounts of the wartime roles of Beriya, Kaganovich, Khrushchev, Malenkov, Mikoyan, Molotov and Voroshilov, are given in Medvedev 1983 and Volkogonov vol 2(i) 1989. Voznesenskii's role is described in Harrison 1985. For contrasting descriptions of Kosygin, see Granin 1988 and Kravchenko 1947.

PART TWO

Soviet Society at War

CHAPTER FOUR
Mobilisation

'ALL FOR THE FRONT!'

Despite the shock of an invasion that its government had declared impossible up to the last moment, and despite Nazi Germany's record of military triumphs in western and central Europe, the Soviet population initially reacted to the outbreak of war with calmness and confidence. Inevitably there were exceptions. At the front, as the German forces poured across the frontier, although some units fought heroically, confusion and panic gripped many soldiers and civilians. In policy-making circles, officials who had vainly warned of Germany's preparations for an all-out attack on the USSR now watched in dismay as their worst fears were realised. Reports from regional Party committees to the Central Committee about the population's responses to the war mentioned cases of anti-Soviet statements, drunkenness and arson.[1] But among the population as a whole, most people believed what government propaganda for years had taught them to accept unquestioningly: that in the event of enemy attack, the superiority of socialism and the invincibility of the Red Army guaranteed a speedy Soviet victory. The question in many people's minds was not whether the USSR would win, but how soon; not how far the Red Army would retreat, but how far it would carry the war into enemy territory.

'Who do they think they are attacking? Have they gone out of their minds?' . . . 'Of course, the German workers will support us, and all

1 For reports from the front to Stalin and the high command in the first days of the war, see *Nachalo voiny* 1990: 196 ff.

59

other peoples will rise up' . . . 'Our men will hit them so hard, it will all be over in a week', said one worker. 'Well, it won't necessarily be finished in one week', answered another. 'They've got to get to Berlin . . . . It will take three or four weeks.'[2]

Official statements at first reinforced this optimism. In his broadcast to the population on 22 June, Molotov confined himself to expressing the government's outrage at Germany's perfidious attack and its certainty of victory. 'Our cause is just. The enemy will be beaten. We shall triumph.' Stalin himself initially believed that Hitler had committed an incredible blunder.[3] For several days bulletins from the front reported only that the Red Army was inflicting heavy casualties on the enemy, giving no indication of the disasters overwhelming Soviet forces.

Ordinary people meanwhile rallied to their country's defence with a rapidity which showed that years of Stalinist controls had not destroyed their capacity for independent action. Although 22 June was a Sunday and the majority were not working, many people spontaneously went to their factory or office after hearing Molotov's broadcast. There they held meetings, pledged their loyalty to the motherland, the Soviet Union and Stalin, and in many cases worked an extra shift. Without waiting to be called up, large numbers of reservists immediately reported for military service. Many others whose age, profession or gender exempted them from conscription volunteered to go to the front none the less: 100,000 in Leningrad alone by the afternoon of 23 June, and 212,000 by the end of the first week.[4] In the town of Krasnoyarsk, 2,632 volunteered on 26 June, including 1,162 women.[5]

Despite its slowness to grasp the scale of the conflict now unfolding, the country's leadership lost no time in introducing emergency measures of mobilisation. On 22 June, a decree of the Supreme Soviet called up all reservists born between 1905 and 1918, except those from Central Asia, Transbaikal and the Far East (the 1919–22 cohort was already in the armed forces). On the same day, martial law was declared in regions close to the front line; two days later it was extended to the entire European part of the USSR. An emergency labour draft was also decreed on 22 June. All able-bodied men aged between 18 and 45 and women aged between 18 and 40 who were not already employed were ordered to work eight hours a day on defence con-

2 Kulagin 1978: 17, cited in Kozlov VA 1989: 128.
3 Volkogonov vol 2(i) 1989: 154 ff.
4 Bidlack 1987: 50.
5 Nachalo voiny 1990: 210.

struction.[6] At the same time, government bodies were given the power to transfer employees to work in war industry. On 26 June, the length of working time was significantly increased. Overtime of up to three hours a day (or two hours for juveniles aged between 12 and 16) was made mandatory if required by management, and leave and holiday entitlement were cancelled.[7]

These were serious measures; but their initial implementation was piecemeal, as managers and workers attempted to come to terms with the new situation. In some factories, workers stood idle, waiting for new assignments. As news of the Red Army's retreat trickled back from the front, however, optimism changed to alarm and the sense of crisis deepened. On 29 June a joint resolution of the Sovnarkom and Central Committee signalled a clear change in the official line on the war. Attacking complacency, it called for the total mobilisation of the country's resources, a scorched earth policy and partisan warfare in the enemy's rear. But for most people, Stalin's broadcast on 3 July was the first public confirmation of the gravity of the crisis. It was not merely by addressing his listeners as 'brothers and sisters' as well as 'comrades and citizens' that Stalin broke with the past; more important, it was by confronting the population with the stark reality of the situation.

> the enemy continues to push forward . . . A grave danger hangs over our country . . . It is essential that our people . . . should appreciate the full immensity of the danger that threatens our country . . . The issue is one of life and death for the Soviet state, for the peoples of the USSR; the issue is whether the peoples of the Soviet Union shall remain free or fall into slavery ... All our work must be immediately reconstructed on a war footing, everything must be subordinated to the interests of the front and the task of organizing the demolition of the enemy.[8]

The broadcast was undoubtedly a turning point. Although it demanded heavy sacrifices from the population, it had a vital rallying effect: 'it raised the morale of a whole country.'[9] It unified the government's and the public's perceptions of the war. 'The truth he uttered was a bitter truth, but at last it was uttered, and people felt they stood more firmly on the ground.'[10]

From now on, the principle of 'all for the front' determined the lives of all members of Soviet society. The mobilisation decrees of the first days of the war were urgently implemented. Millions of people

6 Mitrofanova 1984: 167.
7 Resheniya vol 3 1968: 37–8.
8 Stalin 1945: 9–14.
9 Karol 1986: 76.
10 Konstantin Simonov, cited in Werth 1964: 166.

were conscripted into the armed forces, or enrolled in para-military units, or drafted into defence industry, or sent into the countryside in a desperate attempt to bring in the harvest before the Germans arrived.

One of the most striking forms of civilian mobilisation in the summer and autumn of 1941 was the mass employment of labour conscripts in building defence fortifications. Hundreds of thousands of inhabitants of cities in danger of being taken by the Germans were dispatched to nearby areas to dig trenches, bunkers, tank-traps, or erect pill-boxes, fire-points, observation points, barricades. From the end of July to the end of August, up to 1 million Leningraders, at least one-third of its working-age population, were employed on defence construction, mainly along the Luga Line.[11] In Belorussia, at the beginning of September there were said to be over 2 million people engaged in such work, though without any engineers to help them.[12] Similar large-scale efforts occurred at Kiev, Moscow and other major cities. Some of those involved were workers released from their factories for this high-priority work; but many, probably most, were housewives or young people still at school or college. Drafted at a day or two's notice, provided with minimal food or shelter, and ill-equipped, they worked, often round the clock, for days or weeks on end until their assignments were completed. Sometimes close to the front line, always in danger of being bombed or strafed by enemy planes, they suffered casualties as well as hardships.[13] In the event, their efforts often failed to stop the enemy; but at least they bought valuable time by slowing the pace of its advance and exacting a higher price for it.

Despite the substantial mobilisation of the work-force in the first months of the war, the deterioration of the economic situation by the end of 1941 forced the government to take on still greater powers to cope with the high labour turnover and manpower shortage. To the right to direct labour where most needed was now added the ability to keep it there. A decree of 26 December declared all employees in the defence industry, and in enterprises supplying it, mobilised for the duration of the war. They were now explicitly 'tied to the enterprises employing them'. Leaving employment without permission was punishable by imprisonment for five to eight years.[14] Seven weeks later, the labour draft was widened still further. A decree of 13 February mobilised all able-bodied men aged between 16 and 55 and women

11 Bidlack 1987: 107.
12 *Izvestiya TsK KPSS* (10) 1990: 210.
13 See for example Werth 1964: 241.
14 Kozlov VA 1989: 134.

aged between 16 and 45 (later changed to 16–50) not already working in state enterprises or establishments for work in industry or construction.[15] Only 16–18 year olds receiving vocational training, students in higher or secondary education, and mothers with several children were exempted. Avoidance of the labour draft was now a criminal offence. The mobilisation of the urban population for agricultural labour was also extended in spring 1942. Local authorities were given powers 'at the time of most intensive agricultural work' to mobilise 'all categories of the population whose absence would not negatively affect industrial production.'[16]

By September 1942, however, even these measures would seem inadequate to a government facing the prospect of defeat. With the Germans at Stalingrad and in the Caucasus, a decree was issued which paralleled on the home front the draconian Order No 227 of 28 July to the Red Army. Employees in all state enterprises and establishments 'located close to the front' who left their jobs without permission were now declared 'deserters', to be tried by military tribunal. In April 1943, the work-force on the railways was also placed under martial law, as was later that on river and marine transport.[17]

Thus was the labour draft reinforced by the threat of summary justice and the Gulag. Such was the legal framework within which the Soviet population was mobilised for the war effort.

DISCIPLINE

An essential precondition of successful mobilisation was political and social stability; but in the first year of the war this was put in serious jeopardy by military defeat and by the steep decline in the living conditions of the population. There was a real danger of the state's authority collapsing and society descending into chaos. The German invasion had created a major crisis of legitimacy for the government. Why should people obey rulers who had proved incapable of protecting them from the ravages of war? Why should they continue to follow leaders whose ability to carry the war to a victorious conclusion was so much in doubt? The disasters of 1941 and 1942 provided fertile soil for the growth of defeatist attitudes. With German military supe-

15 Kozlov VA 1988: 147.
16 Kozlov VA 1989: 147, 291 n.z.
17 Conquest 1967: 106.

riority apparently so obvious, resistance could easily seem pointless. A letter to the Soviet president, Mikhail Kalinin, from a woman teacher in summer 1941 reflected the confusion and despair which were then widespread.

> Thousands of mobilised men from various places which have already been captured and from near the frontline zone go from place to place. They lack any purpose, any sense of order. They have no uniforms, twenty per cent are barefoot . . . Some say 'we have no arms or equipment, German technology is invincible. Share out the grain, it will be wasted otherwise, share out the cattle.' People are extremely worried. The leaders are leaving . . . and they are abandoning us to ruin.[18]

The ultimate effect of such attitudes, as the authorities were well aware, could be not simply a weakening of people's willingness to work and fight for victory, but the complete breakdown of law and order. Nowhere was this danger more clearly shown than in Moscow in the middle of October 1941. As the Germans approached the capital, most government and Party organisations hurriedly began to evacuate their personnel. With officials and their families leaving Moscow in droves, looting and food riots broke out, and a spontaneous exodus took place. For three or four days, Moscow was in the grip of mass panic verging on anarchy. At its root was the fear that the government had abandoned the population to its fate – which was not far from the truth. The situation at the headquarters of the Soviet government on 16 October was described many years later in the reminiscences of Alexei Kosygin, in wartime a Deputy Chairman of Sovnarkom.

> The Sovnarkom building was empty – the doors of offices swung open, papers blew around and rustled underfoot, everywhere telephones rang. Kosygin ran from room to room, answering the phone. No-one spoke at the other end. Silence. He understood: they were checking whether there was anyone in the Kremlin . . . One of those who rang identified himself. It was a well-known person. In a businesslike way, he enquired, 'Well then, are we going to surrender Moscow?'[19]

Eventually the situation was brought under control by the heroism of the Red Army and people's militia divisions defending Moscow and by the ruthless punishment of looters. But the panic in Moscow was not a unique phenomenon; it would be repeated elsewhere, nowhere more dramatically than in Rostov-on-Don on the eve of its capture by the Germans in July 1942.

The government fought the danger of a collapse of morale and

18 Cited in Volkogonov vol 2(i) 1989: 215.
19 Granin 1988: 122.

authority with weapons well tested in the prewar years: tight control over information and severe repression of any suspected threat to public order. From the outset it established a monopoly over the public dissemination of news, and used it to withhold any information which might damage morale. An order was immediately issued for all private radios to be handed in to the local authorities. The only regular source of information about the war was Sovinformburo (the Soviet Information Bureau), whose main function was to relay communiqués from the Stavka. Like any government-run news agency in wartime, it consistently minimised defeats and exaggerated successes; but it did so to an extent that often completely concealed the true state of affairs. Major disasters were glossed over or even portrayed as Soviet successes. Reports that fighting was taking place 'in the direction' of a particular city in 1941 and 1942 frequently meant that the latter had already fallen to the enemy. And official estimates of Soviet and German casualties bore little relation to reality, such as the claim in June 1942 that the Germans had lost 10 million killed or wounded over the previous year, compared with Soviet losses of 4.5 million.[20] At no time during the war was the public given an indication of the real losses suffered by the Red Army or the scale of civilian suffering and deaths. News about conditions in besieged Leningrad, for instance, where hundreds of thousands of people starved to death in the winter of 1941–2, was totally suppressed until the following spring, and even then the tragedy was only hinted at. The titanic battle at Stalingrad was reported in minimal detail until the late stages when Soviet victory was assured. Foreign reporters were able to give their readers and listeners a much fuller picture of events at the front than the Soviet population was allowed.

Attempts to prevent bad news reaching the public had limited success. Although the private circulation of news was also restricted – personal correspondence was censored, private telephones were disconnected, and anyone making unguarded remarks ran the risk of denunciation for anti-Soviet propaganda under Article 58 of the RSFSR Criminal Code – it was impossible to prevent news spreading by word of mouth. Refugees from the occupied areas were inevitably bearers of information about Soviet defeats, which was one reason why they were banned from entering Moscow and Leningrad in 1941. Wounded soldiers convalescing in the rear were well able to contradict official communiqués about Soviet successes.[21] Although it might take

20 Werth 1964: 401–2.
21 Karol 1986: 131.

some time for news to reach the provinces – it would be two months before people in Kislovodsk in southern Russia heard about the Moscow panic, for example – it usually got there in the end.[22]

The price of tight censorship was public scepticism about official communiqués and the spread of rumours which could be even more threatening to morale than the truth would have been. The panic in Moscow was fuelled by wild reports that there had been a coup, Stalin had been arrested, German parachutists had landed in Red Square, and German troops were in Moscow wearing Red Army uniforms.[23] Concealing the real state of affairs at the front from the public could also have dire consequences for people living in areas close to the front line. Unaware of the closeness of the German army, many lost the opportunity to escape, and were condemned to live (and die) under German occupation. In the case of Leningrad, the government delayed recognising the seriousness of the threat to the city until it was far too late to save its inhabitants or to let them save themselves. The order to begin evacuating women and children was given on 29 August 1941, the day before the rail link with the rest of the country was cut and only a week before the city was completely encircled.[24]

Fear of a fifth column and apprehension about a general breakdown of discipline resulted in the immediate repression of anyone suspected of endangering public order. In his speech of 3 July 1941, Stalin demanded a ruthless fight against 'all disorganizers of the rear, deserters, panic-mongers, rumor-mongers'. He declared that 'all who by their panic-mongering and cowardice hinder the work of defense, no matter who they may be, must be immediately hauled before the military tribunal.'[25]

This was no empty threat. Even before Stalin's speech, the NKVD had rounded up people with a record of political opposition.[26] The first execution for spreading rumours was reported in Leningrad at the beginning of July.[27] According to one source, thousands were shot in Moscow alone during the first six months of the war.[28] This is not impossible: confronted with the crisis in the capital in mid-October 1941, the government resorted to extreme measures. A state of siege was declared, while a decree issued on 19 October stated that all

22 Karol 1986: 100.
23 Kravchenko 1947: 375.
24 *Izvestiya TsK KPSS* (9) 1990: 211.
25 Stalin 1945: 14–15.
26 Beginning on 22 June itself, according to Kravchenko 1947: 355.
27 Bidlack 1987: 69.
28 Kravchenko 1947: 356.

breaches of law and order were to be dealt with by emergency tribunals, and that 'all provocateurs, spies and other agents of the enemy are to be shot on the spot.' With the NKVD given the leading role in implementing the decree, it is likely to have been carried out to the letter.[29]

Ruthless as this was, it was in line with the general policy of severe retribution for any behaviour, whatever its motive, which in any way might help the enemy. In this respect, civilians and soldiers were treated alike. Just as surrender was regarded as a betrayal of the motherland, just as 'special sections' were stationed behind troops to arrest or shoot any who retreated without permission, just as officers who retreated without permission were handed over to military tribunals for punishment,[30] so civilians whose actions weakened the collective will to destroy the enemy were also liable to extreme penalties.

A typical example of this attitude can be seen in Stalin's order of 21 September 1941 to the Leningrad command. He denounced as 'more dangerous than German fascists' those who declined to open fire on captured Soviet civilians who were being forced to plead for peace.

> It is said that the German scoundrels approaching Leningrad are sending ahead of their troops old men and old women, women and children, delegates from areas occupied by them to ask the Bolsheviks to surrender Leningrad and make peace. My advice is: don't be sentimental, but hit the enemy and his auxiliaries, willing or unwilling, in the teeth. War is merciless, and it will bring defeat in the first instance to him who shows weakness and vacillation . . . No mercy to the Germans and their delegates, whoever they may be.[31]

Whatever their drawbacks, the controls imposed on the civilian population helped to prevent the breakdown of morale and public order in the most critical periods of the war – although less by crushing the panic-mongers depicted in propaganda than by demonstrating to the population the leadership's determination to achieve victory whatever the cost. This may well have also had a positive effect on popular attitudes to the country's leaders. Ultimately, however, it would be the hard-won victories of the Red Army and the productive achievements of the home front which would preserve both national unity and the legitimacy of the government.

---

29 Kravchenko 1947: 377, Werth 1964: 241.
30 See Stalin's Order No 270 of 12 August 1941, in *Izvestiya TsK KPSS* (9) 1990: 202.
31 Volkogonov vol 2(i) 1989: 64.

PROPAGANDA

The powers of control and coercion at the disposal of the authorities only partly explain the successful mobilisation of the Soviet population in wartime. People's contribution to their country's struggle for survival went far beyond what they were obliged by law to do. Much more than fear of punishment caused millions to make great sacrifices, endure terrible hardships, work to the point of exhaustion, fight on despite the hopelessness of the situation. Motives were many, including patriotism, political conviction, kinship, determination to liberate their native region, hatred of the enemy, desire for revenge – and simply the wish to survive. In essence, these were spontaneous reactions to war. But they were also strongly affected by the government's efforts to influence people's perception of the war, of what was at stake in it, so as to achieve maximum popular participation in the war effort.

From their earliest days, Bolsheviks had stressed the importance of propaganda in developing the consciousness of the masses and after the Revolution had created a wide variety of mechanisms to assure their ideological hegemony. By 1941 the government had at its disposal many effective means of communicating its policies to the public. The most important was the agitation and propaganda apparatus of the Communist Party. As one of the main functions of the Party, agitprop was provided with personnel at every level of its organisation: activists with special responsibilities at the grass-roots level of the Party cell, and departments, secretaries, officials, full-time agitators and propagandists at the higher levels. With Party cells in virtually every factory, farm, office and institute organising meetings and lectures, with 'Red Corners' providing literature and visual materials, and with regular visits by mobile agitprop brigades, Soviet citizens were exposed to a continual stream of Party propaganda. And this was not all. Other organisations, notably the trade unions and the Komsomol, were equally active at the work-place; while the press, radio and cinema, all subject to close government control and censorship, occupied a substantial proportion of most people's leisure time.

From the very beginning of the war, the central theme of Soviet propaganda was defence of the motherland. This immediately took precedence over all other subjects which had earlier predominated – socialism, Marxism-Leninism, the Party, internationalism, anti-imperialism, even anti-fascism (the latter in any case had been dropped after the signing of the Nazi–Soviet Pact in August 1939). In the first issue of *Pravda* following the German attack, the term 'patriotic war' (*otechestvennaya voina*) was used in several articles. One by Emel'yan Yaroslavskii, a leading Party propagandist, was actually entitled 'the Great Patriotic War of the Soviet People', the name by which the war would eventually come to be officially known.[32] This suggests that whatever illusions may have briefly lingered in Stalin's mind, it was quickly apparent to those responsible for gauging and influencing public opinion that the war was going to be fought on Soviet territory, at least for the foreseeable future. In this situation, appealing to the population to resist the alien occupation of its native land was likely to generate greater support than repeating conventional political slogans.

Patriotic themes had been conspicuous in ideology and propaganda from the mid-1920s onwards. Stalin's policy of 'Socialism in One Country' had given Bolshevism a markedly nationalist content, while in the years immediately preceding the war, the terms *rodina* (motherland) and *otechestvo* (fatherland) had come back into official usage. None the less, the impassioned reiteration of the patriotic theme after 22 June 1941 was unprecedented. Calls to 'rise to the defence of the motherland' echoed through every speech, meeting, broadcast and article. 'The motherland summons!' (*rodina-mat' zovyot!*) ran the slogan of the most famous Soviet recruiting poster of the war, designed by I M Toidze in 1941.[33] From the German invasion until the victory at Stalingrad, 'the motherland in danger' was the main focus of Soviet propaganda. Communism, by contrast, featured minimally in official exhortations.[34]

The exact character of the patriotism to which propaganda appealed varied, from 'Soviet patriotism', loyalty to the USSR, commitment to defending its territory, population and way of life, to a local patriotism focusing on people's native district, city or region. But by far the greatest emphasis was on the Russian motherland. With Russians comprising a substantial majority of the population engaged in the Soviet war effort, particularly after the German occupation of Belorussia, the Ukraine and the Baltic republics, this was natural, however much it might diverge from Marxist-Leninist doctrine. In private, Stalin was typically forthright on the subject. The Russian people, he told Averell

32 *Pravda* 23 June 1941.
33 White 1988: 123.
34 An analysis of agitation and propaganda speeches, brochures and articles in a Leningrad newspaper between December 1941 and January 1943 shows that the Party and Communism constituted only 13 out of the 328 topics covered. Much more common were such topics as the city's heroic traditions, great figures of the past, the exploits of the Red Army and German atrocities. Bidlack 1987: 231.

Harriman in September 1941, 'were fighting as they had "for their homeland, not for us", meaning the Communist Party.'[35]

The result was a conscious return to the Russian past for patriotic inspiration. Heroes of epic victories over foreign invaders from Dmitrii Donskoi and Alexander Nevsky onwards were presented as models for emulation. When new orders to mark military distinction were created in July 1942, they were named after great Russian commanders of the Tsarist period, Mikhail Kutuzov, Peter Nakhimov and Alexander Suvorov. The achievements of Russian culture were endlessly evoked as evidence of national greatness. Most striking of all in its break with former policy was the rehabilitation of the Orthodox Church. Stalin's reception of its head, Metropolitan Sergei, in the Kremlin in September 1943 and his approval of the revival of the Synod marked official recognition of the Church's importance as a symbol of continuity with Russian tradition, and of its substantial contribution to mobilising patriotic support for the war effort.

Contemporary themes also featured prominently in Soviet propaganda. The heroic feats of the Red Army and the partisans, together with the production achievements of workers and peasants, were given huge publicity; and the contribution of the Soviet Union's allies was periodically highlighted. The evil enemy inevitably provided one of the main subjects of propaganda. For a brief period a distinction was drawn between the Nazi regime and the German people. As evidence mounted, however, of the wanton destructiveness and brutality of the German army, especially with the Red Army's recapture of Soviet territory during the battle of Moscow, this gave way to hatred of Germans and a call for vengeance – for, in the words of the poet, Alexander Tvardovsky, 'death for death! blood for blood! grief for grief!'[36]

But one subject was continually to the fore. Just as in the 1930s, Stalin had been presented as the personification of Soviet socialism, so during the war he was made the symbol of the patriotic cause. Even in the first days of the war, when he made no public statement, let alone appearance, his name was invoked as the prime source of reassurance and inspiration. 'With Stalin's name we have triumphed, with Stalin's name we will triumph', was a typical headline. The public was exhorted to follow the example of 'our great leader, comrade Stalin', not least in being ready to confront the enemy: 'the great Stalin has continually taught our people mobilisation preparedness'. As early as 24 June, a report from the front quoted the battle cry which would be

35 Cited in McNeal 1988: 241.
36 Quoted in Piper 1984: 148.

attributed (albeit questionably) to Soviet soldiers throughout the war – 'for the motherland, for Stalin! (za *rodinu, za Stalina!*).'[37] His broadcast of 3 July was given much publicity; but this was exceeded by the paeons of praise with which the press greeted his appointment as People's Commissar of Defence on 19 July. 'The genius organiser of our victories', 'the great captain of the Soviet people' was now hailed as the 'symbol of great victories, symbol of the unity of the Soviet people.'[38]

It was as leader of the country, of the people as a whole, rather than as Party leader that Stalin appeared before the Soviet population during the war. Attention was focused on him far more as Chairman of the GKO, Chairman of Sovnarkom, Commissar of Defence and Supreme Commander in Chief than as General Secretary of the Party. The amount of publicity devoted to Stalin varied according to the progress of the war. While his image never disappeared from the press, it was less conspicuous when the Red Army was in retreat in summer and autumn 1941, and again in summer 1942, than when its fortunes were rising in the winters of 1941–2 and 1942–3, and thereafter. Stalin was careful to be identified with victory, not defeat. And at all times he went out of his way to associate himself with patriotic themes. In his 3 July broadcast he spoke of the 'patriotic war' and recalled Russian victories over the armies of Napoleon and Wilhelm II. In his speeches of 6 and 7 November to mark the anniversary of the Revolution, he went further, referring to 'the great Russian nation' and to 'our great ancestors – Alexander Nevsky, Dmitrii Donskoi, Kusma Minin, Dmitri Pozharsky, Alexander Suvorov, Mikhail Kutuzov.'[39] And after the victory at Stalingrad, he increasingly identified himself with the country's military achievements. Until this point references to the fact that Stalin was Supreme Commander-in-Chief had been few, and orders of the day, though composed by him, had often been signed by senior military figures. Now references to 'Stalinist strategy' and 'the Stalinist school of military doctrine' became common. He took the title of Marshal of the Soviet Union, and henceforth mainly appeared in public in military uniform. With its string of major Soviet victories, 1944 would be called the year of 'the ten Stalinist blows'. And at the end of the war Stalin's identification with the military reached its apogee with his assumption of the title previously awarded

37 *Pravda* 24, 27 June 1941. For an emphatic denial by the doyen of Soviet historians of World War II that Soviet troops did in fact charge into battle shouting this slogan, see Samsonov 1988: 142.

38 *Pravda* 20 July 1941.

39 Stalin 1945: 38.

only to the greatest Tsarist commanders, 'Generalissimus'.

The propaganda treatment of Stalin's image in wartime had much in common with that in the prewar period. In both cases the aim was to create what would later be called the 'cult of the personality'. There was, however, an important difference. During the war Stalin was identified with a cause commanding nearly universal support, and for the first time he gained real and widespread popularity. He became a focus for popular patriotism and a means of unifying the population. There were undoubtedly still many people who were hostile or indifferent to Stalin; and whatever positive effects his image may have had, it did not prevent people panicking or troops surrendering. Yet his image of strength and will projected through propaganda, as well as his specific actions, clearly had a great impact on morale at crucial moments. The significance of his Order No 227 in July 1942, at one of the worst moments of the war for the USSR, for example, is acknowledged even by a harsh critic of Stalin's wartime leadership. 'The Order was of course extremely severe, but necessary at that terrible moment. And the people themselves saw precisely the necessity and not the cruelty. For the first time for many years, people heard the truth.' And this historian quotes a soldier's account of his own reaction:

> All my life I will remember what Stalin's Order meant . . . Not the letter, but the spirit and the content of this document made possible the moral and psychological break-through in the hearts and minds of all to whom it was read . . . the chief thing was the courage to tell people the whole terrible and bitter truth about the abyss to whose edge we were then sliding.[40]

Stalin's effect on Soviet people's morale in 1941–2 was not unlike that of Churchill on the British population in 1940. He represented toughness, will and hope – hope of survival, hope of victory, hope against hope that the fate of millions of ordinary people mattered to those in power. Ilya Ehrenburg later recalled his own state of mind in July 1941. 'I believed in victory . . . because I needed to believe.'[41] For the same reason, people believed in Stalin – a feeling poignantly captured in Konstantin Simonov's poem 'Bleak anniversary', written at the beginning of November 1941. 'Comrade Stalin, do you hear us? You must hear us, we know this.'[42] Whatever the gap between image and reality in Stalin's role as war leader, his impact on people's beliefs

---

40 Cited by A M Samsonov in Istoriki 1988: 327.
41 Ehrenburg 1964: 11.
42 Simonov 1990: 316.

and attitudes, on their psychological mobilisation, was undeniably substantial.

THE PEOPLE'S MILITIA

Although separate processes, civilian and military mobilisation in practice overlapped in several areas, and nowhere more so than in the people's militia. Before the war, the idea of recruiting civilian volunteers into locally based military units (*opolchenie*) intended to provide the Red Army with support had played no part military planning. While civil defence would be organised locally, it was assumed that all military activities would come under the aegis of the Commissariat of Defence and the NKVD, and that all fighting would be done by the armed forces. The idea of volunteer military units was condemned as totally ineffective, as betraying a lack of confidence in the Red Army. In September 1939, Marshall Voroshilov recalled the fate of the 'weak and utterly untrained' Civilian Volunteer Army in World War I: 'it showed that hasty preparation in time of war was not very effective. Completely untrained people were sent to the front, and all of you know how it ended.'[43] In the event, such units came into existence almost immediately following the German invasion. Huge numbers of civilians volunteered for military service, and responsibility for their recruitment, organisation and equipment was assumed by local Party and soviet officials.

In the first instance, the formation of the militia was the result of popular patriotism and local initiative. Leningrad led the way. Thousands of the city's inhabitants volunteered to fight in the first days of the war, and on 27 June the local authorities took the decision to set up a volunteer army. Within three days, its commanding staff had been appointed, the selection of recruits from the masses of volunteers was under way, and the first units were being created.[44] By 8 July over 100,000 people had been enrolled in the militia, and by 10 July the first three volunteer divisions, with a fighting strength of over 30,000, were in existence.[45]

The idea was soon taken up in the capital, where the realisation that the war would stretch the Red Army's reserves to the limit was

43 Cited in Kravchenko 1947: 360–1.
44 Kolesnik 1988: 14.
45 Kolesnik 1988: 17.

rapidly dawning. In Moscow, the first formal steps to organise a local militia began on 2 July. The following day, in his broadcast to the nation, Stalin made the establishment of the militia official policy.

> Side by side with the Red Army, many thousands of workers, collective farmers, intellectuals are rising to fight the enemy aggressor. The masses of our people will rise up in their millions.
>
> The working people of Moscow and Leningrad have already commenced to form vast popular levies in support of the Red Army. Such popular levies must be raised in every city which is in danger of enemy invasion.[46]

Over the following weeks, the mass recruitment of volunteers and the organisation of militia units went ahead in every city in the European part of the USSR. From Murmansk to Krasnodar, from Smolensk to Stalingrad, hundreds of thousands of civilians were enlisted. (Eventually the militia would be raised everywhere except Central Asia, Kazakhstan and the Far East.) Manual workers provided the majority of volunteers – whole regiments being formed at major factories, such as the Kirov plant in Leningrad – but large contingents of white-collar workers, professional people, intellectuals and students were also recruited. The numbers involved were huge: by autumn 1941, there are said to have been over 4 million *opolchentsy*, on paper at least. Women as well as men volunteered: in Gor'kii, for example, the 60,000 volunteers by the end of the second week of the war included 16,500 women. In practice, there were neither fitness requirements nor official age limits on eligibility (in Moscow and Leningrad, limits of 17 to 50 and 18 to 55 were applied, but these were hardly restrictive). Previous military experience or training were certainly not conditions of entry: in Leningrad, virtually none of the recruits had served in the Red Army, and only half had even had elementary military training before enlisting.[47]

It is highly unlikely that all the 'volunteers' joined voluntarily. While the early ones almost certainly did, the situation changed once the establishment of the militia became official policy. Local Party organisations came under pressure to form militia units, and they correspondingly put pressure on potential recruits, particularly members of the Party or Komsomol, even when they were skilled workers specifically exempted from military service because of the economic importance of their work. Recruitment often took place at open meetings in factories, where the collective's influence on the individual could be decisive.[48] But the pressure was far from all one way. On one hand,

46 Stalin 1945: 16.
47 Kolesnik 1988: 10–11, 28, 51.

many civilians continued to be strongly motivated to volunteer for the militia. On the other hand, local Party officials, who were also responsible for seeing that production targets were met, could well understand that the loss of skilled personnel would damage plan fulfilment. Army recruitment desks at factories were said to be beseiged by workers insisting on joining up, despite the pleas of their managers and Party officials. Sometimes workers had to be literally dragged off trains taking them to the front.[49]

Few of the initial volunteers could have anticipated being involved in military action, at least in the immediate future. Anyone who volunteered in areas close to the front line, such as Smolensk in early July 1941, must have expected to see active service; but in the rear, volunteers would probably have envisaged themselves joining a home guard, which would be used in combat only as a last resort, in the unlikely event that the enemy had penetrated deep into Soviet territory. The *opolchenie* was indeed primarily intended to have an auxiliary role, training future Red Army conscripts, or providing the 'destruction battalions' (*istrebitel'nye batal'ony*) to defend factories, military installations and administrative centres from surprise attack by enemy saboteurs and parachute troops.

In the event, many volunteers found themselves sent to the front line within a few weeks or even days of enlisting. The first three Leningrad *opolchenie* divisions were almost immediately thrown into the battle along the 'Luga line' some sixty miles from Leningrad. The first division was sent to the front six days after being formed, the second two days, the third on the same day. Altogether they comprised roughly half the Soviet forces engaged in the desperate attempt to halt the German advance.[50] Their training had been minimal; sixteen hours was the norm, and this involved only basic tactics.[51] The first 'training' most volunteers received on a regimental or divisional scale was in battle itself. Officers and NCOs had little more experience than the rank and file; only a small proportion had served in the Red Army. There was also a serious lack of equipment. As locally raised units, the militia were supposed to be supplied from local resources, but these were rarely adequate. Automatic weapons and artillery were in particularly short supply. Early in July 1941, Khrushchev reported to Stalin from the Ukraine that while large numbers of volunteers had

48 For a description of a factory meeting to mobilise volunteers for the militia, see Kravchenko 1947: 361.
49 Kozlov 1988: 133–4.
50 Bidlack 1987: 56.
51 Kolesnik 1988: 51. For later units the norm was 60 hours.

been mobilised, they had no weapons. [52] While the deficiencies were sometimes made good from Red Army supplies, the *opolchentsy* often had to go into battle unable to defend themselves against enemy tanks or planes, or the crack Wehrmacht divisions confronting them.

The results were heroic but tragic. At Leningrad, the first three militia divisions were wiped out, as was a fourth soon afterwards. [53] In the desperate conditions of summer and autumn 1941, however, this did not prevent further *opolchenie* divisions being thrown into the battles to defend the approaches to Moscow, Leningrad and Kiev. Their fate in the battle of Moscow is laconically described by a Soviet historian. One division 'broke out of the encirclement, but its losses were so heavy that it had practically ceased to exist'; another was cut off and 'only a few managed to break out'; in the case of a third, 'its losses were so great that only small fractions remained of its regiments.'[54]

Whether the *opolchenie* achieved much of military value is doubtful. They marginally added to the obstacles facing the Germans, but it is highly unlikely that their contribution was in any way decisive. What is certain is that their heavy casualties meant the loss of much skilled labour which was urgently needed and hard to replace. The lesson was not lost on the government. After 1941, workers in reserved professions were more strictly excluded from military service, while the militia was more selectively employed. Sixty divisions altogether were formed during the war, of which thirty-six took part in fighting; altogether some 2 million civilian volunteers are said to have seen active military service. [55] But never again would their lives be squandered on the scale that they were in 1941.

The *opolchentsy* of the early months of the war reflected the best and the worst features of Soviet society's wartime mobilisation. Patriotic enthusiasm and local initiative were combined with central direction and administrative pressure to produce, with amazing speed, a mass organisation not even envisaged before the outbreak of war. It was employed at first with a profligacy and lack of rational calculation which was no less astonishing. Yet it survived, even if many individuals in its ranks did not, to make a significant contribution to mobilising the Soviet population for the task of winning the war.

52 *Izvestiya TsK KPSS* (7) 1990: 198.
53 Erickson 1975: 149.
54 Kolesnik 1988: 124–5, 130.
55 Kir'yan 1988: 303.

CHAPTER FIVE

Subsistence and survival[1]

SUPPLYING THE POPULATION

The population of the Soviet Union was probably better prepared by its past than that of any other belligerent country in World War II to endure the material hardships of war. Soviet citizens were no strangers to hard times. In 1941 the majority could recall the chronic shortages of World War I and the struggle for survival during the Civil War. Still more vivid were their memories of the industrialisation drive and the collectivisation of agriculture, when workers' real wages had plummetted and millions of peasants had died of famine. Food rationing, introduced in the cities in 1929, had ended only in 1935. Although there had been a significant improvement in the standard of living from 1932–3 onwards, the recovery had ended after 1937; and even by then it had not regained the 1928 level. Between 1937 and 1940, largely under the pressure of rearmament, living standards had declined, per capita household consumption falling by between 4 and 8 per cent.[2]

The Soviet population was thus familiar with shortages and experienced at coping with the effects of economic crisis. The severity of World War II's impact on living standards, however, was unparalleled

---

1 Standard Soviet works of reference, but limited mainly to the supply of the urban population, are Chernyavskii 1964 and Lyubimov 1968 (Lyubimov was wartime Commissar for Trade, responsible for food rationing). Valuable microstudies of blockaded Leningrad are Pavlov 1965 (Pavlov was in charge of food rationing in Leningrad) and Salisbury 1971. An excellent, new and original account of the whole subject is to be found in English in Moskoff 1990. The authors are grateful to William Moskoff for permission to make use of his book while still in typescript before publication.

2 Bergson 1961: 252.

even in Soviet history, and it far exceeded that felt in the other major countries involved. It was not simply that war meant a massive transfer of resources from consumption to production, from the civilian to the military sector of the economy; not simply that the Red Army's vast requirements necessarily deprived individual consumers of everything from food and fuel to transport and medical services. What made the Soviet Union's experience uniquely traumatic was that it had to wage total war largely on its own territory, with all the devastation that implied; and with substantially diminished industrial and agricultural capacity, due to enemy occupation of the western part of the country. Inevitably, the consequences for Soviet living standards were severe in the extreme. And this in turn had potentially grave consequences for the Soviet war effort. Hunger, cold, malnutrition and disease were almost as great threats to the survival of the USSR as German military power.

The wartime crisis in living standards may be illustrated by the cost of bread. This was by far the most important part of the urban population's diet, the main source of calories. It was literally 'the staff of life'. With it life could go on, without it life faded away. People worked and struggled, fought and stole for it. For most of 1942–3, the standard daily bread ration for the Soviet industrial worker was 600 grams – a loaf of bread. In Leningrad in spring 1942, the price of bread on the black market reached 60 roubles for 100 grams – equivalent to nearly five days' pay for an industrial worker in 1940. The latter's *monthly* wage would hardly have been sufficient to buy the *daily* ration of bread then being received by workers in other Soviet cities.

The decline in living standards was rapid and steep, soon reducing much of the population to a level barely above subsistence. Between 1940 and 1942, the population under Soviet control fell by one-third. But the output of light industry (mainly clothing) fell by one-half, while that of agriculture and food processing fell by three-fifths. In 1942, as Table 1 (p. 213) shows, Soviet citizens received one-third less household durables than in 1940 and two-fifths less food. The per capita supply of basic goods – such as cotton and woollen cloth, grain and potatoes – was halved. Access to education, health care, housing and other services suffered a similar squeeze. In 1943, the output of civilian industry increased, but so too did the population under Soviet control. In some respects supplies got even worse. There were 25 million homeless people to be fed and housed. The inhabitants of the liberated territories, moreover, represented urgent demands for goods and services, which had to be diverted away from consumers in the interior. In 1944, the situation marginally improved. Daily energy consumption of the urban population, having fallen from an average of 3,370 calories per head in 1940 to 2,555 calories in 1942, reached 2,751 calories in 1943 and 2,810 calories in 1944.[3] But up to and beyond the end of the war, living standards remained well below the prewar level.

Per capita figures are misleading, for in wartime as in peacetime not everyone got the same. In conditions of extreme shortage, harsh choices had to be made. Given the overriding importance of defeating the enemy, soldiers and workers in war industry were given the highest priority. Their living standards were protected at the expense of others – manual workers in civilian industry, white-collar workers, peasants, old age pensioners and children. (Members of the political and military elite, it is true, did not generally suffer material deprivation, although in many cases the pressures on them took a heavy physical toll.) Among the less privileged, there were also degrees of economic status. It was better to live in the interior than near the front line, better to be in the prime of life than to be very young or very old. For a twelve-year-old, to be dependent on official rations in Leningrad in the winter of 1941–2 meant certain death.

What determined individuals' access to food and consumer goods? The key factor was whether or not they were supplied from official government stocks. Most workers in state enterprises and establishments (which meant most of the adult urban population) were; most of the rural population were not. The former were guaranteed basic rations, although these were often insufficient to keep them alive. The latter had to rely on unofficial sources of supply. On the operation and interraction of these two systems of distribution depended the survival of the population.

RATIONING

The severe reduction in the supply of basic necessities, above all food, made some form of rationing inevitable. In theory, the Soviet government could have continued the prewar practice of regulating the distribution of goods by a system of 'first come, first served', by means of queuing – but besides the huge waste of time this involved, it potentially constituted a serious threat to public order. As Bolsheviks, the Soviet leaders were unlikely to forget that the 1917 Revolution had

3 Chernyavskii 1964: 179.

begun with bread queues in wartime Petrograd turning into anti-government demonstrations and riots. The government could also have brought demand into line with supply by increasing prices or reducing wages. But this would have meant substantial inequality in the provision of goods and great suffering for the poorest section of the population. The damage to civilian morale and national unity likely to result was so obvious that for the greater part of the war official prices for essential goods rose little if at all.[4] The only significant price increases were for alcoholic drinks; and even taking into account a six-fold rise in the price of beer, wine and spirits, official retail prices in state and cooperative stores in Moscow in 1942–3 were altogether only 80–90 per cent above the July 1940 level.[5]

Like other countries in World War II, therefore, and with the same aims of establishing equality of sacrifice, achieving national priorities, and maintaining morale, the Soviet Union introduced a rationing system. It emerged in stages between July and November 1941. A Sovnarkom resolution of 18 July ordered rationing to be implemented in Moscow, Leningrad and towns in the surrounding districts. It covered bread, flour, cereals, pasta, butter, margarine, vegetable oil, meat and fish, sugar and confectionery. On 20 August, bread, sugar and confectionery rationing was extended to 200 towns and industrial settlements of central Russia and the Urals. In November, the rationing of these products was extended to all urban areas; and cereals, pasta, fats, meat and fish began to be rationed in forty-three of the largest industrial cities in addition to those in the Moscow and Leningrad districts.[6]

Rationing now covered most of the urban population, though only a minority of the rural population. Workers on state farms and motor-tractor stations, and other non-agricultural workers living in the countryside, were included in the rationing system, but collective farmers were not. In 1942, about 62 million people received rationed bread, approximately two-thirds of them urban inhabitants; by 1945, with the liberation of formerly occupied territory, this number had risen to over 80 million.[7]

For people on rations, the system was both simple and complex. The simple fact was that bread was all-important. As Table 2 shows, bread provided all categories of consumers with not less than four-

4 Meanwhile the wage of the average public sector employee rose from 330 to 435 roubles per month between 1940 and 1945 (Mitrofanova 1971: 498). In key industries, the increase was considerably greater. The wages of coal-miners in the Kuzbass, for example, rose from 363 to 797 roubles per month (Bukin 1985: 28).

5 Zaleski 1980: 452.

6 Chernyavskii 1964: 70–1.

7 Moskoff 1990: 137–8.

fifths of the calories and proteins they received from rations. Whereas other foodstuffs were issued three times a month, bread was distributed on a daily basis. Whereas the full norms for other foodstuffs were often not honoured, the bread ration was distributed in all but the most desperate circumstances. Every breach in the supply of bread rations was subject to immediate police investigation.[8]

The main complicating factor was the differentiation between different groups of the population, which increased as time went on. Initially, there were four categories – manual workers, white-collar workers, dependants, and children of 12 years or under – to which a new first category, consisting of people employed in important war industries, together with scientists and technicians, was added on 1 February 1942. (Able-bodied adults who were unemployed received no rations.) But these categories soon acquired many internal gradations. Some reflected obvious needs. Babies, for example, were entitled to more milk in place of solid food. People living in the far north, where alternative sources of food supply were extremely limited, received higher rations than those elsewhere. Other differences served as incentives to stimulate high output or attract labour into particularly important occupations or encourage volunteers for vital activities. Those working in particularly hard or dangerous conditions (such as miners, steel workers, oil industry workers) received supplementary rations and free meals at work, as did shock-workers and Stakhanovites.[9] Blood donors were given a worker's ration card in addition to their own card, as well as various supplementary coupons.[10]

Official ration norms remained largely stable. Those for sugar and confectionery were cut on 1 April 1942 and the bread ration was reduced on 21 November 1943; otherwise norms were unchanged throughout the war. Table 2 shows those which applied in the interior of the country from November 1943 to early 1945. (In the two previous years, bread rations had been 100–200 grams more than that shown.) The extent of differentiation was such that the most privileged received four or five times as many calories and grams of protein as the least privileged. Official norms, however, did not necessarily bear a close resemblance to what was actually distributed. Sugar, meat and butter were often unobtainable, and though substitutes might be

8 Chernyavskii 1964: 70–1.

9 Coal-miners in the Kuzbass who fulfilled their norms, for example, from June 1943 received breakfasts of 100–200 grams of bread, 30–50 grams of fat, and 10 grams of sugar, and hot meals consisting of 60 grams of meat, 10 grams of fats and 10 grams of groats. Bukin 1985: 29.

10 Moskoff 1990: 149–50.

provided (such as jam or cake for sugar, salted fish or powdered eggs for meat, vegetable oil for butter), these were frequently inferior both in volume and nutritional value.[11]

Rations played a vital part in helping to keep millions of Soviet people alive during the war. But they could not guarantee survival. The government did not have enough food at its disposal to feed adequately even the minority of the population entitled to rations. Only combat soldiers and manual workers in the most difficult and hazardous occupations received sufficient rations to maintain health. Table 2 shows that most people's rations fell well short of minimum nutritional levels. The shortfall was particularly marked for white-collar workers and for dependants, particularly children over 12 years old.[12]

In deciding who was to get what, the rationing authorities were faced with hard, sometimes tragic choices. In an extreme case such as Leningrad during the blockade, they were in effect exercising powers of life and death. There the lowest point was reached in the month from 20 November to 23 December 1941, when workers' daily bread rations were cut to 250 grams and even front-line soldiers were allotted no more than 500 grams; for everyone else, the ration was fixed at 125 grams. These were starvation levels. Although rations in Leningrad were marginally increased thereafter, their very low level combined with the lowered resistance of the population spelt death for hundreds of thousands of people.

The rationing system in the USSR during World War II was thus not simply a matter, as elsewhere, of distributing the available food in such a way as to achieve a balance of economic efficiency and social fairness. It also meant the authorities being forced to take decisions about whom to preserve and whom to abandon of a kind comparable only with those familiar to food relief workers in the midst of major famines today.

LOCAL RESOURCES

Since rations supplied by the state were insufficient to sustain the lives of all but a minority of those entitled to them, and since over half the population did not receive rations at all, almost everyone had to resort

11 Moskoff 1990: 143.

12 As a result, many children over the age of 12 chose to work, illegally, thus qualifying for larger rations.

to local and unofficial sources of supply. In this respect, food supply in wartime reflected a basic feature of the Stalinist economic system in general. Although decision-making was highly centralised, local authorities were often left to their own devices when it came to obtaining the means to implement the government's decisions. Since centrally allocated resources were inadequate to meet all the claims upon them, high-priority sectors such as heavy industry and defence would have their needs for steel, power, components, and foodstuffs met, while others would be given advice instead of supplies. Managers, workers and consumers would be urged by the centre to look to 'local resources'.

Where food supply was concerned, this meant produce from sideline farms belonging to factories and institutions, from the allotments of urban residents, and from the collective farmers' private plots. Already before the war, these had been seen as playing an important role in protecting living standards from the pressures of rearmament.[13] During the war, they would play a vital part in the survival of the majority of the population.

The importance of such resources even for people receiving rations was substantial. They could make the difference between starvation and survival. Table 2 showed that in 1944 rations for most employed adults provided between 1,000 and 2,000 calories a day. But in 1944 the average daily intake of an urban adult was 2,810 calories. Of this, 69 per cent came from central or local government stocks. The remaining 31 per cent came from local resources, in the following proportions:[14]

	Per cent
Auxiliary farms of enterprises and institutions	4.5
Private allotments	12.4
Collective farm market purchases	14.5

What did these local supplies consist of? First, nearly all enterprises and many other institutions developed their own sources of auxiliary food production. Through their 'departments of worker supply' (ORSy), they organised farms on local wasteland, usually specialising in relatively labour-intensive activities – cultivating potatoes and vegetables, rearing pigs and poultry. In 1944, auxiliary farms in the most important branches of industry yielded more than 2.6 million tons of potatoes

13 See, for example, the government decree of 7 January 1941 calling on local authorities to supplement consumer supplies from local resources. Resheniya vol 3 1968: 5–14.

14 Chernyavskii 1964: 179, 186.

and vegetables, equivalent to roughly 250 calories per worker per day.[15]

Second, individual workers were encouraged to produce food on private allotments. In wartime, the government specifically extended the right to have an allotment from the rural population to the whole population. Urban allotments became an even larger source of supply than auxiliary farming. By 1944, some 16.5 million workers were producing more than 9 million tons of potatoes and vegetables. This represented more than 200 calories of daily energy intake per member of the family with an allotment.[16]

Third, collective farmers brought their private produce to market for sale at unregulated prices. The collective farm market was the most important unofficial source of food for the urban population throughout the war, providing up to one-seventh of the energy content of the average diet.[17] The collective farm markets' share in all food sales by value rose from 20 per cent in 1940 to 51 per cent in 1945.[18] Unofficial did not mean illegal; the collective farm market had been introduced by the government in the mid-1930s as a concession to the peasants and as a means of alleviating food shortages. It meant that prices there were unregulated and, since demand vastly exceeded supply, far greater than official prices. A year after the beginning of the war, the overall index of collective farm market prices had risen eight and a half times, and by mid-1943 it was nearly nineteen times the July 1941 level. For the two main items in the population's diet, potatoes and bread, prices rose respectively twenty-six times and twenty-three times.[19] Although prices declined slightly thereafter, it was not until the second half of 1944 that increased food production, together with the government's introduction of special 'commercial' shops selling goods at prices close to free market rates, brought about a substantial fall in collective farm market prices. By 1945 they were five to six times the prewar level.

The high prices at the collective farm market greatly restricted the

15 For total output of auxiliary farms, and for supplies per workers in nine branches of munitions and heavy industries, see Lyubimov 1968: 150–1. Calories per worker are calculated from the unweighted average of the nine branches, assuming 0.75 cals per gram.

16 Mitrofanova 1971: 510. According to Mitrofanova, this represented some 544 kg of potatoes and vegetables per family annually. We assume 0.75 cals per gram and up to five family members.

17 Chernyavskii 1964: 186.

18 Moskoff 1990: 153.

19 Moskoff 1990: 154. According to Voznesensky 1948: 102, however, collective farm market prices peaked in 1943 at twelve to thirteen times the 1940 level.

ability of most ordinary people to supplement their diets by purchases at the market. While they had to spend much of their income on food, it would not have bought a great deal. In Rostov-on-Don, according to K S Karol, his friend's salary of 300 roubles a month enabled her to buy no more than three extra kilos of bread.[20] The collective farm market may have made a crucial difference to many people's chances of survival, but only for the best-paid workers and employees can it have added substantially to official rations.

No one was more dependent on local resources than the peasant. Over half the population had to survive without any rations. How they did so is one of the least investigated aspects of the history of Soviet society in wartime. The problem was not just that food supplies per head of the population had fallen disastrously. Food output per collective farmer had also fallen seriously, while the share of total grain and meat output taken by the government had risen.[21] Collective farmers were thus left with a reduced share in a much smaller total than before the war.

Even before the war, the attitude of the procurement authorities to the needs of the farm population had been harsh and arbitrary. Compulsory purchases from the collective farms had been based on official assessments of potential farm capacity, not real farm output. Payment of grain by collective farms to the state-owned machine-tractor stations in return for their services had been calculated as a percentage of the crop before harvesting, not after it had been gathered and stored in barns.[22] In wartime, arbitrary confiscation of food from farm stocks was intensified. Right up to 1944, procurement campaigns were waged in what Soviet sources refer to as a 'battlefront atmosphere'.[23] While peasants may have accepted the need for sacrifices in order to feed the non-farming population, including their own relatives who had left to fight at the front or to work in towns, the state's extraction of their produce was sometimes accompanied by conflict and violence.

During the war, the main source of food for the peasants became their private plots, and the main crop they cultivated became potatoes. What bread was to the urban worker, the potato was to the peasant. Per head of the peasant population, the consumption of potatoes more than doubled, rising to 800–50 grams (600 calories) daily. Meanwhile, bread consumption fell to no more than 300 grams (650 calories) per head per day. 'They ate potatoes for breakfast, for lunch and for tea;

20 Karol 1986: 251.
21 Harrison 1990b: 84n.
22 Arutyunyan 1970: 196–7.
23 IVOVSS vol 3 1961: 187–90, vol 4 1962: 602–3; IVMV vol 7 1976: 51.

they ate them all ways – baked, fried, in potato cakes, in soup, but most often simply boiled, with a salted cucumber or pickled cabbage.' Everything else of importance came from milk – proteins, fats and vitamins. And if there was no bread, milk or potatoes, peasants ate nettles, grass and acorns.[24]

Those whose plots yielded a surplus, however small, sold it at the collective farm market to supplement their meagre diets, buying food unavailable on their farms, including bread. Many also disposed of their produce on the thriving black market, bartering it for other foodstuffs, or for jewellery, clothing and manufactured goods offered by town dwellers desperate for food. The resulting flow of assets from the urban to the rural population partially compensated for the state's ruthless extraction of resources from the countryside. Some peasants acquired substantial wealth in the process, and there were even rouble millionaires (although the value of their cash hoards would be wiped out by a currency reform two years after the end of the war). But these were rare exceptions; for the overwhelming majority, the war meant grinding poverty and a continuous struggle to survive.

HUNGER

Of all the wartime hardships suffered by the Soviet population, malnutrition stands out as the most pervasive. While many people experienced violence, injury, bereavement and homelessness, all but a small minority went hungry for much of the time. They lost weight, grew weaker and more tired, and became vulnerable to illnesses of all kinds. Productivity as well as health inevitably suffered. That even so the Soviet work-force was capable of the productive effort achieved reflects both the effectiveness of its mobilisation and its commitment to the common cause.

At its most extreme, malnutrition culminated in death by starvation. Loss of weight and metabolic decline were followed by the fall of blood pressure and pulse rate, the wastage of the heart muscle and the atrophy of internal organs. Past a certain point, the effects were irreversible. Many victims of starvation would linger, only to die months after the arrival of food relief and medical help. In the final stages of starvation, despite retaining their intellectual faculties, people's person-

24 Arutyunyan 1970: 361. We assume 2.15 cals per gram for bread and 0.75 cals per gram for potatoes.

alities were liable to disintegrate. Losing all awareness of the plight of others, they would steal even from their closest relatives.[25] The largest concentration of deaths from starvation was in Leningrad, where around 1 million people, approximately 40 per cent of the prewar population, died of hunger and hunger-related causes during the blockade, the majority in the winter of 1941–2;[26] but deaths from starvation also occurred in the interior of the country. In 1942, according to Victor Kravchenko, 'the sight of men and women falling dead of starvation on Moscow streets became too commonplace to attract crowds.'[27]

Conditions during the war were highly conducive to the spread of disease among the civilian population. Reduced nutritional standards lowered people's resistance to illness. The high level of mobility of the population, involving millions of troops, evacuees and refugees, facilitated the spread of disease from one area to another. The death and destruction resulting from military combat and enemy occupation was also a potential source of epidemics. In Kalinin region, for example, the incidence of typhus was eighty-eight times higher in 1942 than in 1940, and affected 7 per cent of the population.[28] Over the country as a whole, the incidence of typhus, typhoid fever and tuberculosis rose sharply in 1942.[29] The ability of the Soviet health system to respond to the extra demands on it from civilians, meanwhile, was reduced by the draft of medical personnel into the Red Army. In 1943 hospitals in industrial cities were 20 per cent understaffed for doctors and 27 per cent for surgeons.[30]

The threat posed by disease to the war effort was taken extremely seriously by the government. The GKO assumed direct responsibility for all work to prevent epidemics, and G A Miterev, People's Commissar of Health, was made a GKO plenipotentiary, with wide powers to take necessary measures.[31] Strenuous efforts were made to combat the spread of disease. Individuals were subject to regular medical examinations, and their living quarters to regular hygiene inspections. The number of 'disinfection points' to treat accommodation, clothes and people doubled in the RSFSR during the war. There was an 88

25 For a description of the clinical features of undernourishment, see Davidson *et al* 1979: 240–1. For an account of the physiological and psychological decline of Leningrad's population in the winter of 1941–2, see Salisbury 1971: 434–51.

26 Salisbury 1971: 610–12.

27 Kravchenko 1947: 413.

28 Alekseev, Isupov 1986: 133.

29 Arutyunyan 1970: 363–4.

30 Alekseev, Isupov 1986: 127.

31 Alekseev, Isupov 1986: 133.

per cent increase in the number of epidemiological stations; the networks of malaria stations and centres to treat tuberculosis also expanded. Sanitation control points were set up at 275 major stations on the railway network to check passengers and carriages for signs of disease. A large-scale immunisation programme was put into effect, with 250 million innoculations between 1941 and 1943. Altogether, the budget for health care was increased in cash terms from 9 billion to 10.2 billion roubles between 1940 and 1944,[32] although this probably represented a cutback after taking inflation into account.

Thanks to these efforts, there appear to have been no major epidemics during the war, except in occupied territories. While the incidence of infectious disease rose in the first two years of the war, the battle to contain it seems to have been largely won by the end of 1943. Official statistics show that in that year the incidence of diphtheria was reduced by one-quarter, typhus and scarlet fever by half, measles by two-thirds[33] – no small achievement, given that nutritional standards were then at their lowest.

Mortality also rose in the first two years of the war, although the available data provides a far from complete picture of the war's impact on the civilian population. Overall, the death-rate is reported to have risen from eighteen per thousand of the population in 1940 to twenty-one per thousand in 1941, and twenty-four per thousand in 1942, before falling to nine per thousand in 1945.[34] These figures, however, are said to relate to the population as a whole, including the armed forces. Somewhat more informative are the following statistics for reported deaths per thousand of the population in Siberia, 1941–5.[35]

	Urban	Rural
1941	24.1	19.7
1942	29.6	21.3
1943	27.2	13.6
1944	17.3	10.6
1945	12.2	7.4

These also show that the death-rate peaked in 1942. The absence of data for the last full year of peacetime makes it difficult to estimate the whole impact of the war, although the mortality level in Siberia in

32 Alekseev, Isupov 1986: 126, 132–7.
33 Alekseev, Isupov 1986: 137. The statistics do not, unfortunately, show what level had been reached during the first two years of the war.
34 Narkhoz 1960: 45; Alekseev, Isupov 1986: 114.
35 Alekseev, Isupov 1986: 117.

1940 is unlikely to have been substantially different from that in the country as a whole. (Infant mortality is said to have doubled between the end of 1940 and the end of 1941, and to have declined from 1943 onwards, reaching a level in 1945 30 per cent lower than in 1940.)[36] The marked discrepancy between urban and rural mortality levels presumably reflects worse hygienic and nutritional conditions in the towns. It is doubtful, however, whether the decline in mortality in the last two years of the war can be attributed to improved health care. It is more probable that many vulnerable members of society (old people, children, the sick and injured) had perished in 1941–3, and that those who remained were stronger and more likely to survive.

Not surprisingly, the chronic shortage of food drove people to crime – and created many opportunities for some to exploit the desperate needs of others. As in all countries where there was wartime rationing, the system was open to abuse. The rationing authorities themselves were liable to corruption. Ration cards were sold illegally, inferior items were substituted for scarce foodstuffs which were then sold on the black market, shop assistants pilfered food from stocks or gave short weight to customers. Consumers also took advantage of the system's defects, using dead people's cards or registering under false names at more than one address. Ration cards were forged, stolen, bought and sold on the black market.

Abuse of the system were not so widespread, however, as to prevent it from working. This was at least in part because the consequences could be very severe, for victims and perpetrators alike. In besieged Leningrad, for example, lost monthly ration cards were generally not replaced, in order to prevent false reports of losses. To lose cards or have them stolen more than a day or two before the end of the month could easily doom those concerned, already weakened by months of privation, to death. In this situation, their only recourse was to the mercy and generosity of equally undernourished friends. The extreme gravity of the situation was reflected in the fact that people found guilty of 'food crimes' in Leningrad were shot.[37]

Throughout the country, however, crime increased as food supply diminished. Food was stolen from public and private sources – from factories, farms and shops, from gardens, plots and homes – as were items which could be exchanged for food. Survival rather than personal gain was often the motive of those who stole, and to many stealing must have seemed necessary and justified. By 1943, it had

36 Alekseev, Isupov 1986: 119.
37 Salisbury 1971: 533.

reached a scale which to the authorities clearly threatened the whole system of food distribution, and with it social order. In January, the GKO called for action by the Commissariat for Trade to stop abuses of the rationing system and the stealing of food. In February, the leadership of the trade union movement set up a network of some 600,000 volunteers at canteens, shops, storage bases and auxiliary farms to prevent food theft. And in June, a decree on preparations for the harvest declared that anyone stealing grain and other products would be subject to the law of 7 August 1932 on the theft of public property. This draconian law, introduced at the height of the crisis following the collectivisation of agriculture, had made stealing from state and collective farms punishable by death (or in extenuating circumstances, ten years in prison). That it was revived by the government in summer 1943 indicates the seriousness of the problem.[38]

As a sign of the breakdown of conventional norms of social behaviour, however, the theft of food pales into insignificance besides the cannibalism reported from Leningrad. Corpses assembled for mass burials were commonly found with the fleshy parts removed; murderers butchered their victims and sold their flesh, disguised in various products, on the black market; crazed with hunger, people ate the bodies of their nearest relatives.[39] Given that starvation conditions existed elsewhere, albeit on a smaller scale, cannibalism may not have been confined to Leningrad.

THE FAMILY

Personal relations were no less profoundly affected by the war than material conditions of life. For the great majority of people, war brought prolonged separation from their closest friends and relatives. Millions of men were conscripted for military service, and departed from their towns and villages, many never to return. Millions of men and women were drafted, for periods ranging from a few days to months, into work which took them far from their homes. Millions of youths aged 14 and upwards were mobilised into the State Labour Reserves, taken from their families and sent to live in factory barracks

38 Moskoff 1990: 176.
39 Salisbury 1971: 550–3.

under conditions of strict discipline.[40] In the chaos which accompanied evacuation or flight from areas threatened by the German advance, countless families were split up. Some of their members remained in occupied territory, while others were dispersed to the interior of the country. For weeks, months, even years, millions of parents lost contact with their children (many of whom were on holiday in Pioneer camps, sometimes hundreds of miles away, when war began). Decades later, people would still be searching for (and discovering) relatives lost in the war, through social organisations, newspaper bulletins and radio programmes.[41]

Separation and, still more, bereavement inevitably inflicted heavy psychological strain. And to this was often added the material hardship caused by the loss of a major part of the family income. Particularly at risk were the families of men serving in the Red Army. While they received state allowances and other forms of assistance from local authorities, these were not automatically granted. To reinforce soldiers' motivation to fight, a Stavka decree of 16 August 1941 made the well-being of their families dependent on their own fate. The families of those captured, and thus assumed to have betrayed their country, it was ordered, lost any entitlement to allowances.[42]

The war not only imposed great strains on individual families, but also weakened the family as an institution, albeit temporarily. After a surge of weddings in June and July 1941, as couples about to be parted by the war clutched at the symbol of personal security, the number of marriages declined steeply. In Siberia, it fell from 4.7 per thousand of population in 1941 to 2.7 in 1942 and 2.3 in 1943.[43] With fewer young men and women marrying, the average age at marriage rose sharply. The divorce rate remained unchanged, although the proportion of divorces consisting of marriages ending within a year of taking place rose,[44] a sign of the effect of separation on wartime marriages. The decline in registered marriages may have been associated with an increase in the informal, temporary relationships typical of a more mobile wartime population. Its prime cause, however, must have been

40 For a vivid account of their conditions, see Kravchenko 1947: 406. It may be exaggerated; but the author was directly involved in the supply of labour to industry.

41 For examples, see Maksimova 1988: 235–308.

42 Mitrofanova 1989: 337.

43 Alekseev, Isupov 1986: 101–2. Among the urban population of Omsk region, the marriage rate rose from 8.4 per thousand in May 1941 to 15.3 per thousand in June, before declining to 11.3 per thousand in July and 8.8 per thousand in August. Among the rural population, however, the temporary increase was only slight.

44 In Novosibirsk region it rose from 16.5 per cent in 1942 to 22.8 per cent in 1945. Alekseev, Isupov 1986: 105.

the sudden reduction in the number of men of marriageable age in civilian society. Conversely, demobilisation at the end of the war would be accompanied by a sharp rise in the marriage rate; in Siberia, from 3.6 in 1944 to 6.4 per thousand in 1945.

The decline in births per thousand of the population was even more drastic, as the following figures show:[45]

	Moscow	Siberia
1941	22.2	33.2
1942	17.7	21.5
1943	8.5	12.5
1944	—	12.2
1945	—	15.6

In sharp contrast to peacetime, the birth-rate was consistently higher in the towns than in the countryside during the war (and higher in larger towns than smaller ones). The averages conceal some very large decreases indeed. Among the rural population of the Omsk region, for example, the birth-rate fell from 38.8 per thousand in October 1941 to 6.9 per thousand in December 1943.[46] Altogether, the children born during the war amounted to only half the number which would have been expected in normal conditions – a significant part of the demographic damage caused by the war.

Several factors contributed to this decline. Poor nutrition reduced women's fertility: an extreme example was Leningrad, where the birth-rate in 1943 was zero. The substantial increase in the number of employed women and their heavy work-load also reduced the incentive and opportunity for women to have children. So did the reduced ability of other members of the family to contribute to child-care. Ill-health may have resulted in more miscarriages, and the difficulties of raising children in wartime, particularly for single women, may have led to an increase in abortions (although this is not very likely, given that the harsh anti-abortion law of 1936 was still in effect).

But the prime reason for the lower birth-rate was the relative absence of men. This was clearly reflected in the abrupt decline in the birth-rate within a year of the beginning of the war. Among the urban population of the Novosibirsk region, it fell steadily from 38.4 in January 1942 to 27.7 in April and 19.2 in June. The lowest levels were reached approximately ten months after the battles of Stalingrad

45 Alekseev, Isupov 1986: 88.
46 Alekseev, Isupov 1986: 90–1.

and Kursk, for which heavy additional mobilisation for the Red Army had occurred.[47] The upturn in the birth-rate at the end of 1944 and beginning of 1945, well before the effects of demobilisation could be felt, showed the influence of improved conditions from spring 1944 onwards; but not until 1946 would a substantial increase occur, though the prewar level would never again be attained.

Eventually the drastic impact of the war on the family prompted government intervention to reverse some of its effects. A Supreme Soviet decree of 8 July 1944 introduced several measures designed to increase the birth-rate. New orders of 'heroine-mother' (for mothers of ten children or more) and 'motherhood glory' (for seven to nine children) were created, together with the 'motherhood medal' (for five or six children). A progressive scale of grants to mothers was introduced for the birth of the third child onwards, ranging from 400 roubles at the birth of the third child to 1,300 for the fourth child and up to 5,000 roubles for the tenth. Grants were also introduced for single mothers, and they were given the option of putting their children into state-run children's homes, with the right to reclaim them at any time – a reflection of the rise in illegitimate births in wartime, as well as of the state's desire to encourage a higher birth-rate. Conversely, a tax was imposed on couples with fewer than three children.[48]

At the same time, the decree included a number of measures apparently intended to strengthen marriage as an institution. Unregistered marriages ceased to be legally valid, divorce was made much more difficult and expensive, and a heavy tax was imposed on bachelors over the age of 25. The potential effect of these measures, however, was largely undermined by the provision that only *married* fathers were to be legally responsible for the maintenance of their offspring. Allowing men to have families while avoiding material responsibility for them may have been a retreat from conventional morality, but it was a recognition of demographic realities in a situation where young women greatly outnumbered young men. For a government acutely aware of the massive losses caused by the war, long-term population growth was the top priority.

47 Alekseev, Isupov 1986: 92.
48 Werth 1964: 935–6.

CHAPTER SIX
The social order

During the war, for the third time in a quarter of a century, Soviet society was convulsed by massive population movement and social mobility. As in the two earlier periods – first, World War I, the Revolution and Civil War, then the collectivisation and industrialisation drives – huge numbers of people were on the move from one end of the country to another, and from one social group to another.[1]

Millions of people were evacuated to the east, or simply fled as refugees. Millions of conscripted workers and peasants travelled in the opposite direction, leaving their towns and villages to serve in the Red Army (the results are shown in Table 3, p. 213). The boundaries between urban and rural society were endlessly crossed, as town dwellers travelled to the countryside in search of food, or were sent to reinforce the depleted work-force on the farms; as peasants were mobilised to work in factories and on building sites; as prisoners were dispatched to industry and agriculture, as well as to the front. Although the authorities were able to maintain more control over this mass movement of people than on previous occasions, it again placed enormous strains on the social and administrative structures, while its impact on both classes and individuals was deep and lasting.

WORKERS

The War saw the Soviet working class transformed for the second

---

1 For a vivid description of Soviet society 'in flux' in the late 1920s and early 1930s, see Lewin 1985: 209–40.

time in little over a decade. During the 1930s, a new working class had been created. While many experienced 'cadre' workers had been promoted into management, millions of recruits, particularly from the countryside, had flooded into the factories and mines, into transport and construction. By the mid–1930s those who had begun work before the beginning of the industrialisation drive were only a small minority of the labour force. But the speed of this transformation would be dwarfed by the dramatic pace of change in the composition of the working class under the impact of war. Within a year or two of the outbreak of war, new recruits again comprised the majority of Soviet workers.

The main causes of change were the loss of territory where a substantial part of Soviet industry and its work-force was based, and the conscription of millions of workers into the armed forces. Many others were killed by enemy action or died from the privations of wartime. The result was a large reduction in the number of workers employed in the economy in the first year and a half of the war. This was partly mitigated by the evacuation of workers from the occupied areas to the rear and by the recruitment of new workers, which together with the gradual liberation of occupied territory resulted in a steady increase in the number of workers from 1943 onwards. Even so, the immense scale of Soviet military and civilian losses, and the large-scale destruction of industrial plant as the Germans retreated, meant that at the end of the war there were still fewer Soviet workers than there had been on its eve.

The number of workers employed in large-scale industry in wartime as shown in Table 4 (p. 216) varied as follows (in millions):

1940	1941	1942	1943	1944	1945
8.3	7.8	5.5	5.7	6.4	7.2

These figures conceal the scale of the precipitous change in the number of workers in some branches of industry in the first part of the war. In the crucial iron and steel industry, for example, the number in June 1942 was only half what it had been a year earlier.[2] The number of workers employed in the defence industry, on the other hand, rose immediately – partly through the redistribution of labour from non-defence sectors, partly through the recruitment of new workers, partly through the transfer of whole factories from civilian to war production. As a whole, the number of workers in heavy industry fell less

2 Mitrofanova 1984: 361.

than that in light industry, reflecting the economic priorities of the war effort.

Recruits to the work-force came from a variety of sources. Many came from the families of workers mobilised to fight: partly out of a desire to identify with the husbands, fathers or sons at the front, partly to provide much needed income for the remaining family, partly because of legal and moral pressures to work. There were continuous campaigns to attract housewives, pensioners and adolescents into the work-force. White-collar workers and people in service industry were drafted into production. The Commissariat of Defence sent conscripts unfit for military service to work in factories, on building sites, or on transport, and often reallocated wounded servicemen to production after recovery. In the last year and a half of the war, skilled workers and engineers were released from the armed forces to return to work, particularly in the newly liberated regions.

But as in the early 1930s the countryside increasingly became the main source of new workers during the war. While millions of its inhabitants were drafted into the armed forces, millions of others – kolkhoz and individual peasants, artisans, young people – became workers. Between 1942 and 1944, a wartime Committee for Registration and Allocation of Labour Power (hereafter Labour Committee) mobilised 3 million people for permanent work in industry, building and transport, of whom 49.6 per cent were from urban and 50.4 per cent from rural backgrounds. As time went on, the countryside became ever more important as the source of new workers, accounting in 1942 for 23 per cent of the total, in 1943 for 59 per cent, and in 1944 for 62 per cent. Much of this increase came from the population of the liberated regions. [3]

The state of flux in the working class was not confined to the movement of millions of people in and out of the industrial work-force. Many others changed their position within it, either geographically or professionally or both. In the early stages of the war, hundreds of thousands of workers moved eastwards from the war zones to the rear. Whereas in 1940 the eastern areas of the country had accounted for 37 per cent of workers and employees, in 1942 this figure had risen to 70 per cent. [4] Skilled workers in particular were evacuated with their factories to the Urals, Siberia or the Far East. Many more made their own way to the rear as refugees. Later there would be large-scale movement in the opposite direction, as workers were sent

3 Mitrofanova 1984: 353–4.
4 Mitrofanova 1984: 365.

into the liberated territories to rebuild what had been destroyed and to get factories working again.

The most conspicuous features of Soviet workers in wartime were their youth, their inexperience and the great preponderance of women. In many factories the majority of workers were under 25;[5] in the newly built or restored engineering factories by the end of the war, they comprised up to three-quarters. In Leningrad, according to one report, by June 1943, 80 per cent of all factory workers were 23 years or under.[6] The proportion of juveniles under 18 in the work-force rose substantially, from 6 per cent of workers and employees in industry in 1940 to 15 per cent in 1942. Many workers were very young. Of 2,460,000 workers under 18 in 1944, 712,000 were only 14 or 15 years old.[7] Official figures do not reveal the number who were younger still, but there were certainly many. At the age of 12 a child became a 'dependant' and his or her food ration was reduced accordingly. Where food was scarce, sheer hunger, or the need to provide for other members of the family, thus forced children to seek work; and though it was illegal for an employer to hire anyone under the age of 14, children often found work.

The influx of new workers into the labour force produced a corresponding fall in its average *stazh* (length of employment). This was particularly true of the priority sectors, such as defence industry and engineering, where expansion was greatest. In Leningrad, three-quarters of the workers in defence industry at the end of 1942 had begun work since the beginning of that year.[8] By the beginning of 1943, 60–70 per cent of all Leningrad workers had a *stazh* of between six months and two years. By the end of the war, most had not more than three years, and many had only one year. There was still a nucleus of older workers, but it had shrunk enormously. At the Kirov works in Leningrad at the beginning of 1943, 18 per cent of workers had a *stazh* of ten years or more. In 1945 only 25 per cent of Kuzbass miners and 16 per cent of Karaganda miners had been employed since before the war.[9] Inevitably the reduced length of work experience, combined with the much shorter amount of time devoted to training, resulted in lower skill levels.

Women's participation in the work-force had been a conspicuous feature of the industrialisation drive of the 1930s, as it had also been of

5 Mitrofanova 1984: 373.
6 Bidlack 1987: 249.
7 Mitrofanova 1984: 373.
8 Bidlack 1987: 222, 239.
9 Mitrofanova 1984: 381.

Russian industry during World War I. But in World War II it rose to new heights (Table 5, p. 216). 'Men to the front, women to the factories!' was a familiar slogan in the early part of the war; the appeal to women to replace the conscripted male members of their families, together with the mobilisation of women for work which allowed few exemptions, produced an influx of women into the work-force. If they had comprised 41 per cent of workers and employees in 1940, they were 52 per cent in 1942 and 53 per cent in 1943–4, declining slightly to 51 per cent in 1945. In many factories women soon comprised the majority, and sometimes the overwhelming majority, of workers. In light industry, where they had always predominated, 80–90 per cent of the work-force were generally women. But their proportion in heavy industry rose very sharply. In 1942 over half of all turbine operators in power stations were women, and over a quarter of all workers in coal-mining. By the end of 1944, they comprised 41.5 per cent of workers in the restored Donbass mines.[10]

Close to the front line, the female proportion of the work-force was even greater. In Leningrad, merely between July and October 1941 in two major engineering factories, it rose from approximately one-quarter to three-quarters. At the giant Kirov works, two-thirds of workers by January 1943 were women. By the end of 1942, 80 per cent of all Leningrad industrial workers were women, and by February 1943, 84 per cent.[11]

Like all Soviet citizens, workers saw their conditions deteriorate sharply during the war. At work they faced a longer working day and compulsory overtime, the end of leave entitlement, continual pressure to meet higher production targets, obligatory military training or civil defence duties, the virtual suspension of labour safety regulations, and a lack of adequate heating, lighting and ventilation. At home, the scarcity of food and other basic necessities was a continuous and often extreme feature of their lives. Worst off were workers in cities close to the front line (and above all Leningrad), to whose hardships was added the threat of death from enemy action, and evacuated workers, provision for whom tended to be minimal.

Yet workers were also to some extent cushioned against the worst effects of the war. Their rations were higher than non-manual employees, let alone adult dependants, while peasants on collective farms received no rations at all. Factory canteens, shops and allotments were also a vital source of food. The support available at the work-place,

10 Mitrofanova 1984: 376–7.
11 Bidlack 1987: 119, 223.

however, went well beyond this. Many workers and their families lived in factory barracks, or even in the factories themselves; cramped though conditions were, at least heating and lighting were more likely to be available there. Factories also provided clinics, nurseries, launderies, baths, libraries, reading rooms and other amenities. In Leningrad, brigades of young workers organised at factories by the Komsomol took responsibility for taking food and fuel to sick people, cleaning apartments, and even burying the dead. Working-class solidarity and mutual aid, empty phrases for many years, took on new meaning in wartime.

PEASANTS

Despite the large increase in the urban population during the 1930s, the majority of Soviet citizens in 1941 still lived in the countryside and worked on the land. Peasants, mostly consisting of collective farmers, but including a small proportion of individual farmers, together with manual and white-collar workers on state farms and motor-tractor stations, comprised 60 per cent of the population.[12]

Collectivisation of agriculture had given the state decisive influence over the organisation of production, allocation of labour and distribution of produce – and it would use these powers to great effect in harnessing the resources of rural society to the war effort. But the new order was far from firmly rooted in the countryside by the time of the German invasion. Much of the peasantry was embittered and alienated, while many officials in positions of responsibility were inexperienced and insecure. The countryside, moreover, remained to a large extent a world apart. Collectivisation had not abolished the large cultural and material differences between town and country, any more than it had ended the isolation and remoteness of rural society from the urban centres of political, economic and cultural life. If any class constituted the weak link in the Soviet war effort, it was the peasantry; although in fact its contribution was to be substantial. At the same time, it would be more damaged by the war than any other section of society.

The war saw a mass exodus from the countryside, above all of young able-bodied men. More than 60 per cent of the Soviet armed forces in World War II came from the countryside.[13] In absolute

12 Narkhoz 1960: 10.
13 Nove 1985: 78.

terms, the latter's population bore the brunt of the fighting and casualties. Large numbers were also drafted into war industry, transport and building. Agriculture thus lost the youngest and fittest part of its workforce, at the very least for the duration of the war, and in millions of cases permanently. Those who left also included many of the most technically qualified cadres, much sought after by the armed forces and industry alike. Even highly valued personnel such as tractor and combine harvester drivers were liable to military call-up or the labour draft; there were no 'reserved professions' in agriculture until 1944. As a result of this exodus, the number of able-bodied collective farmers fell by 19 million (over 50 per cent) between 1941 and 1944 (see Table 6).

Replacements for those who left came from a variety of sources. Women who had previously worked part-time or not at all were pressed into service. So were disabled ex-servicemen, pensioners, juveniles and even children, as is shown in Table 5. Many evacuees were resettled on collective farms. And for sowing and harvesting, large numbers of urban residents were temporarily drafted into the countryside. The extent of the labour shortage in the countryside is shown by the fact that at such times on some collective farms they constituted up to 80 per cent of the work-force.[14]

The task facing this depleted and weakened class was daunting in the extreme: to feed the vastly expanded armed forces, as well as the urban and rural populations. It is true that the number of people who needed feeding had fallen between 1940 and 1942 by one-third, because of German occupation of much of the European part of the USSR. On the other hand, the lost territory included some of the best agricultural land in the USSR, as well as a significant section of the work-force. The result was that the gross output of agriculture and food processing fell by three-fifths.

The conditions in which the rural population lived and worked rapidly deteriorated. Literally vital though supplying food to the population was, the needs of agriculture were a lesser priority for the government than those of the armed forces and war industry. Agriculture was thus starved of investment. One effect was that mechanisation, which had been one of the few positive features of Soviet agriculture in the 1930s, was halted, indeed reversed. Tractor factories were converted to tank production, and the supply of agricultural machinery to the countryside abruptly ceased, to resume only in 1944 – and even then mostly to the devastated liberated areas. Tractors, lorries and cars

14 Aniskov 1966: 142.

were widely commandeered by the Red Army; and those which remained were often immobilised by the dire shortage of spare parts, the
lack of technicians in the MTSs, and the shortage of fuel. Agriculture
once again became an overwhelmingly manual occupation. In 1942
only one-fifth of the grain was harvested with the help of machinery;
most was brought in by manual labour and horse power.[15] But horses
were also taken by the Red Army on a large scale, their draught
power being replaced by that of cattle or human beings.

A decline in labour productivity and output was the inevitable consequence of these developments. In 1943, the worst year of the war
for agriculture, total output fell to a mere 38 per cent of the 1940
level.[16] The authorities tried to reverse this trend by various administrative means, including the reintroduction of the political departments
of motor-tractor stations and state farms in November 1941. The *politotdely*, whose predecessors had been instrumental in pushing through
the policy of collectivisation a decade earlier, comprised a vanguard of
7,200 organisations which, until their abolition in May 1943, played a
key role in implementing official policies in the countryside.[17]

Some policies, however, only exacerbated the situation. Drives to
expand the sown area, launched with all the publicity and contrived
enthusiasm of socialist competition campaigns, resulted in lower yields,
given the lack of sufficient labour to ensure proper cultivation. Farms
which boosted grain collections at the expense of keeping sufficient
seed paid the inevitable price the following season. An early casualty of
excessive state procurements was livestock. Shortages of feed resulted
in increased slaughtering; as did the pressure put on peasants during
the first year of the war to sell their private livestock to the collective.
Peasants also came under direct pressure to work harder. In April 1942
their compulsory work norms were increased. Failure to achieve the
set number of *trudodny* (workpoints) rendered culprits liable to punishments ranging from compulsory labour with deduction of earnings to
loss of private plots. It may be true, as some Soviet historians argue,
that most peasants were already overfulfilling their norms, and that this
measure was directed only against the most indolent among them, or
more likely against those who were devoting themselves too much to
their private plots and too little to work on the collective. It appears
that sanctions were rarely applied even when norms were not fulfilled.
But the mere threat that they might be probably provided sufficient
incentive for almost all to comply.

15 Nove 1985: 82.
16 IVOVSS vol 6 1965: 45.
17 Savel'ev, Savvin 1974: 39.

A different kind of pressure was reflected in the economic relationship between the state, the collective farms and the peasants. The prices paid by the former for the latter's produce was purely nominal. This had already been the situation before the war. What changed in wartime was that quotas for obligatory deliveries by the collective farms of key crops such as grain and potatoes were increased, leaving them with less to distribute to their members in payment for workpoints. Some distributed nothing at all. Since the state took no responsibility for feeding the rural population, which was not covered by the rationing system in force in the towns, but in effect left it to its own devices where food was concerned, the peasantry's situation was extremely precarious. What averted disaster was that during the war the government put the imperatives of survival before the dictates of ideology in its policy towards the peasants. It suspended its hostility to private production and the market, turned a blind eye to the peasants' informal and theoretically illegal economic activity, and so enabled most of them to stay, however precariously, above subsistence level.

The key to survival on the collective farm during World War II was the private plot. Small though it was (on average, little over a quarter of a hectare),[18] it provided, either directly or indirectly, the majority of the peasants' food. For most peasants it was not, as officially described, their 'subsidiary holding', but their main source of subsistence. Even for hard-working collective farmers earning over twice the obligatory norm of workpoints on the collective farm, it accounted for two-thirds of their income.[19] And this despite the fact that the private plot was often cultivated by older members of the family. From it, peasants obtained potatoes and cabbages (for most, the main elements of their diet), as well as other vegetables, eggs, milk and meat. The larger part of the produce of their plots they consumed themselves themselves; but the shortage of basic necessities forced them also to produce for the local market. There they traded their surplus, either for cash or, by barter, for bread, salt, fuel and the many other items essential for daily life and work, from tar to axle grease, unobtainable from the state.[20]

With the temporary revival of the market, private trade revived for the first time since the end of NEP. Besides allowing peasants to acquire basic necessities, it also served the function of partially compensating them for the state's extraction of their surplus for the benefit of the armed forces and the urban population. Town inhabitants regularly

18 Arutyunyan 1970: 352.
19 Arutyunyan 1970: 350.
20 Arutyunyan 1970: 334, 353.

travelled to the countryside in search of food, or bought it at markets in or on the edge of towns, paying high prices in cash, clothes and valuables of every kind. In this way, substantial amounts of cash and assets were transferred from town to country.

In the process, individual peasants acquired considerable wealth. One indication is the size of purchases of bonds for the Red Army Fund or the Victory Fund. Hundreds of peasants bought bonds for sums ranging from 30,000 to 100,000 roubles; the maximum recorded was 400,000 roubles.[21] How voluntary such purchases were is hard to say. While they may have been motivated by patriotism or by identification with relatives and friends at the front, pressure may also have been put on people (as it was on workers to subscribe to industrialisation 'loans' during the first Five Year Plan) to pay what was in effect an additional tax. The important point is that some peasants were in a position to hand over very large sums of money to the state. Its origin, in any case, was probably often dubious from an official point of view. The remoteness of many collective farms made close supervision of their activities by the authorities difficult, and this gave considerable scope for corruption. Goods could be distributed to members, for example, not only on the basis of labour points earned, but also on the order of the kolkhoz chairman. The same person could allow the rent or even sale of collective farm land to individuals.[22] Whether by legal or illegal means, even during the war, some people in the countryside prospered.

But they were very much the exception. For the vast majority of peasants, who had neither the entrepreneurial talent, nor the fertile land, valuable produce or advantageous geographical location of these fortunate individuals, life in wartime was hard. On average, they ate even less than their urban counterparts, with hunger, malnutrition, disease and premature death the inevitable consequences.

The Soviet state's treatment of the peasantry in World War II, measured by its extraction of food from the countryside, was certainly harsher than its Tsarist predecessor's in World War I (which had helped to precipitate a revolution), and probably even more ruthless than its own policy of requisitioning during the Civil War (which had ended with the peasantry in virtual revolt and the Soviet government forced into the retreat of the New Economic Policy). So why did Soviet peasants not react against the hardships imposed on them in World War II?

21 Aniskov 1966: 337.
22 Arutyunyan 1970: 348.

The explanation given by some Soviet historians, that the peasantry was already strongly committed to the Soviet order and above all to the collective farm system, is very dubious. There is abundant evidence that many peasants hoped the war would result in decollectivisation, and for this reason welcomed or looked forward to the Germans' arrival. From the western border to the Volga, peasants are said to have planned the redistribution of land once the collective farms were dissolved. Soviet historians themselves allude to this, noting the growth of 'petit-bourgeois individualistic attitudes' among peasants during the war.[23] There seems little reason to doubt that the peasants' loyalty to Soviet power would have been severely shaken had the Germans returned the land to them.

But the collective farm system was retained in the occupied areas, which, together with the Germans' barbaric treatment of the Soviet population, destroyed any illusion peasants might have entertained about their conquerers' intentions. Patriotic resistance to the invader remained their only realistic option. Moreover, by 1941 the Soviet state's capacity for combatting internal and external threats to its authority was far more formidable than two decades earlier. Ultimately, however, the main factor which preserved the peasants' loyalty to the Soviet state was the latter's perceived ability to maintain order in the rear and to lead resistance to the foreign invaders at the front. It demanded heavy sacrifices of them, and at the same time it offered them the prospect that their patriotism would not be in vain.

The war not only imposed great burdens on peasants as individuals, but also contributed to their decline as a class. Many millions of young males died or were crippled; many others, both male and female, never returned to the countryside, choosing, after demobilisation from the armed forces or after the end of their drafted employment in war industry, to settle in towns. The war thus accelerated the shift of population from the countryside to the town, at the same time setting the condition of Soviet agriculture back several years and widening the gap between agriculture and industry.

INTELLECTUALS

Unlike the working class and the peasantry, the smallest of the three social groups included in the official description of Soviet society's class

23 Aniskov 1966: 303.

104

structure saw its position improve during the war. While as individuals the highly qualified, professional specialists in various cultural, scientific and technical fields who comprised the intelligentsia often suffered hardships similar to those experienced by workers and peasants, as a group their role and status was significantly enhanced by the war.[24]

The contrast with the prewar period was striking. In the 1930s the size of the intelligentsia had grown substantially, and economic growth had opened up new professional and material opportunities. But the price had been a heavy one. The intelligentsia was heavily purged in the late 1930s, and the context within which its members had to work was ever more restrictive, with a party line laid down in every sphere of science and culture. Nor had repression ceased with the end of the Ezhov purges. While the number of arrests fell sharply after 1938, and while some people were freed, others continued to suffer. The great aircraft designer, A N Tupolev, for example, was arrested on the eve of the war, as were several other leading specialists, and forced to continue research in captivity. The war changed this situation radically. Pasternak's remark that, compared with the 1930s, 'the war came as a breath of fresh air, an omen of deliverance, a purifying storm',[25] applied to no group so much as the intelligentsia. For a time at least, its interests coincided with the regime's. That the leadership's basic distrust of the intelligentsia had altered little was reflected in Stalin's characteristic jibe, in his Red Square speech of 7 November 1941, that 'The enemy is not as strong as some terror-stricken would-be intellectuals picture him.'[26] But the need for the intelligentsia's expertise was urgent as never before; and there were obvious limits to the efficacy of coercion in gaining its cooperation. Without abandoning the controls established over the preceding years, the regime had to apply them more selectively, and give intellectuals greater scope to contribute to the war effort.

Not that they lacked incentives to do so. While their responses to war were determined by the same range of motives, from patriotism to self-preservation, as those of others, they were well placed to grasp the full extent of the threat posed by the German invasion to national independence, to Russia's cultural heritage, and to the social and economic gains of the Revolution. They were also prepared, organisationally and psychologically, by developments over the previous de-

24 For an analysis of the composition and role of the intelligentsia in Soviet society, see Churchward 1973: 1–15.

25 Pasternak B 1985 *Doctor Zhivago,* translated by Hayward M and Harari M, London. Cited by Piper 1984: 131.

26 Stalin 1945: 37.

cade to meet the demands now placed on them. Whatever the damage inflicted by the purges, and whatever the intellectual drawbacks of centralised organisation, the creation of large networks of scientific research institutes and powerful unions in virtually every branch of cultural life over the past decade undoubtedly facilitated collective action on the intelligentsia's part. And the regime's continual demand that theory be linked with practice, that intellectual work be relevant to the needs of society, had tended to inculcate the value of a practical orientation for science and culture. The difference now was that the intelligentsia could have no doubt about the legitimacy or the necessity of the cause it was called on to serve.

Soviet intellectuals' participation in the war effort involved a great range of activities. For scientists and technical specialists, these included the development of weapons and communications systems, the provision of medical services for the armed forces, the fight against epidemics at the front and in the rear, the evacuation and reorganisation of industry, the struggle to feed the population. Much of this activity was channelled through bodies designed to link the academic world with production. In many cities 'committees of scholars' were set up which brought scientists, engineers and 'practical' specialists together to work on concrete tasks, such as saving materials, energy and fuel, and improving production technology. Another vehicle for applying science to the needs of industry was the 'factory laboratories', some of which evolved into large, factory-based research centres.[27]

Members of the 'creative intelligentsia', engaged in art, culture and the humanities, were no less involved in the war effort. Their main contribution was in focusing the public's attention on the nature and aims of the war, and in maintaining popular morale. Historians wrote on military and patriotic themes and stressing continuity between the Russian past and the Soviet present (for example the works of E V Tarle and R Vipper, and the histories of the Russian Army and Navy published by the Academy of Sciences Institute of History). Composers depicted the people's heroism (as in Shostakovich's 'Leningrad' symphony, Prokofiev's opera *War and Peace*, Kabalevskii's suite 'The avenging people'). Film-makers produced dozens of war epics, including *The German Soldiers' Defeat at Moscow, The Battle for Sevastopol, She Defends the Motherland, Stalingrad* and *Berlin*.

Most influential of all were writers. Some gained enormous popularity for their expression of intense feelings of pain, patriotism, fortitude, hatred and revenge. At the front, in factories, in besieged

27 Savel'ev, Savvin 1974: 78–9.

Leningrad, poets read their work to huge audiences. Prominent writers became war correspondents, and the reports, pamphlets and fictional works of the best known of these, such as Il'ya Ehrenburg, Vasilii Grossman and Konstantin Simonov, had a massive circulation. The main themes of wartime literature were predictable, but no less effective for that – revenge, as in Ehrenburg's article 'The justification of hatred' or Simonov's poem 'Kill him!'; heroism, as in Margarita Aliger's 'Zoya', about a young partisan executed by the Germans; defiance in adversity, as in Olga Berggolts's 'February diary', describing Leningrad in the blockade; and the resourcefulness of ordinary Russians, as in Alexander Tvardovskii's immensely popular poem 'Vasilii Tyorkin'.

The intelligentsia's wartime activity also brought about its greater involvement in decision-making, as well as greater official recognition. Leading scientists were appointed to government posts. Academicians I P Bardin and B E Vedenev were Deputy People's Commissars for the Iron and Steel Industry and Electrical Power Industry respectively, while academician S I Vavilov served as a GKO plenipotentiary. Several other academicians, including P L Kapitsa, A F Fersman, A F Ioffe and A N Bakh, had key assignments from the GKO, Gosplan or specific commissariats.[28] GKO and Sovnarkom meetings were frequently attended by academic experts. And far from scientific activity declining, new institutions were created during the war. These included the Academy of Medical Sciences and the Academy of Pedagogical Sciences, the Azerbaijan, Armenian, Kazakh and Uzbek Academies of Science, and the western Siberian and Kirgizia branches of the All-Union Academy of Sciences.[29] In practice, these were mainly upgraded versions of previously existing institutions, which would not have involved a substantial commitment of resources. Even so, they reflected the importance accorded to science by the government during the war.

None of this prevented a worsening of the physical conditions in which many intellectuals lived and worked. Like others, they were called on to dig trenches or bring in the harvest or volunteer for the *narodnoe opolchenie*. Like others, they were exposed to danger, even death: 417 writers alone were killed at the front.[30] Many academic and cultural institutions were evacuated to distant locations, where their personnel suffered the same cramped conditions and material shortages

28 Savel'ev, Savvin 1974: 64.
29 Savel'ev, Savvin 1974: 95.
30 Brown 1985: 243.

as other evacuees. Some, however, saw an improvement in their relative situation where food was concerned. Initially the rationing system had four categories, with intellectuals, classified as white-collar workers, placed in the second category. In February 1942, a new first category was introduced for people working in war industry and for scientific and technical personnel. At least this section of the intelligentsia was considered sufficiently important to be given the highest rations.[31]

But more significant was the general intellectual atmosphere which prevailed during the war. While the authorities continued to issue directives and criticisms, and while censorship continued, the extent of official interference was substantially reduced and the scope for creativity and self-expression considerably widened. Conformity with doctrine was less important a criterion of intellectual work than its potential contribution to the war effort. In both the academic and cultural spheres there was a greater degree of freedom than at any time since the 1920s. Towards the end of the war, ideological orthodoxy began to be reimposed. Even so, it was possible, as the war ended, for theoreticians to advance diverging views on the role of the Party and state, the organisation of the economy, the treatment of the peasantry and Soviet foreign policy.[32] And many people, particularly among the intelligentsia, looked forward with optimism to a postwar society which would be very different from the Soviet Union of the 1930s. Utopian as such hopes might later seem in retrospect, they were a projection of real trends in Soviet intellectual life in wartime.

OFFICIALS

Of all groups in Soviet society, the one with the greatest immediate stake in defeating the Germans was the political and administrative elite, the *nomenklatura*. For the officials of the Party and state apparatus, the senior personnel of all economic, social, military and scientific institutions, the 'leading cadres' who ran the 'administrative-command system', the war was literally a struggle for survival. It was not only their powers and privileges which could depend on the outcome. So also could their lives – as the Germans' merciless treatment of captured Soviet officials indicated. This, as well as traditional Bolshevik disci-

31 Moskoff 1990: 138.
32 Hough 1985: 253–81.

pline and fear of retribution for disloyalty, helps explain their unity in the face of disaster. Though the succession of calamities which followed the surprise attack on 22 June 1941 must have destroyed many illusions within the elite about the leadership's infallibility, there was no indication of a split in official ranks, still less of a fifth column or a peace party. Officials were no more immune from panic than ordinary citizens, as the behaviour of many of them showed when Moscow seemed about to be captured in October 1941, showed. But even among those members of the Soviet elite captured by the Germans only a small minority attempted to organise opposition to Stalin's government, in the form of General Vlasov's 'Russian Liberation Movement'; and its appeal for support evoked no response within the Soviet establishment.

Like other groups, the size and composition of the *nomenklatura* was radically affected by the war. A large number of Party and government cadres were immediately drafted into the armed forces to fight or serve as political commissars, or administer the vast logistical operation of keeping a modern army in the field. In Leningrad, for example, 96 per cent of Party branch secretaries left for the front in the first weeks of the war.[33] Local government was also hard hit. In Perm' region, 80 per cent of the chairmen of rural soviets had resigned by March 1942.[34] Altogether, 70 per cent of local soviet officials left to serve in the armed forces.[35] At the centre, vacancies were fille relatively quickly, but at the local level there was a major reduction in administrative personnel. In many departments and enterprises it fell by one-third or one-half.[36]

This did not always have negative results, given the swollen size of the bureaucracy in many organisations. Sometimes it may even have increased efficiency by forcing unnecessary procedures to be dropped. At the giant Magnitogorsk metallurgical plant, for example, more than 600 types of written report had been eliminated by March 1942.[37] But inevitably the inexperience of many of the replacements of those who had left for the front adversely affected the quality of administration.[38]

Particularly in the first year and a half of the war, the pressures on officials were enormous. In a situation where the territory and resources under Soviet control were substantially diminishing and the enemy

33 Bidlack 1987: 62.
34 Kumanev 1988: 111.
35 Mitrofanova 1989: 247.
36 Kozlov V A 1988: 132.
37 *Trud* 10 March 1942, cited in Kozlov V A 1988: 132.
38 Mitrofanova 1989: 247.

was inflicting heavy losses on Soviet forces, the organisational tasks of supplying the front with sufficient material and manpower, of extracting maximum output from industry and agriculture, of maintaining an overloaded transport system, and simply keeping order in the civilian population, were massive.

In addition there was the political leadership's relentless demand for action and results, combined with the threat of dire punishment for failure. The *nomenklatura* had had over a decade to become accustomed to a 'voluntaristic' style of government, to orders being issued regardless of the objective possibilities of achieving them. But the early period of the war in particular produced ultra-voluntarism in the leadership, with the desperate situation investing all orders with absolute force. Voznesenskii's reply to a group of experts from the People's Commissariat of Armament in July 1941, who were trying to convince him of the impossibility of increasing the output of 37mm guns sixfold in a week, is typical: 'The fascist horde has swooped down on us; to discuss a lesser plan is impermissible. Propose any measures, and the government will endorse them, but we will not reduce the plan by one item.'[39]

In this sense, the command character of the system was strengthened in the war. Values of discipline and obedience, already prominent, became even more pronounced, and the hierarchy even more explicitly militarised. In transport, military officers were actually put in charge. Kaganovich was replaced as Transport Commissar first by General A V Khrulev, then later again by General I V Kovalev. More generally, as a corollary of the militarisation of labour introduced in 1941–2, factory directors were often given military ranks to emphasise their authority.

At the same time, the *nomenklatura* was granted more autonomy in carrying out orders during the war than before it. In the interests of speed and efficiency, the government gave its officials greater scope for using their initiative. In some cases this was specifically reflected in their increased status. Leading designers and directors of major plants were made deputy people's commissars, with substantial powers over the distribution of labour and material resources. Many officials were appointed plenipotentiaries of the centre, exercising substantial authority on behalf of government or Party organisations. But more generally the need for effective action and the inability of central government to provide detailed instructions resulted in greater freedom for officials to take decisions themselves. At the same time there

39 Cited in Kozlov V A 1988: 130–1.

110

was a marked reduction in the use of punitive sanctions. While officials were still criticised and dismissed, there was less tendency to interpret failure or mistakes as sabotage. Compared with what had preceded and what would follow the war, it was a period when officials were relatively immune from terror.

In material respects, too, the *nomenklatura* cannot be said to have suffered unduly, though its standard of living was certainly affected by the war. A middle-ranking Soviet diplomat, Nikolai Novikov, was one of many officials evacuated to Kuibyshev.

> The food ration for the family was so meagre that it wasn't even enough to feed the children enough, let alone the adults. We had to exchange all the things from our wardrobe which had any value, one after the other, at the market for butter, meat and milk.

Fortunately, 'catastrophe' was avoided, thanks to the 'supplementary feeding' he received now and then at diplomatic banquets.[40] In general, those responsible for running the system managed to look after themselves and their own. Even during the starvation winter of 1941–2 in Leningrad, special 'directors' cafeterias' were provided for senior factory personnel, while at Party headquarters in the Smolny, officials ate well throughout the siege.[41] Victor Kravchenko, head of a department at the RSFSR Sovnarkom in Moscow, soon discovered the difference between the conditions of the elite and those of its subordinates. After his breakfast ('two eggs, some stewed meat, white bread, butter, a glass of hot tea, several lumps of sugar, a few cookies'), what was left every day fed his secretary, his waitress and her two children; its market value was two-thirds of his secretary's monthly wage.[42]

Inevitably, the behaviour of the regime's representatives varied greatly. Self-sacrifice coexisted with self-interest, probity with corruption. Many displayed extreme courage and commitment to the common cause at moments of danger. Others showed great devotion to saving their own skin. In the panic which accompanied the evacuation of much of the Party and state apparatus from Moscow in mid-October 1941, members of the elite were to the fore:

> Small, medium and even high Party or non-Party officials who felt that Moscow had become a job for the Army, and that there was not much

---

40 Novikov 1989: 118.
41 Bidlack 1987: 164, 209.
42 Kravchenko 1947: 396–7.

that civilians could do . . . with regular passes, or with passes of sorts they had somehow wangled – or sometimes with no passes at all . . . fled to the east.[43]

Nepotism and political influence, according to Kravchenko, decided who got permission to leave.

For the first time in twenty years . . . I heard open cursing of officialdom . . . as if to taunt the miserable mobs, comfortable caravans of official motorcars streamed out of Moscow, loaded with the families and household goods of the elite.[44]

For all this, the fact remains that it was the *nomenklatura* which organised the war effort, which provided the coordination and leadership on which victory depended. It was responsible for the system's success in defeating the enemy, for what was arguably its finest hour. And it did not go unrewarded. For years, even decades after the war, the generation of officials which had governed Soviet society in wartime would remain in power enjoying the fruits of victory.

NATIONALITIES

When Nazi Germany invaded the USSR, it went to war with the most ethnically diverse country in the world. While Russians accounted for over half the population, and Slavs (Russians, Ukrainians and Belorussians) three-quarters, the remaining quarter was composed of more than a hundred distinct nationalities. In theory, Soviet citizenship and a common sense of Soviet patriotism united all the peoples of the USSR. In practice, feelings of ethnic identity had a strong influence on their attitudes and behaviour. The consequences for the Soviet war effort were serious.

Some were positive. For many Russians, as already mentioned, traditional patriotism played a major role in mobilising resistance to the invader. And members of all the non-Russian nationalities participated, some on a large scale, in the struggle to defeat Nazi Germany. Some indication of the level of involvement is indicated by the death rate among young males. Among nationalities with their own all- Union republics, it was highest among Russians, followed by Ukrainians and Belorussians. It was higher still, however, among Tartars, Bashkirs,

43 Werth 1964: 237.
44 Kravchenko 1947: 373–4.

Chuvash, Mordvinians and other nationalities within the RSFSR.[45] In the occupied areas, particularly Belorussia and the Ukraine, over 1 million partisans inflicted substantial damage on the enemy. More than 25 million people, many from the non-Russian republics, were evacuated eastwards, to continue working or fighting for the Soviet cause. And Central Asia, together with Siberia, played a crucial role in the Soviet war economy.

But the USSR's multinational character was also a major source of weakness in wartime. In many areas, a long history of Russian domination, together with two decades of extreme centralisation and ruthless suppression of 'bourgeois nationalist deviations', or annexation and Sovietisation in the case of the territories incorporated in the USSR under the secret clauses of the Nazi–Soviet Pact (Lithuania, Estonia, Latvia, the western regions of Belorussia and the Ukraine, and Moldavia), had left a legacy of strong anti-Russian and anti-Soviet feeling. When the Germans and their allies invaded, they were greeted by many non-Russians as liberators. In the western Ukrainian city of L'vov, there was an anti-Soviet uprising even before the arrival of German forces. From the western border of the USSR to the Caucasus, nationalists saw the Germans as potential allies in their struggle for independence.

There is little doubt that support for the Germans among the non-Russian nationalities was potentially very large, as some Nazis, particularly in the Reich Ministry for Occupied Eastern Territories, recognised. What prevented it from becoming a decisive factor in the war was the irreconcilable conflict between Nazi ideology and war aims on the one hand and the policies needed to gain widespread support on the other. According to Nazi racial theory, Slavs were sub-human (*Untermenschen*), Armenians biologically related to Jews, and Soviet Asians inferior 'mongols'. (Georgians and Estonians, on the other hand, were classified as Aryans, while Latvians and Lithuanians were regarded as fit for 'Germanisation'.) This strongly conditioned German treatment of the Soviet nationalities, and provided a rationale for the ruthless exploitation of the population of the occupied territories. But while it destroyed the possibility of winning mass support among the non-Russian nationalities, it did not prevent widespread collaboration with the Germans by Russians and non-Russians alike.

---

45 Anderson, Silver 1985: 212–13. Causes of death were not limited to those involving resistance to the enemy. But in the age cohorts mainly conscripted for military service, these are likely to have predominated, particularly among the RSFSR nationalities, whose territory was not occupied by the Germans.

This took both civilian and military forms. Throughout the occupied areas, German administration depended on local mayors, district chiefs and other officials, as well as on police and local security units recruited from the native population to maintain order and defend military installations and railways from the partisans. Hundreds of thousands of people, perhaps more, were involved. Many others participated directly in the German war effort. By late autumn 1941, local volunteers were being recruited into the Wehrmacht as *Helfswillige* (or Hiwis, 'little helpers'), and from the end of 1941 national military units were created from released POWs and indigenous populations to fight alongside the Wehrmacht. These took a variety of forms – including Vlasov's 'Russian Liberation Army', national 'legions' from the Baltic, Georgia, Armenia, Turkistan and the Moslem nationalities of the North Caucasus, and the Baltic and Galician divisions of the Waffen SS. Uncertainty surrounds the numbers involved; estimates involved range from a quarter of a million to over 1 million. It is quite possible that some nationalities were more strongly represented in the German army than in the Red Army.[46]

Overall, the effects of collaboration were limited, mainly because of the hostility German policies provoked among the indigenous population in the occupied areas. The example of the nationalities of the North Caucasus, however, shows what might have been, given different policies. The Germans reached the Caucasus in summer 1942 and were forced to retreat at the beginning of 1943. During this short period, administration remained in the hands of the Wehrmacht; the SS and the German economic agencies responsible for the worst treatment of civilians elsewhere played no role. In these few months, substantial decollectivisation occurred, a significant degree of religious freedom and cultural autonomy were allowed, and minimal use was made of forced labour. The result was a higher level of recruitment for military service with the Germans and a lower level of partisan activity than in any other occupied area. In the Caucasus, as elsewhere (particularly in the Baltic republics and western Ukraine), local anti-Soviet units continued to fight the Red Army even after the Germans had departed.

Retribution was extreme. With the restoration of Soviet rule, not only were known collaborators shot or imprisoned. Although collaboration had everywhere been a minority activity, whole nationalities were declared guilty by association and punished by deportation from their native area. In 1943–4 this was the fate of the Crimean Tartars

46 See Dallin A 1957; Alexiev 1985: 61–74.

114

and five Moslem or Turkic nationalities from the Caucasus (the Chechens, Ingushi, Karachai, Balkars and Kalmyks), 1 million people in all,
who were deported, under abysmal conditions, to Kazakhstan and
Central Asia.

This was not the first mass deportation of non-Russians during the
war, nor the last. In autumn 1941 the German population of the
Volga region, 400,000 people in all, had been deported to Siberia and
Central Asia, more than half to work in NKVD camps.[47] In 1944–5
large number of Balts, Georgians and Ukrainians were exiled, as were
Armenians, Bulgars and Greeks from the Crimea. So too were the
Meskhetian Turks from southern Georgia, even though, unlike other
nationalities, their collaboration, not least for geographical reasons, had
been non-existent.

With the possible exception of the Volga Germans (whose fate had
certain parallels – in the arbitrary and paranoid exclusion of a group
from society purely on ethnic grounds, if not in the conditions experienced – with the wholesale internment of Germans in the UK and
Japanese in the USA), the ruthless treatment of the small non-Russian
nationalities made little political or military sense. Local resistance to
the Soviet authorities after liberation of the occupied areas was small
scale; in any case, those exiled were mainly old people, women and
children. And at a time when the war with Germany was reaching its
climax and the front's demand for manpower was huge, large numbers
of troops had to be employed in the deportations – over 100,000 in
the case of the Chechens and Ingushi alone.[48]

The wartime deportations were essentially an application of Stalinist
policies and attitudes whose origins lay in the prewar period – the
attribution of guilt by association, as seen in the punishment of the
families of kulaks and purge victims; the obsession with the threat to
the unity of the USSR posed by nationalist feeling among non-Russians; and the all-pervasive fear of treason. They must also be seen in
the context of the officially endorsed Russian nationalism, which grew
steadily during the war, reaching a climax with victory. Nowhere was
the supreme importance of the Russian (and by clear inference the
secondary significance of the non-Russian) contribution to the Soviet
war effort more frankly expressed than in Stalin's celebrated toast at
the banquet for Red Army commanders in May 1945. The Russian
people, he said, was 'the leading nation of all the nations belonging to
the Soviet Union.' It had earned in the war 'general recognition as the

47 Litovkin 1990: 17.
48 Volkogonov vol 2(i) 1989: 257–8.

guiding force of the Soviet Union.'[49] The implications for the non-Russian peoples were ominous.

PRISONERS

No account of Soviet society during the war would be complete without mention of those at the very bottom of the social pyramid – the population of the camps and prisons. Less is known about this group than any other. Until recently, it figured in no Soviet statistics or histories of war; even now evidence of its size, composition and conditions is fragmentary. What is clear, however, is that the number of prisoners was substantial and that their already wretched conditions worsened considerably with the outbreak of war.

Estimates of the total number of Soviet citizens engaged in forced labour during the war range from 5 million to over 20 million.[50] This divergence reflects both the lack of firm data and the inclusion of different categories of people. Besides the inmates of prison and labour camps, the figures may, for example, include members of national minorities deported to remote areas as 'special migrants' (*spetsposelentsy*); or people sentenced to compulsory work at their place of employment for breaches of labour discipline. All had their freedom seriously limited in one way or another.

But those sentenced to penal servitude were in a category of their own, and deserve discussing as such. Unlike the others, they had no control over where they lived, or what work they did, or how much. Their freedom was not only restricted; it was in all important respects extinguished. A small proportion served their sentences in prison; but the great majority were in labour camps or labour colonies run by the NKVD's Chief Administration of Camps (Gulag). Much is still unknown about their number and conditions, but statistics recently published in the USSR provide considerably more data than previously available (Table 7). Although they may still be incomplete, they probably indicate the main trends.

Having risen in 1940 (largely because of arrests in the territories newly incorporated in the USSR), the number of Gulag prisoners declined steadily between 1941 and 1944. By the beginning of 1944, it

49 *Pravda* 25 May 1945.
50 See Dallin D J, Nikolaevsky 1947: 84–6. Dallin's own estimate was between 7 million and 12 million.

was reportedly down to three-fifths of the level of three years earlier; although over the following year it appears to have risen sharply again. There appear to have been two main reasons for the decline. First, releases from the camps ran at a high level in 1941–3. At over 40 per cent of the average annual number of prisoners, this was nearly double the rate in the last year of peace. The first release of prisoners was decreed on 12 July 1941; it applied to those in areas near the war zone who had been convicted for relatively minor crimes. The scope of this decree was extended on 24 November, and as a result some 420,000 men were dispatched to the front. Altogether, 1 million ex-prisoners fought during the war, mainly in the 'penal battalions' (*shtrafnye batal'-ony*).[51] Used for the most dangerous operations (clearing minefields, storming well-fortified positions), their casualty rate was the highest in the Red Army. In many cases, perhaps most, release from the camps during the war meant a speedy release from the misery of this world. Even so, many prisoners volunteered for military service, preferring to die on the battlefield rather than in the camps, or clutching at the hope of distinguishing themselves and winning rehabilitation, as some did.

Second, the death-rate in the camps soared during the war. According to Table 7, it rose seven-fold between 1940 and 1942. One in five of the camp population died in 1942 and 1943. The reasons are simple: 'more work and less food and less heat and worse clothes and ferocious discipline and more severe punishment.'[52] In a situation of scarcity, prisoners were the lowest priority, and their rations were reduced accordingly. At the same time, like all civilians they were under great pressure to increase output. Despite their conditions, productivity in the camps increased by 80 per cent between 1941 and 1943.[53] Cold and hunger, malnutrition and exhaustion took their inevitable toll. So bad were the conditions that the Soviet procuracy is said to have made representations about them to Beriya.[54] Solzhenitsyn claims that in the wartime camps during winter 'a death rate of one per cent per day was commonplace and common knowledge.' In some camps at least this may not have been an exaggeration.[55]

One other factor may have contributed to the decline in the size of the camp population in 1941 and 1942, namely the loss of territory,

51 Litovkin 1990: 17.
52 Dallin D J, Nikolaevsky 1947: 119.
53 Litovkin 1990: 17.
54 Litovkin 1990: 17.
55 Solzhenitsyn vol 2 1976: 90. On the other hand, his assertion that 'during the war they buried no fewer dead in the camps than at the front' is highly dubious, unless the highest estimates of the camp population are in fact accurate.

and with it the loss of prisoners. At the outbreak of war, the NKVD decided to evacuate three-quarters of a million prisoners from the western part of the country eastwards. Lacking transport, many had to cover vast distances on foot. But the speed of the German advance prevented this in some areas, particularly in Belorussia, the Ukraine and the Baltic republics. Some prisoners may have escaped, other may have been captured by the Germans. What is certain is that prisoners were often executed by their NKVD guards. The 'L'vov massacre' on 29–30 June 1941 was the first of many such cases.[56]

Despite the fall in the number of prisoners, there was a constant stream of new arrivals. Although it was at its height in the first year of the war, the net inflow of prisoners was never less than a quarter of the average total, and it rose again as the end of the war approached, probably as a result of arrests in the newly liberated areas. This, plus a decline in the death-rate and, in 1944, in the number of prisoners released, produced an increase of nearly a quarter in the size of the Gulag work-force between 1 January 1944 and 1 January 1945.

On the other hand, the number of prisoners actually in the camps stayed relatively low; at the beginning of 1945 it was less than half what it had been four years earlier. The reason for this was the steady shift of prisoners from the camps to Gulag labour colonies attached to factories and construction sites. To cope with the worsening man-power shortage in industry, Gulag prisoners were increasingly used to supplement the free work-force. By 1945 there were more prisoners in the labour colonies than in the camps themselves. According to Victor Kravchenko, 'few industrial enterprises were without slave contingents . . . in dozens of them coerced labor was the principal or sole reliance',[57] and this may well have been the case. The figures in Tables 3 and 7 suggest that prisoners could have constituted around one-tenth of the industrial work-force by the end of the war. They were employed in many areas of industry and construction. The NKVD provided labour amounting to a quarter of a million prisoners for 640 enterprises and building sites belonging to other commissariats. Other prisoners worked for the NKVD itself, in its mines, metalworks, farms, even fisheries.[58]

Not all prisoners were victims of political repression. There were real criminals among them, guilty of treason, collaboration, personal violence, speculation, theft and the whole range of crimes known in

56 Erickson 1975: 166. According to a Soviet source, 3,000 prisoners were shot in L'vov prison alone: 'Red Empire', Channel 4 Television, 19 August 1990.

57 Kravchenko 1947: 405.

58 Litovkin 1990: 18.

every society. But there were also many who were punished on trumped-up charges of desertion from the Red Army, or for minor infractions of the draconian labour laws, or for spreading rumours, for making anti-Soviet statements or for the many other political offences which came under Article 58 of the RSFSR Criminal Code. Guilty or innocent, whether working in factories, mines, forests, building sites, or fighting the enemy, they all contributed to Soviet victory. And they did so in conditions which were extreme even by the standards of the Gulag. As Solzhenitsyn writes, 'whoever didn't serve time in wartime didn't know what camp was really like.'[59]

59 Solzhenitsyn vol 2 1976: 119.

PART THREE
The Productive Effort

CHAPTER SEVEN
Fortresses of the Rear[1]

THE NEEDS OF WAR

What happened to the Soviet economy in wartime? The picture found in official statistics is summarised in Table 8. It shows realistically enough, at least in outline, what happened on the changing territory under Soviet jurisdiction – the initial collapse of capital assets, of the work-force, and of production generally under the crushing weight of the German invasion; the difficulty with which industrial production was maintained; the disaster which struck agriculture and consumer trade, and the long delay in recovery of these sectors. At the same time, however, there was observed a rapidly rising graph of war production in the machine-building and metal-working sector, where munitions capacity was concentrated.

Essential to Soviet victory over Germany in World War II was the latter achievement. One of the most important reasons why the Red Army was able to beat the Wehrmacht was that, in the interior of the country in 1942–3, Soviet factories were pouring out aircraft, tanks,

---

1 On prewar investment policy, and the influence of rearmament, see especially Cooper 1976, Tupper 1981, and a background summary in Harrison 1985: 45–63. For a first, brief official summary of wartime trends we still rely heavily on Voznesensky 1948. Apart from the official histories, an important source on the evacuation of industry is Eshelony 1966 (a collection of essays and memoirs by officials who for the most part were personally involved); also of value are writings of the railway historian Kumanev 1966, 1976, 1988, and a recent survey by Likhomanov *et al* 1985. The relocation process is discussed by Zinich 1971. The evacuation is discussed in English by Lieberman 1983 and Harrison 1985: 63–81. On wartime conversion, and investment policy in general, see Harrison 1985: 81–93, 133–7.

guns and shells at a faster rate than German factories. These factories were the fortresses of the Soviet rear.

The basis of the Soviet Union's wartime economic defences was laid down in the prewar years, during the Stalinist industrialisation drive. The principal objective of this drive was the construction of new capital assets. Soviet economic policy of the 1930s was not directed towards maximising consumer welfare, nor to maximising the rate of growth of national income or of industrial production. Its chief aim was the most rapid possible structural change – the speedy rebuilding of the traditionally agrarian economy on industrial lines through public sector investment.

What did public sector investment come to mean? It meant the initiation and multiplication, by the state, of hundreds – eventually thousands – of large-scale capital projects in heavy industry and transport, new coalfields and oilfields, huge new blast furnaces and metal rolling mills, new chemical and engineering works, great new cities and hydroelectric power stations, new airfields and highways. The whole country was to become a gigantic building site. Success in this historic endeavour would be judged by the sheer volume of activity, not by its quality or results.

The investment policy of the interwar years was responsive to Soviet defence requirements, and influenced the country's war-making capacities in several respects.

First, the drive to build up heavy industries was itself of prime importance, because no country could produce its own modern weapons without steel, chemicals, engineering plant and electric power. Expansion of the heavy industries created a huge potential for domestic production of munitions in the long run. So did investment in scientific and technological research, and in human capital through general and specialised education.

Second, to realise this potential in the form of a ready supply of modern weapons for immediate combat required something more – the development of industrial capacities specialised in the production of components and their assembly into aircraft, armoured vehicles, artillery and shells. There also had to be created domestic resources and institutions for military research and development and its application to production; otherwise, as in the civilian field, the Soviet Union would remain dependent upon foreign technologies and foreign designs, which tended to be already obsolete by the time they had been identified, imported and absorbed. This was also the focus of major efforts in the prewar years.

Third, peacetime investment in specialised defence capacity, even on a substantial scale, would never generate the scale of munitions output required in a real war – first, to replace heavy initial equipment losses; then, to provide additional resources for rapid force expansion. Here prewar policy sought a solution through peacetime creation of reserve capacities for war production which could be speedily mobilised in the event of war. The reserve capacities were of two kinds: in some branches of defence manufacture, for example armament and tank building, excess capacity was deliberately created. In others, for example the ammunition industry where specialised capacity was already at full stretch in the late 1930s, defence leaders tried to build up reserves by subcontracting the supply of parts and assemblies to civilian factories which essentially became part-time defence producers, acquired the equipment and knowledge necessary for defence production and were thereby familiarised with its needs.

The prewar investment policy contained significant flaws which were perfectly visible at the time but which went uncorrected. First, the sheer scale of the investment drive carried significant costs – consumption losses which arose from the need to make weapons instead of consumer goods and services and to invest in defence plant rather than the means for raising living standards. Second, the costs of rearmament were simply piled on top of other investment priorities, rather than being met by scaling others down; in consequence, the economy as a whole was disrupted, and civilian consumption and morale suffered further.

Both of these were consequences of urgency and pressure for quick results, as was a third defect: the need for dispersal of defence plant and strategic industries away from vulnerable regions was ignored. Too much of the defence capacity created in the 1930s lay in western and southern regions close to Soviet borders; by 1942, they would be under enemy control. Undoubtedly, the dispersal of industrial plant to remote regions of the interior was costly in terms of additional investment in duplicating sources of supply and creating new transport and service infrastructures. But so, too, would be the consequences of the Soviet defence industry's acute vulnerability to invasion. Because the dispersal of defence plant had not been undertaken in advance, it would have to be carried out in wartime, under far more difficult circumstances, when fighting had already broken out.

Behind these defects lay the permanent pressure for quick results, which frequently came into conflict with long-range considerations. As seen from the Kremlin, long-range considerations dictated a broad spectrum of investments, spanning the full range of basic and engineering industries and means of transport as well as specialised defence plant. Long-range objectives also worked in favour of a diffusion of defence plant away from traditional centres of industrialisation in the south and west towards the country's main interior regions. Lower down the decision-making hierarchy, pressure for quick results meant that short-run priorities came into conflict with long-run goals, with uncertain results. Economic managers dared not cut back on civilian programmes in order to make way for accelerated rearmament, so that civilian sacrifice was achieved through intensified pressure of work, queues and shortages rather than through markets which found an equilibrium. Leaders of the strategic industries preferred to add to plant which could produce immediately at a high rate, but in the wrong place from the point of view of an immediate war, rather than to incur the extra cost of building new plant in more remote industrial regions, which would add to immediate output only after a delay.

Thus there was pressure for quick results, but the results did not add to the Soviet Union's ability to survive an immediate military struggle. There were results in terms of the volume of output of steel and artillery, and the numbers of aircraft and tanks available for deployment on Soviet frontiers, but this represented the Soviet part in a 'numbers game' aimed at deterring Germany and other potential adversaries from initiating warfare; the numbers were only indirectly connected with the Soviet Union's ability to wage a real war, should war be imposed upon her.

Soviet investment policy in the prewar years laid the foundations of wartime economic resilience. However, just as foundations do not automatically result in a building, the capital construction programme of the Stalinist industrialisation drive did not predetermine the fate of Hitler's adventure in the east. German plans underestimated Soviet war preparations, but aimed in any case to nullify them, no matter how extensive they had been, by seizing the advantages of surprise and pre-emption. Soviet efforts to prepare the economic structure for war contained inherent flaws and, in the initial phase of the war, these flaws might easily have brought the whole Soviet war effort to a standstill. Before the full range of Soviet assets could be brought to bear upon the task of Germany's military defeat, they had first to be mobilised – some to be saved from capture and relocated, much to be converted to new production needs, and all to be brought into wartime commission.

INVASION AND EVACUATION

In World War II both sides attempted by various means to disrupt the adversary's economic effort – naval blockade, aerial bombing, sabotage of production and finance. But the only method that was guaranteed any degree of success was 'the time-honoured strategic concept of invasion of the enemy's territory'.[2]

The Soviet industrial capacities created before the war were highly vulnerable to military occupation. This is shown by the record. On the territory occupied by Germany up to November 1941 had lived two-fifths of the Soviet Union's 1940 population: 78 million people. This was also one of the country's industrially most developed regions. On it had been located more than 85 per cent of prewar aircraft factories, 70 per cent or more of capacity for coking coal and iron ore, 60 per cent or more of capacity for pig iron, coal and aluminium and of factories for making armament and explosive powder (also the country's key plant for nitroglycerine), more than half steel-making and steel rolling capacity (including the country's key rolling mill for armour steel), nine big tank factories, two-fifths of the country's capacity for electric power and for railway freight. The invasion also meant devastating agricultural disruption, since the occupied territories had accounted for nearly two-fifths of prewar grain harvests and cattle stocks, 60 per cent of prewar pig herds and virtually all the country's domestic sugar producing capacity.[3]

With the eastward retreat of the Red Army after 22 June 1941, many of these capacities were simply lost. They could not be moved, or else there was no time to move them. The most that could be done in the short space of time available was to fire crops, burn fuel, blow up bridges and fixed installations (this was the fate, for example, of the famous hydroelectric dam across the Dnepr river), and try to deny to the Germans the assets which they had hoped to capture intact. In some places even the will to carry out such acts of denial was lacking; at first, many Ukrainian and Baltic nationalists welcomed German rule in place of Soviet power. Even where the will to resist was present, sometimes there was little to be done. Stocks of metals and other raw materials were not only too difficult to destroy, but also too heavy and bulky to evacuate without warning. Livestock and farm equipment

---

2 Milward 1977: 298.

3 Voznesensky 1948: 36–7; Kravchenko 1970: 123–4; Cooper 1976: 10–11, 15, 18, 20.

could be driven away but, without fuel and fodder, were soon abandoned or died on the road.[4]

To try to save even a proportion of the productive capacities threatened by occupation required both foresight and will-power. Foresight meant understanding that the Soviet resistance could be sustained long enough for evacuated machinery and production complexes to be re-established in the interior and set to work again and that, with this done, the German war strategy was vulnerable to a sustained productive effort. Will power meant the will to impose these ends, in face of the demoralisation, isolation, deprivation, exhaustion and physical dangers faced by the populations of the front-line regions under enemy fire.

The 1941 evacuation began at the end of June 1941 and continued until the end of December. During the second half of the year, a monthly average of 165,000 railway truck loads of industrial equipment rolled eastwards. Superimposed on this pattern of massive movement were two main peaks of activity – the first in July–August and the second, reflecting the German approach to the gates of Moscow, in October.[5] In 1942 there was another, smaller wave of evacuation in the southern sector as the Germans advanced on Stalingrad.

The first steps towards a programme of evacuation of capital assets were taken in the first days of the war. On 23 June, Stalin ordered the Kirov tank factory in Leningrad to send a delegation to the Urals to find a new location for their factory.[6] The next day, in the name of the Politburo, he ordered evacuation of the Mariupol' tank armour rolling mill in the south.[7] The same day a central Council for evacuation was established, headed first by transport commissar and Stalin's deputy L M Kaganovich, then (from mid-July) by the trade union leader N M Shvernik.[8] Prompt action in setting up an administrative framework to coordinate and manage the evacuation process stands in marked contrast to virtually every other aspect of the war in its first days, where central initiatives were either wrong headed and fraught with illusion, or entirely lacking.

To coordinate and manage the evacuation process – but not to implement a plan, for there were no plans. The need for an industrial

---

4 On the farm evacuation see Arutyunyan 1970: 45–53.

5 Likhomanov *et al* 1985: 81.

6 Salisbury 1971: 176–7n. On its return the delegation opposed immediate evacuation, and Moscow acquiesced.

7 Chalmaev 1981: 151.

8 Nachalo voiny 1990: 201.

evacuation was entirely unforeseen in prewar consideration of the contingency of war, at least after the Red Army purges of 1937. There was no plan for evacuation at a national level where it had been assumed that, within days of a German attack, Soviet forces would be occupying German territory. There were no plans, either, at the level of the industrial branch, municipality or individual enterprise, where plans for wartime conversion were similarly reckoned on a short, offensive war. Thus the evacuation was launched exclusively on a basis of improvisation.

In theory the evacuation was managed from above; the Council for evacuation was supposed to be notified of the situation at the front, to decide priorities, to authorise the decommissioning and dismantling of plant and to allocate freight capacities. To enforce its authority it wielded not only a central apparatus and representation in important ministries and government committees, but also a burgeoning network of local trouble shooters and inspectors with full powers to act on the spot. In practice, the work of evacuation also depended heavily on initiative from below. The latter was most important in the evacuation of farm stocks, but it also operated in the evacuation of industry, the main result being to generate trainloads of equipment without documentation of origin or destination, of which nobody knew how to dispose.

Some decisions were far-sighted – for example the evacuation of the armour-rolling mill from Mariupol', authorised on the third day of the war, and the decision of 27 June ordering evacuation of key aircraft factories from Moscow and Leningrad. But many decisions were taken too late, because the authorities wanted to maintain production for urgent defence requirements up to (sometimes beyond) the last minute. This applied, for example, to many metallurgical, engineering and defence factories which should have been evacuated from Leningrad and from the Donets basin – delayed, according to some, by bureaucratic overcentralisation.[9] Sometimes the dilemma was expressed in obviously contradictory instructions, as when aircraft industry commissar A I Shakhurin was instructed (on 20 July) to evacuate threatened plant 'without violation of the current production plan' – yet by mid-October more than three-quarters of the industry's capacity was in transit.[10]

The operational problems of the evacuation were huge and complex. There was the problem of correct timing. When evacuation was completed successfully, trainloads of equipment and materials were

9 Likhomanov *et al* 1985: 80.
10 IVMV vol 4 1975: 137, 150.

none the less intercepted by the enemy; or they were relocated too close to the rapidly moving front and had to be evacuated repeatedly, or were dispatched thousands of kilometres to the Far East, or were dispatched round in circles by bewildered railways officials trying to clear lines for military traffic, or were dispersed to several different new locations.

As the railways moved deeper into crisis, the turnaround of evacuation trucks slowed down, and this in turn intensified the shortage of freight capacity and imposed additional delays on evacuation from the front. In the short term the only solution was often to dump evacuation freights beside the lines in order to return empty trucks to the front, but a price was paid for this in terms of delayed relocation, physical deterioration of machinery left under the skies, and the need for repeated loading and trans-shipment.

How much was actually evacuated? In the third quarter of 1941 alone, according to official reports, 1,361 large-scale enterprises were shifted; the final total by the end of the year had risen to 1,523. Being large in scale, their economic significance was out of all proportion to their number. For example, included in the evacuation totals were more than 100 aircraft factories; the largest of them, using floor space of 150,000 to 200,000 square metres, meant 25,000 to 30,000 workers and 5,000 to 10,000 pieces of equipment.[11] They filled 1 million ten-metre trucks which, coupled end to end, would have formed a solid line along 10,000 kilometres of track, from the Far East where Soviet territory is separated from Alaska by a few miles of sea, to the Soviet Union's western border with prewar Poland. Nearly half the evacuated factories went to the Urals, the rest to the Volga region, western Siberia, Kazakhstan and Central Asia (a handful travelled still further to eastern Siberia). The whole process involved 8–10 per cent of the country's entire net capital stock (excluding livestock), or up to one-eighth of Soviet industrial assets.[12]

Could more have been evacuated with better management, allow-

11 Shakhurin 1975: 139.

12 According to Lipatov 1966: 187, the value of assets put on wheels exceeded three years' state investments under the first Five Year Plan (1928–32). According to official estimates, between 1929 and 1932 the fixed assets of Soviet industry grew by 3.8 billion roubles annually, or 11.4 billion roubles in three years. This can be compared with the value of all Soviet industrial assets, given as 92 billion roubles in 1941 in ISE vol. 5 1978: 52–3, yielding a proportion of evacuated assets of one-eighth. The lower figure of 8–10 per cent is the result of comparing independent estimates of annual net fixed and total investment (excluding livestock), 1928–32, with net fixed and total capital stock (excluding livestock) on 1 January 1941, whether in prices of 1928 or those of 1937, from Moorsteen, Powell 1966: Tables T-1, T-8, T-24 to T-26.

ing reduced costs and sacrifices? The answer seems to be: probably
not. It is easy to demonstrate that the real process of Soviet industrial
evacuation in face of the enemy (and often under fire) was ill-
prepared, chaotic and costly. It is more difficult to show that there was
some smoother, more coordinated response available under these immensely difficult conditions.

A group of Leningrad historians has argued recently that control of
the evacuation process in 1941 was excessively centralised, resulting in
bureaucratic delays and unnecessary losses to the enemy.[13] It is clear
that some decisions were taken too late, the main reason being the
desire to maintain output up to the last minute. The other evidence is
Moscow's frequent failure to supply sufficient means of transport for
the evacuation of key installations and complexes. However, the latter
evidence can be interpreted just as easily as showing that the main
constraint on timely evacuation was the overall shortage of labour and
transport capacities, which could not have been improved by prompt
administrative action. There was simply not enough labour, fuel and
railway trucks in the country to evacuate everything, and less bureaucracy would probably have made no difference.

The results of the industrial evacuation were of critical importance
for success of the Soviet war effort. It supplied the Red Army with
the essential means of survival in the winter of 1941, without which
nothing could have been done. This was understood not only later but
also at the time; for example, in July 1941, construction industry commissar S Z Ginzburg found himself negotiating with Red Army Chief of
Staff G K Zhukov, who wanted construction workers to help with
building defensive fortifications around Moscow. But all Ginzburg's
reserves were already allocated to the evacuation and relocation of industry. Zhukov said:

> We'll take not one more construction commissariat worker. We'll manage
> ourselves. What you have outlined for the construction commissariat is
> the most important thing for enabling us to fight . . . The construction
> workers . . . are smelting victory side by side with the soldiers at the
> front.[14]

And after the war Zhukov wrote:

> The heroic feat of evacuation and restoration of industrial capacities
> during the war . . . meant as much for the country's destiny as the
> greatest battles of the war.[15]

13 Likhomanov et al 1985: 79–80.
14 Ginzburg 1983: 223.
15 Zhukov 1971: 266.

At the same time, the place of the evacuation in the history of the war has sometimes been overplayed. This is for two reasons – because it was such a good story, and because it was the *only* good story to have come out of the first six months of fighting on the eastern front, other major events consisting of virtually unremitting retreat and defeat. (A very similar role in the British history of World War II is played by Dunkirk, the evacuation of the British Expeditionary Force from the Belgian coast after the fall of France in 1940.)

The fact is that the evacuation of industry was an essential precondition for eventual Soviet victory but, after its completion, the Soviet economy was if anything in a worse state than before. The reason is that, while Moscow's attention was focused exclusively on saving and relocating the country's key basic and military industrial plant, everything else was going under – transport, coal and oil extraction, iron and steel, food supplies. By 1942 shortages in these sectors, not the shortage of munitions capacity, had become the key factors constraining and undermining the country's war effort. It was becoming impossible to fight the war with guns and bullets alone.

The very success of the evacuation, which made possible military survival at the front, made matters worse in the interior. Huge steel works, engineering factories, tank and aircraft assembly plants were being transported to remote regions of the Urals, western Siberia and central Asia. In the space of a few months, many small communities experienced a second or even a first industrial revolution. But as yet there were few or insufficient rail or road links, electric power lines or generating capacity, sources of metals and components, financial and commercial services, homes and services for workers. The arrival of evacuated plant put additional strain upon the established enterprises of the interior, which now had not only to convert themselves to war production but also to service the new needs of relocated enterprises for materials, components and power supplies. Now the price was paid for the prior failure to secure industrial dispersal in the years of peace, when there had still been time to do things properly and in a balanced way. Part of the price was paid immediately, in wartime, in reduced output for increased effort; some of the payment was postponed until it was realised, decades after the war, how the rush to industrialise these quiet backwaters of the Urals and western Siberia had resulted in long-term disruption of the natural environment.

The economic crisis of 1942 reached awesome dimensions before being resolved. The story of its management and resolution is told in following chapters.

CONVERSION TO WAR PRODUCTION

The evacuation of the Soviet Union's vital defence plant was just one of many streams of economic activity which began with the outbreak of war and converged upon a single goal: the most rapid possible increase in the supply of military goods for the Red Army.

No matter how rapidly and efficiently the evacuation was carried out, there was bound to be a period of months in which the burden of military supply must be carried by the productive capacities of the interior.

Moreover, no matter how important were the country's specialised defence industries (counting both the factories of the interior and those evacuated there from the occupied regions) for immediate military supply, they still represented only a fraction of the country's total capacity for production. Therefore, side by side with the evacuation, there proceeded another essential process of gearing up the economy for war: the conversion of fixed capacities in the civilian sector to war production. And since the civilian sector deployed much the larger share of prewar productive capacity, the potential for increased defence output was correspondingly great when compared with the potential of the specialised defence industries already in existence, which was already under strain.

Conversion to war production meant different things in different civilian sectors. For some sectors it meant doing the same things as in peacetime, but more intensively and with a somewhat different balance. The iron and steel industry continued to make iron and steel, but the production of ordinary structural and sheet steel gave way to processes emphasising more the special alloy steels, high-grade and armour rolled steels and fine steel tubes required for the manufacture of armaments. Coal-mines continued to extract coal, and oilfields still gave oil, but in subsequent processing the petrochemicals industry gave more emphasis to high-grade fuels such as aviation spirit. Chemicals plants still made chemicals, but the emphasis shifted to explosives of all kinds.

In the same way transport workers (and in the Soviet Union this meant first of all railway staff) went on transporting both people and goods about the country, but civilian passengers and goods gave way to military traffic and evacuation consignments; the predominant lines of movement changed, too, reflecting the loss of territory, the switch to new sources and lines of supply, and the new requirements of the front. Construction workers went on building, but instead of building new power stations, factories, towns and transport routes listed in Five Year Plans they switched to military construction, such as defensive fortifications and airfields, to the relocation of evacuated factories, and to crash programmes for new railways and oil pipelines in the interior.

In other sectors of the economy, conversion to war needs meant carrying on much as before, but with still less support from the rest of the economy than in peacetime. These were the low-priority branches – light industry, agriculture and household services, sectors which had traditionally suffered peacetime neglect under the Stalinist administrative system. In wartime the neglect of the prewar years was transformed into a policy of actively stripping away these sectors' capacity for other purposes. Clothing, footwear, food and public services were still necessary, of course, but were switched to the supply of uniforms and woollen clothes for winter fighting, army boots, basic rations, care for the wounded, the orphaned and so on.

The most complicated changes were in branches producing machinery and tools. Motor and tractor factories were converted to making military trucks, artillery tractors and tanks. Plant for manufacturing vehicle and tractor parts and agricultural machinery went over to making rifles, artillery and mortars. More generally, the engineering industry was switched to making specialised machine tools for the defence sector, ammunition, equipment for military communications, military engineering equipment and so on. All of these required each factory to adapt or replace its machinery, acquire new technological processes, stock new materials and organise its floor space and working time in new ways.

In most manufacturing branches, conversion of fixed capacities to war production was vitally conditioned by prewar preparation of one kind or another. Conversion of many factories was made easy by their experience of the late 1930s. At this time, rearmament and the rapid expansion of defence requirements had repeatedly overstretched the capacity of the specialised defence industries, and the authorities had responded by opening up civilian factories to subcontracted defence orders. This had been particularly important for expanded production of shells and bullets, and for tank building where not only components but even assembly of finished products had taken place in civilian plant. This policy was implemented, not only in order to solve immediate supply problems, but also to foster the ability of the civilian economy to switch freely between peacetime and wartime specialisations.

Another prewar activity which contributed greatly to the wartime convertibility of civilian industries, and which was carried on side by side with the subcontracting of defence orders, was that of contingency planning. The most important field for this was the factory; major works were all supposed to have plans for war mobilisation, which designated both the kind of war goods the factory should begin to produce on the outbreak of war, and were supposed to maintain special workshops where the necessary preparations could be carried out in peacetime – practising the necessary technological and management skills, studying the necessary modification of machinery, laying in reserves of materials and components. Contingency plans were also drawn up, or coordinated, in the industrial ministries and municipalities, under unified control of a subcommittee for the military industries under the government Defence Committee.

From one point of view the story of industrial conversion in the war's early months is another surprising and outstanding success. When war broke out the years of preparation and contingency planning paid off. Typically, Soviet workers, managers and administrators did not do what the Germans counted on them to do, that is, lose the will to resist, slacken effort and adopt an attitude of 'wait and see'. Instead, at least in the big cities where the major factories were located, officials and managers swung into action and began to implement their contingency plans for accelerated war production.

This is what happened in Moscow: a children's bicycle factory began making flame-throwers. A die-stamping works where teaspoons and paper clips were made switched to entrenching tools and parts for anti-tank grenades. A woodworking shop producing abacuses and screens changed over to making pistol cartridges. A furniture factory started turning out anti-tank mines, cartridge boxes and stretchers. A typewriter works began making automatic rifles and ammunition.[16] In Leningrad, by early July, civilian factories were starting to manufacture tanks, artillery, mortars and flame-throwers. A toy factory and a stove works (among others) were producing grenades; anti-tank mines were being made in place of musical instruments and perfumes.[17] Speedy conversion could also be found on the railways where wartime running was introduced at 6 p.m. on the first day of the war, with new priorities and timetables; 'planned reserves' were brought into operation, and on only one main line was the transition accompanied by any disruption.[18]

At the same time, behind this picture of a smooth conversion of industry to new priorities lay profound difficulties. The fact that there

16 Aleshchenko 1980: 29.
17 Salisbury 1971: 173.
18 Kumanev 1976: 73–4.

was a ready response in the economy to the outbreak of war was of the utmost importance, psychologically as much as materially, because it meant for everyone, no matter how remote from western frontiers, the possibility of fighting back and resisting the aggressor. However, the total of responses at lower levels, when summed across the national economy, did not add up to a coordinated whole. This was for two reasons.

First, the prewar plans for industry were drawn up on the basis of a short, offensive war. This meant that beforehand the likely losses and demands of warfare upon industrial capacity were greatly underestimated; the possible need for air and ground defence of installations, for their temporary decommissioning and evacuation was entirely neglected. It also meant that the plans for different kinds of military goods were unbalanced; for example, the likely rate of expenditure of ammunition was understated in comparison with the need for armament.

Second, there was no ready understanding of the demands that war production would place upon the civilian economy, and of the inroads upon civilian production. According to reports, the first wartime national economic plan (this covered the third quarter of 1941 and was adopted on 30 June) did not even mention the need for further conversion of civilian capacities. Subsequently, when the true enormity of the situation became apparent, conversion of the civilian economy was carried far beyond anything imagined in the prewar period, and was eventually carried too far. This meant that, while attention was fixed exclusively on saving and converting capacities for making military goods, the availability of steel, fuels, foodstuffs and transport services dwindled rapidly. Without these, the acceleration of defence output could not be sustained. For a short time, arms production could be expanded on basis of running down strategic stocks of metals and other commodities, but these soon ran out.[19] Now attention had necessarily to be refocused on protecting and restoring the residual civilian economy.

In the past, Soviet historians have been fond of saying that the conversion of industrial capacity to a war footing, together with the evacuation of assets from the front-line regions, proceeded *po edinomu planu* ('according to a unified plan').[20] In fact there was, to begin with, no effective coordination of the many different streams contributing to the Soviet war effort. And they were certainly not planned, even in

19 Morekhina 1974: 56–7.
20 This was first contended by a leading Gosplan official, Kosyachenko 1944: 5–7.

the most elementary sense of following a schedule laid down in advance. This came eventually, but only after another year of hard struggle in 1942.

CAPITAL CONSTRUCTION IN WARTIME

In World War II the availability of Soviet capital assets went through a violent fluctuation. The official measure shows that at the end of 1942 the stock of fixed assets of the economy's 'productive' sector was reduced to only 68 per cent of the end-1940 level. Even by the end of 1945, when the war had been over for several months, productive fixed capacity was still 12 per cent less than in 1940.[21]

The changes in the country's capital stock were due to three factors. Each can be roughly quantified on the basis of official information and a few assumptions. First and most important was the advance and retreat of the invader. The eastward advance of German troops in 1941–2 may at first have deprived the Soviet economy of about 45 per cent of its fixed capacities of 1940 in rouble terms. When the Germans were expelled, little more than one-quarter of these values was recovered. This implies the second factor – in the process of German aggression and occupation the bulk of the assets involved was permanently lost or destroyed, resulting in a permanent loss of about one-third of the fixed capital stock of 1940. In third place were the wartime efforts of the Soviet investment and construction sectors, which offset the loss of capital assets by building and commissioning new capacity; they contributed approximately one-quarter of the 1940 fixed capital stock.[22]

At the same time, this certainly understates the importance of capital construction for the Soviet war effort. In 1942, for example, almost

21 Narkhoz 1987: 43.

22 These corrected estimates are based on the methodology indicated in Harrison 1985: 158–9n. Official indices of productive and non-productive fixed assets are combined for an estimate of total fixed assets. An official index of investment activity is scaled by means of an official estimate for the share of investment in 1940 national income utilised (19 per cent) and an assumed capital–output ratio (3.0) to provide a measure of the annual change in fixed capacities attributable to investment. (For this purpose, strictly speaking, the investment measure should be corrected by an index of the share of investment representing actually completed capital projects, but this is known only for 1940, 1942 and 1943 and, for our purposes, would not be especially critical.) The difference between this and the actual change in fixed capacities is attributed to territorial changes resulting from movement of the front line.

half the work of capital installation in the first eighteen months of the war was relocating, reconstructing and converting existing equipment for wartime operation, including the 1,500 or so big evacuated factories; this was in addition to the installation of equipment newly produced for war purposes. And again, in 1944–5, two-fifths of industrial investment was being devoted to restoration of 7,500 recaptured large-scale factories in the zones of former German occupation.[23]

The 3,500 big new factories built from scratch during the war years were also a substantial achievement; they represented an annual rate of 780 commissioned plants, only a little less than the 860 per year under the third Five Year Plan (1938–41) or the 900 per year of the second (1933–7), and well above the 375 of the first (1929–32).[24] Probably, however, the new large-scale factory of the war years was smaller and more modest than the grandiose projects of peacetime, and locked up substantially fewer investible roubles.

The capital construction sector had faced the most demanding tasks and circumstances since the beginning of the Stalinist industrialisation drive. War took both tasks and conditions to new extremes. These were seen at their most intense in the process of relocating the evacuated factories in the remote interior regions in 1941–2 and recommissioning them.

The relocation of evacuated plant was undertaken at a speed appropriate to its urgency. Where possible, factories would be moved to existing empty accommodation and space already under construction. Redesign and even rebuilding was usually cheaper than building entirely new accommodation. But everywhere empty space was scarce, and evacuated plant usually had to be broken up into its component technological processes and redistributed among existing defence, engineering and metallurgical enterprises of the interior regions. Only a minority of factories were simply reassembled intact in a new location. Whether this was a rational choice depends on whether the enhancement of the technological capacities of existing factories in the interior was sufficient to offset the lost technological coherence of the evacuated plant and the increased overcrowding of floor space in recipient enterprises.

Where big factories had to be set up in completely fresh locations, the keys to speed were standardisation and simplification of design and building processes, lowered standards (the use of structural steel for

23 Lerskii 1945: 17, D'yakov 1978: 63.
24 Narkhoz v 1960 godu 1961: 603. For the breakdown into different categories see D'yakov 1978: 63.

factory accommodation being prohibited except with express government permission), and long hours of intense labour. Conditions on site
could be frightful. For example, construction commissar S Z Ginzburg
was personally in charge of a project to recommission the big Zapo-
rozhstal' steel works from the Ukraine in Chebarkul', near Chelyabinsk in the Urals – a job which, under prewar circumstances,
might have taken years. They were given seventy-five days, from the
end of December 1941 to mid-March 1942. They had to re-establish
seven main and eleven auxiliary production shops together with railway lines, water supplies, air shafts; all this in 45 degrees of frost, with
the soil frozen to a depth of two metres. They had to heat the
ground, drill it and break it up with explosives, keep the concrete
from freezing, working round the clock, often holding production
conferences at 2 and 3 a.m. The job was finished ahead of schedule, in
six weeks.[25]

It was claimed at the time that most evacuated plant had restarted
production within six to eight weeks of evacuation, but in retrospect
this seems a minimum, not an average. The Khar'kov tractor factory,
evacuated in mid-October 1941, dispatched its first trainload of T-34
tanks to the army on 8 December: 'Front, accept a New Year gift!
Motherland, accept the first tanks from the Urals!' But relocation of
the armour rolling mill from Mariupol', the evacuation of which had
been ordered at the end of June 1941, took four months. Of 94 iron
and steel works evacuated in the second half of 1941, 40 were still not
back in commission by mid-1942. Of the 1,523 big evacuated factories, 55 were still idle at the end of 1942 because a work-force could
not be found to operate them.[26]

Beyond a point, the main constraint on recommissioning evacuated
plant was not the efforts of construction agencies, which usually suf-
ficed in the end, but the capacity of the new environment for supply
of current inputs and labour to the relocated factory. The latter typically required not only ores, metals or components but also fuel and
power, water, transport and communications, food and accommodation for the work-force, frequently a new work-force as well. The
proportion of its original work-force which the typical evacuated enterprise retained while in transit to the interior was traditionally given
as 30–40 per cent,[27] although a recent estimate is as low as 20 per
cent; the failure to find a new work-force under conditions of mount-

25 Ginzburg 1983: 228–31.
26 Ginzburg 1983: 234, D'yakov 1978: 47, Kravchenko 1970: 115.
27 Tel'pukhovskii 1958: 32; IVOVSS vol 2 1961: 150.

ing labour shortage is offered as the main reason for delayed restoration of output.[28]

When we turn to survey the whole field of wartime capital construction we find big changes which in some ways reinforced the peacetime pattern, and in some ways reversed it. The pattern of bias towards heavy industry was intensified. The defence industries, iron and steel, engineering, the fuel and power sector all received still higher priority in allocation of investment funds. The defence and heavy industries together accounted for more than two-fifths of all public sector investment in July 1941–5 compared with less than one-third in 1938–June 1941, and nearly 60 per cent in 1942 alone.[29] On average the new capacity commissioned annually in wartime in steel-making, coal-mining and electricity supply substantially exceeded the prewar norm.[30] Meanwhile, other sectors were starved of resources.

A second dramatic change was to be found in the regional pattern of investment. The prewar pattern of concentration of new capacities in the traditional regions of industrial development was suddenly disrupted. In 1940, more than half of public sector investment had gone to the main regions threatened by war. In 1942–3 their share would be reduced to one-fifth. In 1940, the Urals and western Siberia received less than one-seventh (13 per cent) of investment funds; in 1942–3 their share would rise to two-fifths (39–40 per cent). The south-eastern region, safe behind the Volga River, would also receive a bigger share together with Kazakhstan and Central Asia. At the other end of the country, eastern Siberia and the Far Eastern region would receive still less.[31]

In a third respect, the prewar pattern would be reversed. This was the pattern of investment project completion. In the Soviet economy, as everywhere, the volume of investment activity rarely corresponded with the volume of new capacity becoming available within a given period of time. This was partly inevitable, and it arose because projects took a long time – often years, not months – to carry through from first foundations to a finished factory able to receive workers and materials and to start work. But the period of each project's gestation was often lengthened by the fact that the economy as a whole was under strain, even excessively mobilised, and unable to supply every project simultaneously with power, machinery, building workers and foodstuffs. When this happened, projects were temporarily frozen, and

28 Likhomanov *et al* 1985: 111.
29 Harrison 1985: 136.
30 Kapital'noe 1961: 136.
31 Sokolov V 1946: 20.

construction agencies had to mark time until supplies could be secured again.

Here was one of the most important problems of prewar capital construction. In the years of greatest strain (1931–2), one-fifth or one-quarter of all investment activity simply added to unfinished projects, without adding useful capacity to the economy's assets. In the late 1930s, when overstrain was felt again, 13–15 per cent of annual investment was regularly reflected in accumulating stocks of unfinished capacity. When war broke out, however, the volume of investment was drastically cut back. The 5,700 capital projects envisaged in the third Five Year Plan (1938–42) were almost all cancelled immediately, only 614 still being allowed to go ahead.[32] Available resources were concentrated, as we have seen, on defence and heavy industry objectives in the interior regions; within this restriction, available resources were committed primarily to the installation of new equipment in preference to new construction; construction methods were simplified and speeded up, as we have seen. As a result, in 1942–3 the volume of new capacities commissioned *exceeded* the volume of investment activity, while the backlog of unfinished capacity, representing 'tens of billions of roubles', was halved.[33]

In 1943, with the recapture of significant territory, the perspectives of capital construction began to change. The recaptured territories represented new resources, but also new demands. Each region was populated by human beings and assets which had once formed an organic part of the economy. But now everything was in ruins. Most enterprises were damaged or dismantled. The population itself was homeless and dispossessed, stripped of its most productive members. In Belorussia, the Ukraine and the occupied part of the Russian Federation, four in every five industrial enterprises had been put out of commission, and five of every six industrial workers dispersed.[34] Even the fields were contaminated by the debris of war. Thus the promise of restoration could not be realised without new resources.

The balance of investment resources began to shift westward once more. In 1943 the commitment to reconstruction was still slight – only 16 per cent of total investible resources. But in 1944–5 the proportion rose to two-fifths of the total, including two-thirds of invest-

32 IVOVSS vol 2 1961: 142.

33 Lerskii 1943: 40, Sokolov V 1946: 25–6. An estimate for the backlog of unfinished capacity of 31.5 billion roubles at historic cost on 1 January 1940 is available from Davies 1984: 178. By comparison, gross investment for 1937 (the last prewar year for which investment data are officially reported) is given as 32.5 billion roubles.

34 Tel'pukhovskii 1968: 31.

ment in the basic industries (iron and steel, electricity supply, railway transport).[35] Significant resources were also committed to the food and housing needs of the liberated population. At this stage, however, with the war still in progress, the main priority was to restore the recaptured territories' ability to supply the war effort with metals and munitions, rather than to restore their civilian economy as such.

35 Prikhod'ko 1968: 16–18.

CHAPTER EIGHT

Labour: The 'Ultimate Bottleneck'[1]

THE DEGREE OF LABOUR SHORTAGE

The capital assets with which the Soviet economy entered the war were only one of the constraints limiting the Soviet war potential. Others included the availability of strategic materials, especially high-grade fuels, steels and rare metals; the abilities and skills of industrial organisers, engineers and skilled workers; food stocks, and many others. In the short run these factors were expressed in intense shortages of food and fuel, metals and components, skilled engineering and munitions workers and machinery with which to employ them.

All of these factors, however, had one feature in common. Given time and effort, they could be added to and improved, even in the middle of a bitter war. Old factories could be converted and reconstructed, and new factories built. New sources of scarce materials could be developed, or substitutes found. New entrepreneurial talent could be encouraged and new skills formed through education and training. In the long run, therefore, each of these limits on warmaking capacity could be relaxed – subject to one condition. This was the availability of enough workers, regardless of skill and qualification, to build and rebuild, to explore and develop, to learn as well as teach.

The factor ultimately constraining the war potential of the major economies on both sides in the long run proved to be the sheer num-

1 The chapter's title, and much of the analysis, belong to Kaldor 1946: 34. Mitrofanova 1971 provides the standard work of reference on the subject of this chapter.

ber of workers available. In World War II it was labour of all kinds which proved the 'ultimate bottleneck' limiting the capacity to make war. As long as additional supplies of labour were available, unskilled workers could be trained and promoted, construction workers could build new fixed capacity, scientific workers could develop new processes and products. Once available supplies of additional labour were exhausted, however, very hard choices would present themselves.

The different great powers entered World War II in quite different states of labour mobilisation. In Britain and the United States of America there was still mass unemployment in the first year after entry into the war. In fact, with millions of workers out of work and idle factories everywhere, the first stages of rearmament had been accompanied by job creation and rising prosperity, and in the United States this would continue to be the case until 1944.

In contrast both the German and Soviet economies were already fully employed in the peacetime sense, although in both countries this was consistent with a great deal of normal slack and wastage. As additional military priorities arose, they could be met only at the cost of reduced investment, public services, civilian consumption, or idle time on the job or at leisure. In the late 1930s, German living standards stagnated, while Soviet living standards fell.

By 1942, the British and Soviet work-forces had reached a stage of full war mobilisation. Wartime conversion was complete. No further resources of any kind were to be found for the war, and the 'ultimate bottleneck' had been encountered. Among civilian employments, only those essential to the war effort remained, and inessential ones had been eliminated. Each new military objective was met only by sacrificing an existing one. Germany reached this stage only in 1944; so great was the wealth of American resources that it is debatable whether the United States reached it at all.

Under full war mobilisation, the biggest danger was one of going too far. It turned out to be possible to put too many workers into the front line, as Germany would find out after June 1944. Too many soldiers meant that, once existing stocks had been used up, the supply of both guns and food would dry up. Everyone would fight to the last bullet and ration, after which resistance would cease. It was also possible to have too many soldiers and war workers combined, as the USSR would discover in 1942; at any moment, the war factories would be in danger of grinding to a halt because of shortages of metals, fuel, power, transport services and food rations. The work-force could be mobilised at this level only for a short period, unless external supplies of industrial goods and foodstuffs were brought to bear.

A final qualification is that the labour bottleneck, although 'ultimate', was not absolute. It reflected not just the physical number of workers multiplied by the hours available in the working day, week and year, but also their morale and productiveness. The constraint could be relaxed to a limited extent if labour productivity could be lifted by longer hours and increased intensity of effort, or by better organisation of machinery and materials. Foreign supply would also prove to be an important mitigating factor.

WARTIME LOSSES AND MOBILISATION NEEDS

The first impact of the war was a radical change in Soviet priorities. Overnight, the economy was pitched from a state of full peacetime employment to one of intensive mobilisation for combat. There was an immediate requirement for millions of soldiers. There were already 5 million soldiers in the Red Army; 5 million more would be mobilised from the civilian population in the first week of the war.[2] And this was just the first of several multimillion drafts eventually required to replace wartime losses and to expand force levels. In the economy the production of guns, bullets, shells, tanks and aircraft received the top priority, together with the provision of other means of military operations and construction — fuel, cement, machinery, transport and building services; in comparison, nothing else mattered. In employment policy, therefore, the critical task became to mobilise further millions of workers into the expanded production of military goods.

In the west, many still thought of Russia as a country of 'inexhaustible reserves' — reserves of human labour and energy as well as of natural resources. Russia's reserves existed, as the war would prove, but they were far from endless; on the contrary, they were completely inadequate to the needs of the situation.

The main reserves were 'disguised' unemployment among able-bodied adults, and those who in peacetime would be considered too young or too old to be employed — older school students and pensioners. There was no 'open' unemployment of men and women seeking jobs and unable to find them, and there had been none for more than a decade of rapid industrial expansion and public sector job creation.

Disguised unemployment fell under several different headings. Most widespread was underemployment of the farm population, which still

2 IVMV vol 4 1975: 53.

made up half the total. For example, it was normal for the collective farm peasant to work a shortened working year of 200 days or less, rather than the 250 days or more worked by city dwellers, because of the shortage of work in the countryside (especially in the winter months). Other kinds of disguised unemployment were to be found in the urban economy. Employees in factories and offices worked a longer, fuller year, but here too disguised unemployment could be found in the form of idle time on the job. Factory work, in particular, often came in bursts. On the surface this was partly because of numerous breaks, meetings and other excuses for not working; partly because of poor organisation of supplies; partly because the division of working time into planning periods (ten days, a month, a quarter, a year) resulted in periodic surges of effort to overcome the results of previous idleness and still meet the official target for output within the alloted span of time. (Deeper underlying causes are surveyed in Chapter 9.)

Another significant source of disguised unemployment of the urban population was the lag of women's participation in paid employment behind men's. In 1940 women still accounted for only two-fifths of public sector employment – a higher proportion than in Germany, Great Britain or the United States, but still well below the 50 per cent which formed a notional target and which would actually be achieved in the postwar years.

These reserves, with the reserves of school students and pensioners, shared one important feature. They could not be drawn upon freely and unconditionally. To bring them into employment required breaking down one kind or another of social restraint. To turn agrarian underemployment into hands freed from agricultural tasks and ready for combat or war work meant that those remaining in the village must be prepared to work much harder at ploughing, sowing and harvesting in the months of peak effort; at this time their leisure would entirely disappear. To mobilise reserves of underemployment in the factory and office meant that workers and managers must go over to working at maximum pace, regardless of traditional breaks, working practices or safety regulations. For women to leave the domestic sphere and take the place of men sent to the front from the office and factory bench meant either that they would bear an intensified 'double shift' of paid work coupled with unpaid house-work and child-care, or that society must take on more responsibility for family meals and looking after children. For the sake of a national cause the whole of society must stand ready to give up precious rights, if workers were to give up leisure, if children were to give up their education and if old people were to give up a peaceful retirement on pension.

Soviet labour reserves were already limited on the outbreak of war, but now something else made matters far, far worse. This was the catastrophic loss of population and other assets on the territory occupied by the invading forces. The military disasters of 1941–2 cut the working population from 85 million to 53 million (Table 9). At the same time the additional requirements of wartime mobilisation would reach 12 million to 13 million. Proportionally, losses had been heaviest in the armed forces, the war effort's cutting edge. The Soviet defence commissariat would have not only to replace early losses but also to find, in addition, 6 million to 7 million more men and women to lift Red Army numbers to the 11 million of 1942. At the same time the defence industry commissariats were screaming for more workers. The number of specialised munitions workers would increase in 1940–2 by at least 1 million, but this was just the tip of the iceberg as far as war work generally is concerned. The number of other war workers supplying the means of munitions production, military construction and military operations may have risen by 5 million. The *unsatisfied* demand for labour of the main defence, engineering and metallurgical industries in early 1942 amounted to nearly half a million workers.[3]

Soviet reserves of unutilised labour would be mobilised to the full, but there was not the slightest possibility of meeting this demand out of reserves alone. A huge blow would fall on existing employment in production of civilian goods and services. The number of such jobs would fall from roughly 72 million in 1940 to perhaps 28 million in 1942. This was a shock of unprecedented scale.

THE MOBILISATION PROCESS

Where would the 13 million new soldiers and war workers come from? Initially reserves were mobilised from the urban population. Thus in the second half of 1941 half a million unemployed women volunteered for war work, together with 300,000 school children between the ages of 12 and 15, and thousands of students and veterans. In 1942 more than half a million more were found for war work from the same groups.[4]

At the same time, the unemployed reserves of the urban economy were slight by comparison with the huge requirements of the war.

3 Kravchenko 1970: 109, Mitrofanova 1971: 189.
4 Mitrofanova 1971: 186, 190

The main source of additional war workers and soldiers was necessarily those already employed in the town and countryside.

As far as recruitment to war work was concerned, much of it did not require anyone to change their place of work or residence; it took place automatically, as a result of the conversion of civilian enterprises to war production. Steel-workers went on making steel, but their steel went to armour tanks rather than to plate road vehicles. Engineers continued to build machines, but the machines were for warlike not peaceful use. However, there was still a need to find many new workers for such enterprises because established workers joined the armed forces or were promoted to administrative grades. For this reason, and because of the need to expand converted defence factories and create new ones, there was also significant recruitment into war work out of light industry and services – 130,000 under the auspices of the wartime Labour Committee just in the second half of 1941.[5] In subsequent years this channel would be greatly enlarged; in 1942–5 the Labour Committee directed nearly 12 million workers into war work or training, and half of them came from the urban economy.[6]

The last major source of recruitment to the war was the rural population. Three-fifths of the Red Army's wartime strength (11.6 million at its peak) were of rural origin. Rural conscripts judged unfit for combat duty were directed by the defence commissariat into war work – 700,000 just in the second half of 1941.[7] Of those mobilised in later years by the Labour Committee, a growing proportion was of rural origin; in 1943–4 three-fifths came from the countryside.

These recruits helped to fill the places of existing workers, mainly young men, taken into the armed forces. The result was major change in the composition of the Soviet work-force. The share of women in industrial employment, which stood at two-fifths in 1940, rose to over half during 1942 and nearly three-fifths in 1943. In beleaguered Leningrad, where virtually all male workers were enlisted in combat units, women's share in the factory work-force rose to 80 per cent or more.[8] Age was affected as much as gender. In the public sector as a whole, the combined employment share of the very young (under 19 years) and the relatively mature (over 50) rose from one-sixth in 1939 to more than one-quarter in 1942.[9] It is hardly an exaggeration to picture

5 ISE vol 5 1978: 203.
6 The total is derived from Mitrofanova 1971: 193, 428, 433; for shares of the urban and rural populations in recruitment in each year, see ISE vol 5 1978: 203.
7 Kravchenko 1970: 110–11.
8 Rogachevskaya 1977: 183.
9 Voznesensky 1948: 90, IVMV vol 5 1975: 50, IVMV vol 7 1976: 43.

the typical Soviet work-place collective in wartime as schoolchildren, grandparents, mothers and aunts.

The impact on rural employment was also predictable. Young men vanished from the countryside. The total rural work-force on Soviet-controlled territory fell disastrously, and not just because of the loss of huge territories behind German lines. In the Soviet rear, in regions untouched by occupation, villages were stripped of working hands; there, the collective farm working population fell by more than one-third – in the Ural region and Siberia, by 45 per cent. Agriculture became the preserve of women, children, pensioners and evacuees.[10] In the prewar village, women already formed a majority of the collective farm work-force (this is explained by the rapid prewar recruitment of young men from the village to new jobs in industry and construction during rapid industrialisation). The war sharply intensified the trend. By 1944 able-bodied women outnumbered men in the interior regions by almost four to one.[11]

The destination of those mobilised was either military service or service as a war worker. On the whole, war work meant one of five different kinds of employment. There were millions of new jobs in *defence plant* making guns, shells, tanks and aircraft. War work could also mean employment in civilian *heavy industry* – in engineering factories, iron and steel works and chemicals plants, in coal-mines, oil-fields and power stations, producing the essential inputs for the manufacture and arming of weapons. Other branches of war work included *construction* – work on defensive fortifications, as well as building or rebuilding factories, power stations and railway lines. *Transport* itself became a branch of war work, with its immense significance for supply of the front, as well as of production. Lastly, there were times when even *agriculture* was given the status of war work because, without bread, meat and fats, soldiers could not fight and war workers could not go on working.

Few of these jobs were unskilled. At least half the unsatisfied labour requirements reported by the defence and heavy industry commissariats early in 1942 were for skilled workers, and in the aircraft and tank industries the proportion rose to two-thirds. At this early stage of the war, the skill deficit probably seemed much more alarming than the short supply of labour generally. To assemble modern aeroplanes and armoured vehicles demanded the steady hand and stamina of experienced craft workers in the prime of life, rather than housewives in

10 Vinogradov 1976: 12, 86.
11 Uchastie 1962: 29.

middle age who had never seen the inside of a factory workshop, or raw youths from remote villages. At the same time, the skills shortage was being aggravated by the uncoordinated mobilisation process which was stripping away the existing work-force from munitions factories, especially those in the front-line regions.

As long as more unskilled workers were available, however, the skill deficit could always be overcome. There were many traditional ways of adapting skilled occupations and the industrial environment to the needs of new unskilled war workers, for skilled labour had always been short in backward, agrarian Russia and this was no new problem. Ways of coping ranged from breaking down skilled processes or 'de-skilling' jobs to movements for 'learning by doing' or training on the job.

At the same time, the principal reliance had to be placed on formal schemes for upgrading workers' skills, and the war saw a huge expansion of vocational training. In 1940 a total of 3.5 million manual workers in industry either underwent some kind of induction training on entering the work-force, or else trained for a higher level of skill qualification (this was out of a mid-year industrial work-force of 8.3 million). In 1942, when there were 2.8 million *fewer* industrial manual workers, the number undergoing training actually rose to 3.8 million. In addition, in 1942 some 600,000 school leavers entered full-time vocational training, compared to an insignificant number in 1940. In total, the number training for improved skills during the year was equivalent to fully four-fifths of the 1942 manual work-force in industry, compared to less than half of the work-force in 1940.[12] Industrial training on this massive scale opened up new skilled trades to women.[13] However, the new avenues for female advancement were restricted to the shop-floor; there does not seem to have been any wartime increase in women's share of managerial or administrative posts.

Taking the war years as a whole, therefore, the shortage of skilled labour was acute but could not be decisive. Ultimately, what constrained the Soviet productive effort was the shortage of working hands. Allocating the working population correctly between alternative employments, whether on the front line or in the rear, would help make the difference between defeat and victory.

There was already an absolute shortage of hands when war broke out. However, the civilian economy contained substantial reserves, both of 'disguised' unemployment, and of workers in occupations

12 Kravchenko 1970: 112.
13 Voznesensky 1948: 89.

which would be graded inessential in wartime. These reserves were quickly used up. The drain of workers out of civilian employment into the Soviet Army and defence production was so rapid that soon nothing was left that did not carry the status of war work – even in agriculture. Thus, in connection with the 1942 spring sowing campaign, the Soviet head of state M I Kalinin declared:

> If we evaluate the different kinds of work in our country at present, in the ninth month of the war, then we can rank spring sowing work as of first importance. With it can be compared only the production of ammunition and armament.[14]

Nor was this rhetoric. A month later, a government decree ordered a reverse mobilisation of the non-employed back into farm work.[15]

This was just one symptom of the general situation. The reserves of labour in inessential employment were running out; the remaining kinds of employment were all essential to the war effort, and all carried the highest priority. Construction work meant building war plant. Agricultural work meant growing food for soldiers and war workers. Work in transport meant carrying weapons, rations and machinery and fuel for war production around the country. Work in the clothing industry meant making uniforms for soldiers and work clothes for war workers. The relative priority of these jobs became more and more finely graded and, at times, even outranked the priority of military needs. Thus, in May 1942 the GKO halted the conscription of railway workers and ordered the return to railway employment of Red Army personnel skilled in railway operations.[16]

Thus, during 1942 the Soviet economy moved from full employment in the normal, peacetime sense to full wartime mobilisation. At the same time this was not a smooth, orderly transition. For a start, there was a great difference between the western regions and the interior. In the western regions where the threat of invasion and occupation was immediate, there was no question of a smooth, controlled mobilisation of the work-force for a prolonged war effort. Immediately, combat took priority over production.

In Leningrad, in Kiev and Odessa, in the Donbass, in Moscow and Tula, home defence militias were recruited from the factories. Their formation and training went on at work-places outside working hours.[17] But with the enemy's approach, the workers left the factories

14 *Pravda*, 1 March 1942.
15 Kurskii 1975: 16.
16 Istoriya KPSS, vol 5(i) 1970: 307.
17 Belonosov 1970: 21–36.

to collect spades and rifles, to dig defensive fortifications and to fight the invader. This applied just as much to munitions workers as to teachers and pastry-cooks, and reflected the simple logic that there was no point carrying on war production if the factory could not be defended. (But none of it applied in the Baltic republics and the former territory of eastern Poland, where the mood of the population was anti-Soviet and the fighting was over in days rather than weeks.) The only activity which might be given still higher priority was to fulfil measures for the most desperate eventuality, that of giving up the town. In this case movable assets and civilians must be evacuated, fixed installations and road and rail links mined for destruction and papers burnt.

Thus in the western regions the immediate response was to pitch the work-force into a state of immediate combat mobilisation. This was a state of utter imbalance, a running crisis which could be sustained for more than a few days only by uninterrupted supply of food and munitions from the interior regions. When the enemy came the volunteer divisions, poorly led and virtually untrained, would suffer appalling losses. The casualties would include many skilled munitions, engineering and metal workers, who represented a severe loss to the war economy.

In the interior the situation was better, and the transition to wartime economic mobilisation was smoother, but only by comparison. Near the front line, the problem was that everyone was forced to become a soldier, leaving not enough workers to produce even the military goods, let alone to carry on civilian trades. In the interior, the problem was that, of those not taken by the army, nearly everyone became a war worker, leaving too few to carry on with producing food, fuel and basic materials. In the long run, this was just as threatening to continuity of the war effort. To correct it would take terrific restraint, and the task would occupy most of 1942.

THE CENTRALISATION OF WORK-FORCE CONTROLS

To run the Soviet economy successfully for an all-out war of resources depended on two indispensable conditions. These were mobilisation and coordination. *Mobilisation* meant that all the available resources would be brought to bear upon the enemy. *Coordination* meant that they would be mobilised in the right proportions. With too many soldiers, there would be too few workers left to produce the soldiers' munitions and rations. Too many munitions workers would mean that there would be not enough workers left to make bread, fuel and steel with which to subsist, produce and fight.

To coordinate resources in the right proportions required, above all, centralisation. Only a centralised system of controls could evolve nation-wide priorities, rank the different military and productive requirements for resources, and ensure that everyone followed them consistently. For example, without restraint from central political authority, the claims of the army on manpower would overwhelm the needs of the defence and heavy industries. Someone had to limit the size of the fighting forces, and the limit could be set only at the level of the war cabinet.

Again, even given a limit on military recruitment, priorities within the economy had to be graded nationally. Otherwise, priorities would still be evolved – but at lower levels, and different agencies would operate them inconsistently with each other. For example, the management of an artillery factory might allow its skilled workers to volunteer or be conscripted for the army; at the same time, security police officers might hold on to their cafeteria staff and office boys by declaring them to be 'essential workers'.

Soviet labour administrators were quite unprepared for this task. This may seem surprising for a 'centrally planned economy'. However, the fact is that for most of the prewar period the labour market had been least centralised of the various sectors subject to official regulation.

There were plenty of controls, most of them dating from 1938–40. There was universal male liability to military service. School leavers went on to higher education, or else to semi-compulsory vocational training, although the latter was relatively new. The route from institute or industrial school into employment was also controlled from above; once employed, the worker could no longer freely change employment. The route from the village to employment in large-scale industry and construction was also regulated by government-controlled agencies of 'organised recruitment' which negotiated fixed-term contracts with collective farms for semi-compulsory mass hiring of farm workers for employment in the public sector.

This was a highly restrictive system – in theory, at least. In reality, because labour was scarce and had a high value to employers, workers could exercise considerable discretion in negotiating with officialdom. Even if the theory had been strictly applied, however, it still did not

153

amount to a centralised system. It was mainly regulation for regulation's sake, rather than for the purpose of meeting explicit national
objectives. There were two main symptoms. One is that there was no
system for ranking jobs by priority and directing workers from lower
to higher ones (except for a few highly qualified specialist grades).
Neither was there any system for arbitrating between the claims of the
army and of industry on manpower, in the event of competition between them. Although highly regulated, the prewar labour market was
still basically competitive in the sense that a multitude of regulatory
agencies vied with each other to hire scarce workers, offering inducements or applying moral or (in the case of prison camp labour, administered by the security police) physical pressure to workers to accept
employment and remain in it.

The other symptom is that those outside the urban educational and
industrial system could not be compelled into it. This applied equally
to the non-employed strata of the urban population, and to the much
larger rural population. In theory the latter was liable to 'organised
recruitment', but in reality the system for recruiting labour was a mess,
completely unable to fulfil high-level plans. The underlying reason is
that collective farmers did not necessarily want to travel away to
remote building sites on the terms offered, and were able to make
their preference effective.

The creation of a wartime system for truly national coordination of
labour resources had therefore to be carried out largely from scratch.
The process took nearly eighteen months, and passed through several
stages. The first stage was establishment of a national authority for
mobilisation of the work-force – the Labour Committee, set up on 30
June 1941. Its chief was named as P G Moskatov, previously head of
the state vocational training system set up in October 1940; other
members included officials representing the ministerial apparatus, economic planning and, significantly, the NKVD.[18] But at first the policies
formed by the Labour Committee were backed up neither by laws nor
by administrative powers. In the first half year of the war, the Labour
Committee simply placed its rubber stamp on mobilisations which
would probably have taken place even without it – the flows of volunteers from the urban population and of 'organised recruitment' from
the countryside.

In the winter of 1941, tougher controls began to be enforced. In
December 1941 a decree belatedly mobilised defence industry workers
at their posts.[19] This meant that work on munitions production would

18 Mitrofanova 1971: 187.
19 Mitrofanova 1971: 188.

be treated as equivalent to military service; workers in defence factories were placed under military discipline, with unauthorised departure from work treated as desertion in face of the enemy. Just as importantly, it meant that the Army could no longer conscript them for fighting. And a further decree of February 1942 rendered the entire able-bodied population of the towns not already employed, in training or solely responsible for the care of small children, liable to compulsory mobilisation into war work under the Labour Committee.[20]

Even now, implementation was characterised by long postponements and delays. The decree of February 1942 could not be implemented without local (regional and municipal) labour committees to register and allocate those liable to compulsory mobilisation; these were formed in following months. Nor could it be implemented without criteria laying down which categories of people should be mobilised first and what employments for them should be given first priority. This awaited a government statute issued only in August 1942.[21]

The protection of essential workers from military conscription was also developed belatedly and pragmatically. National policy seems to have been restricted to blanket measures such as the mobilisation of construction and munitions workers at their posts. There was no national scheme for protecting the employment of workers in other key sectors like the steel industry, engineering, chemicals, fuels and power. This was apparently the responsibility of party leaders in ministries and factories who had to choose which categories of worker to exempt from conscription or to be refused voluntary enlistment in the armed forces.[22] They carried out this task in a decentralised way, often in the teeth of military demands; for example, at one unnamed artillery plant, several thousand workers, technicians and engineers were saved from immediate conscription only by the manager's appeal first to the regional party secretary, then to Marshal K E Voroshilov personally.[23]

After August 1942, a nation-wide policy with teeth under the government Labour Committee began to be possible in theory, but still could not be implemented in practice. This is because the new agency had simply been superimposed on existing ones, which continued to operate independently. At least six kinds of agency were still competing in the labour market to determine priorities. At national level, in addition to the Labour Committee (now responsible for mobilising the

20 Resheniya vol 3 1968: 64.
21 Mitrofanova 1971: 189, 191.
22 e g Kravchenko 1947: 360, 362.
23 Olevsky 1983: 19.

urban population into war work) there were two other ministries, the Defence Commissariat (responsible for military recruitment and the allocation of conscripts unfit for military service), and the NKVD (responsible for prison camp labour). Further, there were three different kinds of local government department, responsible respectively for relocating evacuated workers, for 'organised recruitment' of the rural population into industry, and for mobilisation of the urban population into agriculture.

True centralisation was secured only in November 1942, when a government statute resolved the competition in favour of the Labour Committee. The Labour Committee would be responsible for coordinating mobilisation into war work from the countryside as well as in the towns. Moskatov, its first chief was replaced by the politically senior N M Shvernik, head of the Soviet trade unions.[24] Of course conflict between the priorities of the military and the economy, and also between those of the Labour Committee and the still powerful NKVD, remained possible. In such case, they were resolved by decisions of Stalin's war cabinet, the GKO.[25]

One index of change in the degree of centralisation is to compare the changing roles of the Labour Committee and the Defence Commissariat. In the second half of 1941 the Labour Committee drafted 120,000 workers into industry, transport and construction, but this number was dwarfed by the 700,000 'unfit' conscripts mobilised into these branches by the Defence Commissariat. (Lack of fitness was not just a medical condition, and covered many from the western territories absorbed in 1939–40 who had been judged politically unreliable *en masse*.) By 1943 the proportions were reversed; the Labour Committee mobilised nearly 900,000 workers into industry, construction and transport; all other channels of labour mobilisation accounted for less than half this number.[26]

By November 1942 the conditions for successful coordination of wartime labour mobilisation had been met. There was universal service liability of the population. A system for job reservation for essential war workers had been evolved,[27] albeit in a pragmatic way. Centralised coordination and arbitration between competing priorities had also been established through the Labour Committee and, if necessary, the GKO.

24 Mitrofanova 1971: 191, IVMV vol 5 1975: 50.
25 e g Kravchenko 1947: 403–6.
26 Mitrofanova 1971: 187–8, 193, 428, 433.
27 Mitrofanova 1971: 434.

The delay in implementing a centralised system of labour administration in 1941–2 was inevitable to some degree. The rapid movement of the front line made it so. For one thing, it was impossible to draw up and implement nation-wide priorities for the working population when the numbers available were changing so unpredictably and in such disastrous proportions. For another, the mobilisation needs of different regions differed so greatly. It made little sense for anyone in Moscow to add up the labour requirements of war work in the Donbass and the Urals and compare them with the combined labour resources of these regions, when the workers of the Donbass were dismantling their factories one day, fighting German spearheads the next, and under enemy occupation the day after. In fact, the Soviet labour market remained fluid just as long as the front line remained unstable. Stabilisation of labour administration came only with the stabilisation of the Stalingrad front and launching of the successful Soviet counter-offensive in November 1942.

None the less the military situation alone cannot explain the long delay in grasping effective, centralised control over labour resources. There is little sign that those in control of employment policy understood the task which faced them when war broke out. Like others, they had for years underestimated the likely cost and duration of war with Germany and did not understand the difficulties of bringing to bear the country's entire resources under the weight of a deep invasion.

By the end of 1942, everyone in the territories under Soviet control was working for victory in a relatively coordinated way. But a substantial price had been paid for the delay in achieving nation-wide coordination. This was the deep and persistent economic crisis of 1942 which arose from the economy's excessive mobilisation.

During most of 1942 there were too many soldiers and too many munitions workers compared to the few left in the supporting civilian infrastructure. In the absence of effective restraint, the armed forces and munitions industries acted on the economy like a gigantic vacuum pump, sucking up civilian employees and farm workers to replace soldiers and workers lost in the invasion and to meet the huge expansion of demand emanating from the front. Key sectors ranging from steel and transport to agriculture were left critically short of resources. The very foundations of the country's military-economic resistance were undermined. Stricter controls on the mobilisation process and the stabilisation of the civilian economy came more or less together at the end of 1942. Only then could the country turn the corner of its terrible economic crisis.

CHAPTER NINE

'In Labour as in Combat'[1]

PRODUCTIVITY IN PREWAR PERSPECTIVE

The macroeconomic dimension of Soviet labour mobilisation was the subject of Chapter 8. Was the country's working population fully mobilised into employment? Was it employed in fighting, in the munitions industries and in other war work in the right proportions? After this, however, comes the microeconomic aspect. Would each give their utmost – would they work with new discipline and intensity, relentlessly, for hours without any break and for years without any holiday? Would their hard work produce results? For without work effort and productivity, sheer numbers of war workers could not suffice to supply the colossal needs of the front.

The wartime motivation and morale of Soviet workers are best seen against the backdrop of the prewar years, when rapid industrialisation had transformed the economy's structure, replacing agriculture's dominant role with modern industries and services. But labour productivity had not been transformed, and remained stubbornly low. There were two kinds of reasons for this. On one hand were defects of resource allocation flowing from the Stalinist strategy of economic development, especially the neglect of agriculture and living standards. On the

1 On prewar labour policy and mechanisms of labour motivation see especially Barber 1986, Kuromiya 1988, Siegelbaum 1988. For the war period, much valuable detail is again contained in Mitrofanova 1971. Valuable sources on more specialised topics include Rogachevskaya 1977 (socialist emulation), Dokuchaev 1973 (the workforce in Siberia), Zelkin 1969 (the Kuznetsk coalfield).

other hand were social relations of production which had become entrenched in the work-place.[2]

What made up these relations of production? A contingent factor was the work-force's historical background of self-employment in peasant and artisan production, which predisposed workers to a casual attitude to timekeeping, to unsteady work rhythms, and to resistance to management authority. But, in addition, there were influences permanently entrenched in the Stalinist economic system and reproduced by it.

First, the sticks and carrots used by employers in the old, pre-Soviet labour market to discipline the work-force had been weakened. The lack of open unemployment and the high demand for labour meant that workers charged with absenteeism or slacking could laugh off the threat of dismissal. Labour shortage encouraged workers to solve their problems at work by not turning up, or by leaving work and getting another job rather than acquiring skills and seniority while remaining in their posts. Absenteeism and a high rate of quitting work in Soviet industry in the prewar decade notoriously lowered the average level of skill and experience of the work-force and held back the rise of labour productivity.[3] The shortage of available consumer goods also meant that higher wage bonuses, offered in return for increased skill, seniority and effort, could not easily be spent in official shops and were often ineffective as incentives.

Second, managers in Soviet industry had to meet their quotas and satisfy those in authority over them; but, in order to do this, they also had to get along with the workers under them. To secure their co-operation, managers often had to close their eyes to regular absences, and to working practices and traditions established to defend a slow working pace with plentiful breaks. It was better to work for compromise and a quiet life, than create a turmoil and cause a lot of trouble to no effect. If more output was needed, it was easier to hire more workers than to try to make the existing work-force do more work.

2 This explanation begins from Kornai 1980 and his theory of the 'shortage' economy. Kornai's theory stresses underlying social relationships of paternalism between superiors and subordinates and the power of the producer over the user, the producer's 'soft' budget constraint, and the widespread resort to non-price controls. As a starting point I prefer Kornai's theory to the neoclassical Barro-Grossman disequilibrium approach, but the reader will not find any dogmatic exclusion of disequilibrium concepts from this and following chapters. For a technical summary of the two approaches and contrast between them, see Davis, Charemza 1989.

3 Barber 1986: 59–63.

Third, the planning system supplied plenty of 'natural breaks' in production by aiming to run the economy beyond its full capacity, by failing to make available machinery and materials of sufficient quantity and quality on time throughout the increasingly complex industrial economy. This also meant that, if the workers worked slowly and the factory performed badly, it was always possible for managers to blame their suppliers or even those higher up – the planners.

Fourth, firms and managers were rewarded for producing additional output, and achieving this was usually sufficient protection against mild penalties for producing inefficiently. On the other hand, penalties for not increasing output or underfulfilling the plan could be severe. Managers strove constantly to acquire spare capacity, surplus stocks of materials and supernumerary workers which could be mobilised when needed to cope with the rising scale of orders and requirements handed down from above.

Fifth and last, this 'safety factor' of reserve capacity must be carefully concealed from outsiders. Planners must be led to believe the factory needed all its machinery, all its stocks, all its workers to meet just its regular quarterly, annual and five-year targets. Reporting low productivity and exaggerating input needs was the best way of achieving this goal. And the best way of substantiating such reports and claims was to underperform in reality – not to mobilise the workforce, not to achieve full capacity.

The tacit collusion between managers and workers in favour of low productivity and a quiet life could survive by means of a self-sustaining process. The planners wanted higher output from given resources but, as long as they did not know what was truly possible, they were compiling and sending out factory plans in the dark. As long as the factory refrained from heroic efforts and self-sacrificing demonstrations, the factory's low output would continue to seem 'normal' and no one higher up would expect miracles.

In Soviet economic policy discussions the existence of 'hidden reserves' of labour productivity had been long recognised. How could the collusion of workers and managers in order to conceal these reserves be broken? There were three traditional methods of mobilising hidden reserves: political campaigns, legal compulsions and economic inducements.

First came extensive resort to *political campaigns* – most spectacularly, the movement of shock workers under the first Five Year Plan (1928–32), and the Stakhanov movement which began during the second plan period (1933–7).[4] (A G Stakhanov was a coal-miner of the Don-bass region who, in August 1935, set a record by digging 102 tons of coal, 10 times his personal average and 15 times the official norm, in a single shift). These movements sought to combine appeals from leaders to workers' ideals and consciences with moral pressures within the work-force, so that badly-performing workers would feel they were letting the side down. Workers could also be encouraged to blame slack managerial personnel for problems and delays and to denounce them.

But those who did not want to work harder and produce higher output were often in the majority; high achievers, who pointed the way to more intensive and consistent effort, could experience social isolation, and verbal or even physical abuse. Workers and managers alike could readily understand that the better the minority elite of shock workers performed, the more they exposed past underperformance by the work-force as a whole. More hard work would be expected of the workers in the next planning period. Meanwhile, the revelation of 'hidden reserves' would expose managers to criticism for not having uncovered them before.

Second, *legal compulsions* were habitually applied to both workers and managers in order to overcome problems of lateness and absenteeism, drunkenness, resistance to management decisions and so forth. By forcible means the Soviet worker could be compelled to attend work and to remain in post. Managers could be compelled to report offences and punished for condoning them.

Force was a blunt instrument and, on its own, could never guarantee good morale or work efficiency. However, it could effectively reinforce political appeals and make the most of any spirit of voluntary compliance. The exercise of compulsory controls would demonstrate to willing workers that the authorities would not allow the backsliding of others to undermine their increased efforts. Everyone would be willing to work harder if they knew that no one would be permitted a free ride on their backs.[5]

Third, both voluntary spirit and compulsory measures could be further reinforced by *financial inducements* such as wage differentials and 'progressive' piece-rate bonuses. Here, however, another dilemma would be generated.[6] Wage and salary incentives offered the worker the chance to translate higher effort into higher living standards. But

4 See respectively Kuromiya 1988, Siegelbaum 1988.

5 Mills, Rockoff 1987: 209, ascribe popular compliance with British wartime controls to this mix of regimentation with voluntary spirit.

6 Siegelbaum 1988: Chapter 2.

increased earnings contradicted the regime's purpose in stimulating higher output, which was to produce additional resources for public sector investment, not for household consumption. The authorities could avoid a rise in earnings by pushing up work norms to match the higher rates of work, but at the cost of damaging workers' motivation in the future – why work harder, if harder work became a permanent requirement while the effect on earnings was only ever temporary?

Alternatively, policy-makers could allow wage incomes to rise while continuing to steer resources into public investment, not retail supplies. Consumer shortages and queues would result, weakening the attraction of higher pay, which in reality could not be translated into higher consumption. This latter problem was often overcome by administrative rules reserving first place in the queue for particularly scarce items (from meats and textiles to opera tickets and rest cures) for high achievers from the management and work-force. But this, in turn, made the shortages and disincentives still worse for everyone else.

It would be probably be a mistake to see these methods, alone or in combination, as always ineffective, but their influence was hard to disentangle from that of other factors. In the prewar decade the productivity record of Soviet industry was not static.[7] After disappointing results under the first Five Year Plan, there was a big spurt under the second. The spurt was associated with several factors. One was the fruition, at last, of the big capital projects of the first Five Year Plan which now brought a radical reduction in the average age of the industrial capital stock. At the same time the new work-force, assembled in haste during the first plan, now grew less rapidly, so that its average level of skill and experience rose. In addition, there was a return to financial controls and wage incentives. Another factor was the Stakhanov movement, through which the new capital stock and the new work-force were accommodated to each other. But after 1937 there was stagnation once more, which culminated in 1940 in the reinstatement of strict legal compulsions, despite their apparently disappointing record of success in the early 1930s.

In Soviet agriculture output per worker stagnated under the Five Year Plans.[8] Again, it is difficult to disentangle the influence of differ-

7 For competing estimates of change in industrial output per year worked, 1928–40, see Nutter 1962: 173–3. Nutter's own measures show output per worker (1928 = 100) to have fallen to 93 in 1933, rising thereafter to 122 in 1937 and 127 in 1940. Output per hour worked in 1940, however, was no more than 115 per cent of 1928.

8 According to Moorsteen, Powell 1966: 370, labour productivity in agriculture in 1940 was barely higher (1,800 roubles of GNP per 1937 'man-year') than in 1928 (1,750 roubles). It was a little higher than this in 1937, but lower in every other intervening year.

ent factors. Probably the dominant effect was the setback resulting from the widespread destruction of farm animals supplying food and tractive power at the time of collectivisation. This was a legacy which could not be overcome by any inducement or compulsion to labour. But it is also true that in the 1930s the farm population was treated brutally by higher authority, deprived of necessary supplies and offered little incentive to good husbandry and farm management.

When war broke out, the mechanisms sustaining the tradition of low productivity became life-threatening. It was insufficient just to mobilise resources. Resources also had to be used efficiently. Otherwise, even when fully mobilised, the work-force would still produce insufficient means to defeat the enemy. Maintaining and raising its productiveness became a major preoccupation of policy. In wartime all the traditional mechanisms for trying to lever up the intensity and quality of labour were used – forcible constraints, economic incentives and political campaigns. But they were deployed in a different balance from before. First among them were disciplinary measures.

WORK DISCIPLINE (I) – PUBLIC SECTOR EMPLOYEES

Coercive measures were applied very extensively to the work-force. First, under the prewar legislation of June 1940, public sector employees were already liable to strict penalties for minor lateness, absenteeism, and quitting their jobs without official sanction.

Second, a new wartime decree which affected the greatest number of people raised the minimum working week. On 26 June 1941, government measures abolished normal holidays and introduced up to a maximum of three hours' compulsory overtime per day. Overtime was to be paid at the rate of time and a half.[9] The adult public sector employee's normal working week, which had stood at 41 hours until June 1940, and 48 hours (8 hours a day, 6 days a week) thereafter, now rose to 54–5 hours.[10]

Whether this was wise is a good question in itself. The evidence of industrial work in western countries suggests strongly that, when the

9 Resheniya vol 3 1968: 37–8.
10 According to Voznesensky 1948: 91, in 1942 the industrial worker's hours exceeded those worked in 1940 by 22 per cent. If the working week in 1940 stood at 44.5 hours (the average of 41 and 48 hours), then the 1942 figure must have risen to 54.3 hours.

working week stands at 48 hours, weekly output per worker is already at a maximum and that persistently working longer hours does not typically increase total output.[11]

Many, however, clearly worked far more than this. Amid the emergencies of 1941–2 they simply lived at work, slept on site and extended the working week to its physiological maximum. Reports of such cases were common where workers were near to the front line, or were directly involved in munitions work, or in the industrial evacuation, or in trying to replace the output of a fellow worker mobilised for combat.[12] (The quality of work resulting from such long hours is not reported.)

Third, some key workers – on 26 December 1941, the munitions workers, and on 15 April 1943, the railway workers – were conscripted at their posts, which made them liable to arraignment before a military tribunal for virtually any infringement of labour discipline, including lateness and unauthorised leaving of employment.

Absenteeism and departure from employment, made possible by chronic labour shortage, were already established in peacetime as traditional responses of Soviet workers to bad living and working conditions. In wartime, the intense labour shortage and exceptionally poor conditions probably combined to encourage absenteeism and turnover, despite the harsh prohibitions in force. Certainly it seems to be true that Soviet workers frequently failed to measure up to the exacting standards of discipline set by the authorities.[13] During the war years an average of 1 million people were taken to court annually and convicted of absenteeism which, under the prewar decree of 26 June 1940, was defined as leaving one's post or being more than twenty minutes late. In 1942 this meant one in sixteen of the public sector work-force. Their sentence could include six months' corrective labour at work with reduced pay and loss of seniority. Three occasions or more were counted as unauthorised quitting, leading to a prison term of two to four months. A yearly average of 200,000 people (in 1942, one in seventy) were convicted of unauthorised quitting. Further thousands escaped these penalties by going on the run, until an amnesty in 1944.

Those employed in the munitions industries fell under still harsher regulation after the militarisation decree of 26 December 1941. From 1942 onwards a yearly average of 200,000 convictions was recorded

11 Denison 1967: 59.

12 e g Mitrofanova 1971: 101, Rogachevskaya 1977: 189, Tyl SVS 1977: 172, Ginzburg 1983: 230–1.

13 Following discussion is based on Zemskov, 1990.

for unauthorised quitting, which under this law could lead to a five to eight year term of prison or forced labour; it is not certain how many were subject to this decree but, if we compare numbers convicted against estimated employment in military machine building and metal working, then in 1943 it caught one in eight workers. Nearly 300,000 people were sent to the Gulag under the same decree (not necessarily all for quitting) in 1943–5.

These figures show something about workers' failure to work according to the letter of the law. The law was so harsh, however, that they tell us far more about the mistrustful and punitive attitudes of the authorities than about workers' real commitment or underlying effort. When a disrupted bus route could result in hundreds of people facing criminal charges for lateness, an increase in convictions was just as likely to have been caused by more difficult circumstances as by lower worker morale. This means that we learn little from the law enforcement process about workers' underlying readiness to be absent from work, or about real trends in turnover.

Workforce turnover was more meaningfully measured by factory returns on departures from employment. Some of this turnover was seen as allowable in official eyes, but it is confirmed that there was significant unauthorised quitting as well. In 1943–4, in each year, more than one-tenth of the manual work-force of plant operating in the iron and steel industry left work illegally. At steel works under reconstruction in 1944 the rate was even higher – one-fifth.[14] Regardless of legal bans, the prewar labour market was struggling to reappear. Of new workers being taken on at steel works in 1943, the proportion hired by individual application varied between 9 and 16 per cent, but in 1944–5 the proportion rose to one-quarter.[15]

The authorities looked on the revival of voluntary turnover with deep disfavour. In the summer of 1944 there was a renewed clampdown, based on an unpublished decree.[16] Reports for a number of industries suggest that turnover fell after August, and was lower in 1945 than in 1944.[17] But it is hard to say whether this was because the new controls were effective, or because August was anyway by tradition a bad month for workers with family links to farming, or because the country's economic structure was anyway becoming more

14 Sovetskaya ekonomika 1970: 195–6
15 Mitrofanova 1971: 434.
16 Mitrofanova 1971: 436.
17 Sovetskaya ekonomika 1970: 195–6; Mitrofanova 1971: 436.

stable with the restoration of fixed frontiers and the winding down of the war effort.

The difficulty of maintaining labour discipline amid desperate shortages and deprivations was exemplified in the Soviet coal industry. In 1942 coal was desperately short. Invasion had cut the country's coal capacity by nearly two-thirds. At the same time, output from the Kuznetsk and the Karaganda coalfields, accounting for more than one-third of the country's remaining capacity, was falling. Behind falling output lay sharply declining output per worker, with face-workers' productivity in the Kuzbass down by one-quarter in August 1942 compared to the same month in the previous year (in the Karaganda coalfield shift output was down by two-fifths). In both coalfields, face workers' absenteeism on a monthly basis was running at sixteen to seventeen times the level of the previous year. Only half the face workers in the Kuzbass were fulfilling personal work norms, and in Karaganda the proportion was no more than one-eighth. The monthly plans for January to August 1942 were also being underfulfilled for each coalfield taken as a whole – on average, by one-quarter in the Kuzbass, and by 30 per cent in Karaganda.[18] In August–September 1942, the party authorities and war cabinet issued stinging rebukes in turn to the local party organisations for their negligence.

With hindsight it can be seen that poor discipline in the coalfields in 1942 was probably inevitable. The central problem (and this was not a peculiarly Soviet problem, being shared by Great Britain, Germany and Japan) was that mining coal was difficult and dangerous, and when war broke out many experienced miners left willingly to join the armed forces. They were replaced by inexperienced young and women workers in insufficient numbers. Wartime experience in ore mining would show that on average two years' work experience was required for underground workers to build up the skill and strength to fulfil personal work norms. In 1942 the proportion of workers in the Kuzbass with prewar experience fell below one-half. The number of women employees and of employees below normal working age rose both absolutely and even more in proportion to the declining workforce.[19] Absenteeism was doubtless highest among new workers, being promoted both by the unpleasant nature of the job and by sheer physical exhaustion. Productivity decline was an inevitable result. Moreover, low productivity could only be further worsened by the

18 Resheniya 1968: 73–80.
19 Zelkin 1969: 77–80.

absorption of massive drafts of new labour sent to the coalfields in the late summer and autumn of 1942.

Other factors also contributed to low productivity. Piece-rate bonuses were not available to all underground workers. The living conditions of new workers were very poor, and consumer supplies and services had deteriorated. (In August 1942, however, a big wage increase for coalfield employees took their cash earnings above those of even steel workers and munitions industry workers.) The level of coalface mechanisation had fallen. For the sake of quick results, existing seams were being worked to exhaustion while high-level directives to open up new pits were being ignored.[20]

In fact, given the problems besetting the industry, the record of coal-mining in 1942 was probably better than appeared at the time. Official condemnation was largely based on comparing monthly coalfield performance indicators of August 1942 with those of the previous year. But in August 1941 there had been the first flush of wartime enthusiasm, and output from the Kuzbass had broken all records, reaching almost 120 per cent of the 1941 (second quarter) average.[21] If August 1941 in the Kuzbass had been untypically good, August 1942 was unusually disappointing, with much lower performance indicators than either of the adjacent months. In terms of plan fulfilment for individual face workers, and for the Kuzbass as a whole, both July and September would have looked better than August.[22]

Most likely, August 1942 was a bad month in the coalfields, unlike August of the previous year, because by 1942 the mines were full of peasant lads who hated the work, were short of food, and seized the excuse of helping with the harvesting to go home for a few days. The rise in absenteeism and dip in output per worker were maybe only temporary – but just the thing to infuriate Moscow.

The situation in the coal industry was not necessarily typical, but still serves to exemplify the limits to coercion. The nature of the work, interacting with a steep deterioration of living conditions, and rapid turnover and renewal of the work-force, was mostly to blame for poor wartime performance. Against such a set of obstacles the compulsion to work was bound to be ineffective and could not bring about good results.

20 Zelkin 1969: 81–4, 93.
21 Dokuchaev 1973: 126–7.
22 Zelkin 1969: 90–1.

WORK DISCIPLINE (II) – COLLECTIVE FARMERS

Equivalent measures affecting collective farm workers were passed, although after some delay. In May 1939 the minimum number of workpoints to be accumulated annually by each farm worker had been set at 60 in the more industrialised regions, 80 in the predominantly agricultural regions and 100 in the southern cotton belt. Each workpoint was supposed to correspond to a day's labour of average skill and intensity, and each farm worker's accumulated annual total would determine their share in the farm's residual net income after the claims of government procurements, payments in kind to the local MTS, and expenditure on farm investments and social funds had been met. (The fact that compulsory workpoint minima had been already enacted even in peacetime reflects the fact that under Stalinist policies the collective farm's residual net income was typically very small, diminishing the individual farmer's economic motivation to work for the collective by choice.)

When war broke out there was no immediate change in the legal minima; in February 1942, however, new ones were set at 100, 120 and 150 workpoints by region (see Chapter 6). And in wartime each collective farmer did considerably more work than before. Thus, the number of workpoints accumulated by each collective farm worker of the interior regions rose substantially during the war years – from 312 to 344 for men and from 193 to 252 for women.

Despite the higher compulsory minima, the proportions of adult male and female collective farm workers reported for violation were substantially lower in 1944 than in 1940.[23] Everyone did more work, but the main reason for increased work was not the higher minima, which were already far exceeded by most farm workers.

Setting a lower minimum in industrialised regions and a higher minimum in the cotton belt was perverse. In the industrialised regions, agriculture was more diversified, and the possibilities of year-round employment were greater. Here farm workers worked the longest year. In the agricultural regions, and most of all in the cotton belt, farms followed a pattern of increasing specialisation, and employment was more and more seasonal. In the cotton belt it was most difficult to find year-round employment. But this was where the legal hurdle was highest. The excess of average labour inputs over the legal minimum in wartime was greatest where the minimum was lowest. As a result,

23 The following discussion is based on Uchastie 1962, and Arutyunyan 1970: 86–96.

the proportion reported for violating the legal minimum was lowest in the industrialised regions (where the minimum was easy to achieve) at 4 per cent of farm workers in 1944, rising to 12 per cent in the agricultural regions and 15 per cent in the cotton belt where the minimum presented the most difficult hurdle.

The arbitrariness of the law was evidently recognised by judicial authorities, who rarely applied the maximum penalty to violators. When they did, they were toughest on violators in the industrialised regions, where the minimum was easiest to attain. Legal penalties tended not to be applied strictly – even in the industrialised regions, with a relatively easy target to aim at, only some 15 per cent of violators actually suffered expulsion from the kolkhoz as specified in the decree, and the proportion was no more than 3–5 per cent where the hurdle was higher.

The impact of higher compulsory workpoint minima in wartime seems therefore to have been slight or non-existent. If farm workers worked harder in wartime it was because of material circumstances. Agricultural work became more labour intensive, because the countryside was stripped of tractive power – horses and oxen, replacement machinery and fuel supplies. Reserves of underemployed rural labour had been exhausted by recruitment into military uniform and war work, so that the work to be done had to be divided among fewer people.

WORK DISCIPLINE (III) – FORCED LABOUR

In wartime some Soviet labour remained literally forced. In June 1941 there were, according to official figures, some 2.3 million held in prisons and in Gulag labour camps and colonies; the camp population alone stood at 1,501,000 in January 1941. In wartime the latter figure fell sharply to a low of 663,000 in January 1944 (at the end of 1944 the larger category of persons held in prisons, labour camps and labour colonies had fallen to 1,450,000). The wartime decline reflected a mixture of fewer arrests, more releases, and horrifying mortality which reached 20 per cent of the camp population annually in 1942–3.[24]

Long hours and poor conditions of camp labour had already been taken to an extreme in peacetime; the regimentation and punitive

24 Zemskov 1989; Nekrasov 1989.

treatment of prisoners made inevitable their very low productivity.[25] (And the wastage of 'human resources' was doubled by the diversion of personnel and transport capacities on a large scale away from more productive tasks, to processing and guarding the Gulag population and shuffling it round the country.) With the outbreak of war, food rations of the Gulag workers were further reduced. And this further lowered their output. According to Solzhenitsyn, declining output clashed with the need to mobilise camp labour for munitions production and soon forced reversal of the food cuts.[26] The official figures suggest, however, that during the acute labour shortage of 1942–3, when every defence factory and building site in the country was screaming for more workers, hundreds of thousands of Gulag labourers perished from overwork and lack of food.

Yet even there, in the camps, Solzhenitsyn reports how labourers of the Gulag became 'caught up' in work for the front – Coal for Leningrad! Mortar shells for the troops! An attempt to collect money for a tank column (suppressed by the camp authorities).[27]

Again suggestive of the inefficiency of forced labour in wartime is the experience of the 'construction battalions' formed in 1941–2 by the Defence Commissariat from those judged physically – or politically – 'unfit' to serve. The construction battalions helped to fill the labour shortages of the early months of the war, but forced recruitment conspired with a harsh barrack regime to degrade their morale and efficiency. So poor was their performance that they were first transferred from the defence commissariat to the civilian construction authorities in October 1941, then assimilated to a civilian regime in March–April 1942.[28]

In summary, in wartime everyone worked much longer hours. The existence of a framework of legal compulsion was clearly of some significance, more so in the public sector than on the collective farm, but there were also limits to its effectiveness which were set partly by technological and supply conditions, partly by motivation and morale,

---

25 The voluminous western and Soviet unofficial literature on life in the Gulag emphasises the low productivity of camp labour, but sheds little analytical light on its underlying determinants. A model might be elaborated from remarks of Solzhenitsyn vol 2 1976: 147, concerning the 'three pillars' propping up the Gulag system – 'the differentiated ration pot, the work brigade, and the two sets of bosses', to which he then adds a fourth – '*tukhta*' (fictitious output). For some post-Stalin insights on the same problem, see Karklins 1989: 292.
26 Solzhenitsyn vol 2 1976: 118.
27 Solzhenitsyn vol 2 1976: 121.
28 D'yakov 1978: 59–60.

and partly by how much physiological strain the human body could take without loss of productive qualities.

ECONOMIC INCENTIVES

What was the role of material incentives to work harder for a higher income? Economic inducements still operated in wartime, but there was an acute shortage of the real resources required to support them.

Between 1940 and 1942, the population fell by one-third, but food production fell by more than three-fifths. In 1943 things got still worse because the population grew a little (with the recovery of territory from the enemy) while food production stagnated so that food availability per head fell still further – to only half the level of 1940. Supplies of manufactured consumer goods fell sharply, too. Meanwhile, the money incomes of public sector employees rose. As a result of extensive overtime and selective wage increases, by 1944 the average monthly earnings of manual workers in industry were 53 per cent higher than in 1940.[29] Prices in state and cooperative shops rose on average by more – 84 per cent according to official reports.[30] But this was far less than the price increase needed for official shops to absorb consumer purchasing power, given the collapse on the supply side. Instead, in a general context of severe shortages and extensive rationing, material incentives were effective only in limited circumstances.

In theory, one of the most important influences on the willingness of households to supply labour to an employer is their demand for cash. Worker households' demand for cash in wartime may have been relatively limited. Worker households still needed some cash, of course. Basic foodstuffs, especially bread, were rationed to most public sector employees and their dependants, but rationed goods were not distributed free and still had to be bought for cash. Still, the 'official' prices at which they were supplied were relatively low, and remained unchanged until 1944, except for increases affecting alcoholic beverages. Workers' cash needs for these purchases could be thought of, therefore, as fairly limited.

As far as goods off the ration were concerned, state shops were soon emptied of stocks. Worker households had little motive to acquire cash to purchase non-rationed goods from official sources, be-

29 Voznesensky 1948: 94.
30 Zaleski 1980: 456.

cause they tended not to be available at any price. This state of affairs persisted until 1944, with the introduction of 'commercial' shops where scarce goods were offered off the ration at much higher prices.

The most important source of worker households' demand for additional cash was to finance transactions in the unregulated collective farm markets (where collective farmers brought their own allotment produce for legitimate sale) and on the black market (where stolen official supplies were illegally resold). There goods were available off the ration, although at prices many times higher than official levels. At their 1943 peak, collective farm market prices were on average twelve to thirteen times the prewar level,[31] and higher still in some localities. Here was still, therefore, a motive for households to supply additional labour in return for additional cash.[32] This motive was strengthened by the reduction in supplies made available through official shops at low prices when war broke out. However, it was also weakened by the rapid rise in unofficial prices, which made those who turned to the unofficial market more likely than before to turn away without making a purchase at all.

At a certain point, the motive to acquire cash balances in order to turn to the unofficial market probably ceased to operate. At peaks of scarcity, unregulated markets shifted from cash transactions to barter. Sellers of food surpluses would no longer accept money in exchange but demanded household durables – kitchen goods, clothing, watches, jewellery or furniture (for use or for firewood); such transactions became widespread in all parts of the country.[33] Beyond this point, workers' desire to acquire additional cash through harder work must have been almost entirely blunted.

Cash incentives were used for purposes of official policy in wartime. For example, there were increases in wage differentials for those employed in the coal, steel, oil and munitions industries, in railway transport. in mechanical work in agriculture, and to various professional employees.[34] However, the most effective kind of economic incentive in wartime was probably the offer of goods in kind.

Workers were rewarded in kind in both the urban and rural economies, but in different ways and for different purposes. In the public sector rationing of foodstuffs and access to meals at work were used as blunt instruments for differentiation of reward. War workers and workers in heavy jobs received a bigger food allocation than office wor-

31 Voznesensky 1948: 102.
32 e g Nuti 1989: 112.
33 Salisbury 1971: 522, Moskoff 1990: 161–5.
34 Mitrofanova 1971: 498–9, Zaleski 1980: 327.

kers and the non-employed. Provided the increased work was not out of proportion to their increased caloric entitlement, such workers were not only kept fitter but also encouraged to remain at their posts and not to risk dismissal for any reason. In emergencies, rationing was also used in a discretionary way, to pump additional food supplies to particularly crucial groups of workers – railway workers in 1942, or coal and steel workers in early 1943.

The ration could be used as a stick as well as carrot. Able-bodied citizens who evaded work were denied rations of meat and fats. Home-workers received workers' rations only on condition of fulfilment of personal work norms. Forestry workers' rations were made to depend directly upon their productivity in the preceding fortnight.[35] In industry, absenteeism could result in a month's reduction of entitlement (examples specify cuts of 200 grams for a manual worker on 800 grams of bread per day or, for an office worker on 500 grams, a cut of 100 grams), with restoration conditional upon good behaviour in the interim. In the munitions industry similar penalties were inflicted under the militarisation decree of 26 December 1941, for lateness.[36] This was no mean threat, since bread typically accounted for 80–90 per cent of officially rationed sources of energy and protein.

In wartime agriculture the lack of economic reward was keenly felt. Of course, one of the most important sources of low farm yields was the loss of material supplies, which could not be made good by any incentive scheme. At the same time, the decline was compounded by harsh policies of confiscation of surplus kolkhoz output. Economic incentives were mainly offered as an emergency measure at harvest time, when the agricultural labour shortage was at its most acute. For example, in the autumn of 1941 the government promised the farm workers in the front-line regions a half share in the harvest in order to secure the crops before the enemy arrived.[37] In 1942, harvest workers were guaranteed a percentage share in above-plan yields. New systems for payment of bonuses in kind were also developed to cover non-harvest tasks.[38]

These measures represented a big breach in two basic principles of the kolkhoz system – that workers were to be rewarded in proportion to labour input, not output; and that their rewards would be calculated as shares in the residual income of the farm, *after* deduction of

35 Chernyavskii 1964: 75.
36 Lyubimov 1968: 32, Zemskov 1990.
37 IVOVSS vol 2 1961: 165.
38 Vinogradov 1976: 83, 89.

compulsory sales to government agencies, not as shares in the gross harvest before other deductions.

All the same, the loss of resources and their diversion from consumer supply to the war effort made it inevitable that economic motivations would generally play a lesser role than before the war in maintaining labour inputs and outputs.

MORALE AND NATIONAL FEELING

Given the wartime limits to both compulsory and economic stimulation of labour, political campaigns and moral appeals played a weightier role and, arguably, had greater effect. And this was more important than anything in helping to break up the peacetime complicity of workers and managers in the maintenance of low industrial productivity. As a result, hidden reserves were uncovered and set to work for the duration of the war.

An important expression of high wartime motivation and morale was the wide scope of 'socialist emulation'. In wartime old styles of socialist emulation were revived and new ones invented.[39] First came a new movement of the Stakhanov type. The initiators of the new movement were the 'two-hundreders', led by an employee of the Gor'kii engineering factory, F Bukin. There had been two hundreders before the war,[40] but in wartime they emerged under a new slogan: 'Work not just for yourself but also for your comrade who has gone to the front'. Their aim was to fulfil their official shift norms by 200 per cent or more.

The movement spread across the country, reaching most enterprises during the autumn of 1941. In August and September 1941 a movement of 'three-hundreders' appeared and, in February 1942 a movement of 'thousanders'. There had been thousanders, too, before the war, and the first individual thousanders of the war period emerged, like Stakhanov, in the coalfields. The initiator of a new thousanders' movement, however, was D F Bosyi, a milling machine operator sent on party orders from Leningrad to Nizhnii Tagil who, on 12 February 1942 worked a special shift in honour of the twenty-fourth anniversary of the Red Army and fulfilled his norm by no less than 1,480 per cent. By April 1942 there were 107 thousanders in Nizhnii Tagil, and

39 See especially Mitrofanova 1971: *passim*, Rogachevskaya 1977: ch 4.
40 Dokuchaev 1973: 131.

Bosyi's example was becoming the inspiration for a national movement. The thousanders seem not to have been very numerous, however, never growing beyond a small elite. (Meanwhile, however, Bosyi went from strength to strength; his norm fulfilment rose to fifteen, then seventeen times, then on 1 May 1942 to thirty-seven times, and to a record peak of sixty-two times in 1943.)

How was it possible for Soviet workers to achieve double, treble or ten or twenty times the official norm? This depended upon two factors. One was the very low level of the starting point. Official peacetime norms were based on a slow rate of work, allowing for frequent breaks and breakdowns of machinery and supplies. The other was the careful preparation of record-breaking shifts, which depended not only on the individual effort of the record-breaker but also on the organised support of a pyramid of auxiliary workers, suppliers and trouble shooters aimed at securing the best possible conditions of uninterrupted work. Undoubtedly this was Bosyi's secret. Not everyone could work under such privileged conditions and be a thousander. At the same time, however, the thousanders were the ultimate expression of a genuine phenomenon.

The new Stakhanovism was found in most of the war economy's key sectors. Two-hundreders and three-hundreders seem to have been found mainly in engineering and metalworking, including defence production. In steel-making a movement of 'accelerators' worked for high-speed smelting. There were also movements for multi-skill acquisition and multi-machine operation. In railway transport this was based on the prewar method of N A Lunin, which involved teaching locomotive drivers and firemen to substitute for repair gangs and to accept entire responsibility for operation and maintenance of the locomotive. Already in the autumn of 1941 this method was being extended to industry as a whole.[41]

Another development was the Komsomol 'front-line' youth brigades in industry. These, also, had arisen before the war, especially in the coalfields. Now they became a particularly important means of galvanising labour into action, given the rising proportion of youth workers in the heavy and defence industries (in 1942, the proportion under 25 years of age in these branches was typically 40–50 per cent). One special feature was expressed by their slogan: 'From individual records to records of the collective.' The Komsomol brigades were popularised especially in September–October 1941 when the battle for

41 Dokuchaev 1973: 135–6.

Moscow was at its height, by young workers at GAZ (the Gor'kii motor factory) and Uralmashzavod (the Urals engineering factory).

An unpleasant attribute which became especially prominent after the battle for Moscow was the Komsomol brigades' tendency to extreme forms of militarisation. Associated with their designation as 'front-line' brigades, and their slogan 'Work in the factory as soldiers fight at the front', were often a quasi-military hierarchy, military oaths, managerial decisions issued as military orders, and military formation marching. These practices were even endorsed for general use by the central committee of the steel workers' union for the eastern regions in March 1942, before being condemned nationally in June.[42]

In a last category of socialist emulation were the intercity and interfactory all-Union competitions, usually organised by branch of industry, which began in May 1942. In these competitions the workers of a factory promised to overfulfil their plan by a given percentage (or fulfil it early, by a given date, which came to the same thing), and challenged others to do likewise. The first such initiatives came from steel workers in the Kuzbass, and from workers in the aircraft industry. Typically the above-plan output would be promised as an addition to the funds for expenditure on defence. Similar campaigns of socialist emulation were repeated throughout the war.

On the surface, at least, moral incentives played a very important role in stimulating wartime labour. One factor was surely the patriotic motivation of the workers – their desire to contribute to expelling the invader from Soviet territory and destroying the Hitler regime. Soviet people saw that Germany was engaged in a war of extermination against them; working for Germany's defeat was seen as bringing its own reward, not requiring further coercive or economic levers to be applied.

One result was the temporary absence of the most important peacetime obstacles to the spread of Stakhanovite record-breaking. For example, when Stakhanovite workers achieved record-breaking feats in peacetime, resistance was invariably induced among slower workers who did not want to have higher rates of work forced upon them by an upgrading of the output norms required to earn wage bonuses. But in wartime, wage bonuses were less important because basic consumer goods were rationed and little else was available for purchase. There were no reports, then or later, of hostile reaction from within the work-force to the wartime feats of Bosyi, Bukin and their emulators.

42 Dokuchaev 1973: 140–5, also Mitrofanova 1971: 155–7, Rogachevskaya 1977: 196.

The traditional incentives to conceal reserves and hold back productivity had been to some extent neutralised.[43]

Undoubtedly there were many important reservoirs of poor morale in the Soviet wartime economy, and many cases where moral incentives did not give results. Patriotic motivation was not an all-powerful influence, and did not suffice to overcome all obstacles. Low productivity often resulted from supply disruptions and technological constraints which could not be overcome by national feeling. In other cases, low productivity could be blamed with equal plausibility on oppressive government and bad management. Conditions in the coal industry and in railway transport were often particularly difficult. Forced labourers in concentration camps, or deportees and conscripts in construction battalions, had no chance to demonstrate high morale and patriotic feeling.

WARTIME PRODUCTIVITY – SUCCESS AND FAILURE

What actually happened to output per worker in wartime? In the munitions industry there were substantial gains; there, output per worker probably doubled, or even more, between 1940 and 1944 (Table 10). This was an international phenomenon, noted also in German, American and, to a lesser extent, in British war factories.[44] The common circumstance was the changeover to standardised production of parts and assembly of weapons, which allowed transition from relatively slow, non-specialised, small batch production to much higher rates of flow production on conveyor belts, with a much greater division of labour. There was also the fact that in every country munitions factories were guaranteed preferential access to labour and supplies. In the Soviet case, the mobilisation of reserve capacities also played a part. These were both explicit reserve capacities created deliberately in advance for mobilisation in the contingency of war, and 'concealed' reserves of idle time arising out of the peacetime labour–management compact. Such reserves were now exploited.

In the rest of the economy, there was a general productivity setback. Table 10 shows that in civilian branches of industry, output per worker sagged by one-tenth before recovery in 1944 (given the in-

43 Dyker 1987: 309. See also Chapter 11.
44 For evidence, see Harrison 1990a: 576n.

crease in hours, output per hour worked remained below prewar levels). In transport, trade and construction, output per worker probably fell by a third in 1940–2, and its trend continued downward.[45] In agriculture, prewar productivity was already notably depressed, and output per worker fell by a quarter in 1940–2 before recovery in 1944. And this was in spite of the fact that each kolkhoz worker farmed more land than before, and contributed more workpoints.

There were several identifiable causes of depressed productivity. In industry and transport important factors were the loss of economic coordination, and the reduced priority of civilian output, which were both expressed in continual supply interruptions.[46] Excessive working hours, and undernourishment, also played a part. In agriculture the devastation of farm stocks of equipment and animals severely limited the wartime results of farm work. Workers' performance was also strongly influenced by the impact of wartime mobilisation on the composition of the work-force. In all branches it was the young, skilled adult males who were most likely to be mobilised but, relatively speaking, heavy and especially defence industry were most protected so that the most rapid turnover was inflicted on civilian industry and the non-industrial branches. There, the work-force rapidly lost seniority and skill.

In summary, the war was associated with sharp discontinuities in the productivity performance of Soviet workers. It is hard to show that these were influenced by specific policies or institutions. The movements of two-hundreders and three-hundreders, the campaigns of socialist emulation, the 'front-line' youth brigades, had no measurable impact on aggregate statistics of output per worker. There was sharp improvement in output per worker in munitions work, but this happened everywhere – in Germany, in Britain and the United States, not just in the USSR. As for the difficulties of the Soviet coal industry, they too could be matched in any of the warring economies. In the main civilian branches productivity sagged, then either recovered or went on falling, but the identifiable determinants of the productivity setback were the loss of human capital, technological regression and supply interruptions, not deficiencies of law enforcement, motivation or morale.

45 The downward trend, although not the extent of decline, is confirmed by official indices of output per worker in transport and construction cited in IVOVSS vol 6 1965: 142.

46 e g Voznesensky 1948: 91.

Was the Soviet wartime productivity record in any way remarkable? By peacetime standards, or by the standards of the other main war economies – no.

On the other hand, one might take as a standard for comparison the German expectation that under the impact of a deep invasion and devastating military defeat the Soviet will to resist would crumble. In that case, the willingness of Soviet workers to turn up for work and continue to produce *at all* should be considered surprising. The wartime extension and modification of peacetime mechanisms of compulsion, inducement and political mobilisation surely averted this worst possible case of a complete collapse of work effort.

CHAPTER TEN

Production: the power of victory[1]

DEMAND AND SUPPLY

The 'power of victory' in World War II was munitions of all kinds: aircraft, tanks, ships, guns and shells. What won the war for the Allies, in the end, was their ability to produce munitions in greater – much greater – quantity than Germany and Japan.[2] This view is strengthened by the fact that, despite frantic military–technical rivalry, there were no persistent differences in the quality of the weapons deployed by either side during the war, sufficient to make the difference between victory and defeat – at least until the first use of the atomic bomb in August 1945, when the outcome of the war was already decided.

The Soviet Union's contribution to the 'power of victory' was very substantial – at least as much as that of the United Kingdom, and as much as half that of the United States. The quantities involved were fantastic. During the war, Soviet production alone amounted to 100,000 tanks, 130,000 aircraft, 800,000 field guns and mortars and up to half a billion artillery shells, 1.4 million machine guns, 6 million machine pistols and 12 million rifles. (However, the Soviet Union produced hardly any warships, jeeps or military trucks.)

---

1 Available annual and quarterly data concerning Soviet physical output are collected in Harrison 1985: 250–5. For their evaluation, see Harrison 1990a. For revised estimates of munitions output, industrial production and net national product (including employment and labour productivity in different branches) see Harrison 1990a, 1991. Preliminary international comparisons are essayed in Harrison 1988. On the evaluation of mutual aid to the USSR see Harrison 1985: 256–6, 1988: 189–90, and 1991.

2 This was the message of Goldsmith 1946, from which this chapter borrows its title.

The colossal volume of war production on each side demands special explanation. No one expected a war of these dimensions. German leaders did not expect it because they expected to win their wars quickly and without major losses. In particular, in the Wehrmacht they possessed a superior combat organisation which, man for man and gun for gun, consistently outfought the enemy on both fronts.[3] Even beforehand, the Allies knew that to beat the Germans would take time and resources, but they did not understand how much. After the failure of the German *Blitzkrieg* the Allies succeeded in committing increasing resources to the war. But at first they did not understand that Germany, although stalemated and under increasing pressure, was economically far from exhausted. Nor did they anticipate the sustained military resistance of the Wehrmacht which would continue through multimillion losses, years after any chance of German victory had been destroyed.

On the contrary, German leaders had only begun to tap the available resources. From the Soviet invasion to July 1944, Germany's war production trebled. This burst of economic effort was already too late. None the less, when multiplied by the outstanding effectiveness of the Germans in combat, it meant that the Allies, too, were forced to devote absolutely undreamt-of resources to their own war production.

One of the most important factors affecting the supply of munitions in wartime was their rate of loss, both in combat and behind the front line in training and other use. World War II required the expenditure of munitions at unprecedented rates. A Red Army gun would last eighteen weeks in the field. The average life of a Soviet combat aircraft was three months, and that of a Soviet tank was barely longer. At the worst, in the winter of 1941–2, the Soviet front-line forces would be losing one-sixth of their aircraft, one-seventh of their guns and mortars and one-tenth of their armoured equipment *every week*.

This was at the worst, but equipment losses would persist at rates not much lower than this throughout the war. Regardless of whether they were retreating or advancing, defending or attacking, outnumbered or possessing numerical superiority, the Soviet armed forces continued to lose hundreds of tanks and aircraft, and thousands of guns, in each week of fighting.[4]

3 Van Creveld 1985: 4–6.
4 Wartime losses of military equipment are evaluated in Harrison 1985: 110–15, 256–66; Sokolov B V 1988. On Sokolov's doubts regarding the reliability of resulting estimates, see Harrison 1990a.

One reason for this was the relatively intense character of warfare on the eastern front. Much more than the British and the Americans, the Russians were faced with a war of national extermination. They carried on fighting under conditions in which soldiers of other nations might have given ground, and their losses were correspondingly heavy.

Another reason was the profound disadvantage of the Soviet soldier when it came to handling the equipment of modern war. Soviet pilots and tank or gun crews lacked the training, experience and battle hardening of the Wehrmacht, especially in the early stages. The threshing of Red Army personnel, first by Stalin in 1937–8, then by Hitler in 1941–2, ensured this. The typical Soviet army man of 1942 was very young and green, as likely to write off his brand new Il-2 on the airfield as under enemy fire. The Luftwaffe rated the Soviet air forces much lower than their British and American counterparts, and 'used Russia as a school for inexperienced pilots. There they could build flying and fighting skills before being thrown into the cauldron of western air battles.'[5]

But these are not the only reasons, for they do not explain the continuation of heavy losses, which probably far exceeded German losses, even when the Soviet forces' personnel had stabilised, and when they were clearly winning the war. Here the reasons for such heavy losses must include harsh and wasteful military policies, which set too low a value not only on conserving equipment but also on human casualties. Thus Soviet tanks were squandered inappropriately in many battles, including assaults on large cities, right through 1945; as a result 'the Soviet tank forces suffered impossibly heavy losses throughout the war.'[6] When planning military operations, it seems likely that high officials generally did not take into account the likely losses of equipment, and also ignored the possible human casualties. This habit was formed in the desperate days of 1941, and it persisted through the war into the period when there was no compelling need to spend resources so carelessly, reinforced by the low valuation which Stalinist ideology placed on the human 'cogs' which made up the military and economic machine.[7]

Soviet war industries thus faced a double task of daunting magnitude – to make good the losses inflicted by the enemy (sometimes invited or magnified by Soviet decisions), under conditions which were far from ideal in the first place, and further to supply additional resources for the huge expansion of the armed forces which the war required.

5 Murray 1988: 371.
6 Shlykov 1988: 112–13.
7 Istoriki 1988: 314.

PRODUCTION FOR WAR

Soviet munitions output had jumped in the years prior to the outbreak of war. In 1937 the Soviet Union was already producing a full range of modern weapons on a scale exceeded only by Germany. By 1940, Soviet munitions output had grown to nearly two and a half times the 1937 level. Table 11 shows that, between 1940 and the peak of the war effort in 1944, Soviet munitions output quadrupled again. By this time, monthly Soviet output would stand at 3,400 aircraft and nearly 1,800 armoured fighting vehicles, 11,000 guns and mortars, 200,000 rifles, and 19 million shells, mines and bombs.

Behind the figures lay two main phases of wartime development. In the first phase, the expansion was extremely rapid, even violent. It included the transition from peace to war and lasted through to the winter of 1942–3. It resulted in the doubling of munitions output in a single year, comparing 1942 with 1941 as a whole.

The great expansion was very costly. Neither the defence industries nor the rest of the economy were ready for it. As a result, different lines of war production were not kept in proportion with each other, nor was war production as a whole coordinated with developments in the rest of the economy. Thus, in the early months of the war the supply of ammunition began to lag behind the availability of guns and other military hardware; by the winter of 1941 on some fronts guns were being limited to one or two shots per day.[8] The shell famine would persist right through 1942. Again, in the winter of 1941, the production of aircraft and armour faltered. This is because, on one hand, prewar reserves of metals and fuels had been quickly used up; on the other hand, an increasing proportion of defence plant was being decommissioned and put on wheels for transfer from battle zones and relocation to the interior regions. Measured by the width of the chasm by which military needs exceeded available supplies of war goods, the winter of 1941 was the worst moment of the war.

Moreover, the expansion of war production was completely out of phase with what was happening elsewhere in the economy. While defence output climbed, everything else pointed to economic collapse. The output of coal, steel, electric power and industrial machinery plummeted. Temporarily, new supplies of non–ferrous metals and ball–bearings, absolute essentials for war production, almost disappeared. Part of this was simply because of the Wehrmacht's success in slicing up Soviet territory, but the pursuit of war production at any price

8 Arsen'ev 1972: 20.

took additional resources out of the civilian economy. In early 1942 the meteoric rise of war production would be resumed, but to draw the civilian economy away from the brink of the precipice would take until the end of that year.

In the second phase, which lasted through 1943–4, disproportions between different lines of war production were rectified and war production as a whole was brought back into balance with the rest of the economy as the civilian infrastructure began to recover. Defence output rose towards its 1944 peak. Some military needs – e g for guns and mortars – were filled, and some lines of output could be cut back, though others continued to grow.

On the whole, enemy action affected Soviet war production mainly by conquering and losing territory, and by diverting workers from production to the battleground. However, in June 1943 there were at least two German attempts to destroy Soviet war industries by means of long-range attack from the air. The Luftwaffe launched both area and precision bombing raids first on Gor'kii, home of a big tank producer, the Gor'kii motor factory (GAZ); then on Yaroslavl', site of the country's first synthetic rubber factory (SK-1). Under repeated attack both plants were knocked out, with significant loss of output. SK-1 was recommissioned in mid-September, GAZ not until the end of October.[9]

CIVILIAN INDUSTRY AND TRANSPORT

Without a minimum level of civilian output, there could be no war production. For the country's defence plant to operate, they needed metals, fuels, machinery and electric power. They also needed workers. The workers could not live without food, clothing and shelter. The munitions factories and their work-force also required a multitude of civilian services – transport, training, scientific and financial services, information and entertainment.

The civilian economy was crucial in another way as well. The army needed not only munitions, but also huge quantities of petrol and aircraft fuel, transport services, building materials and so forth – the means without which military construction and operations could not take place.

9 Ginzburg 1983: 261–3.

What happened to the Soviet civilian economy during the war is, in outline, simple. In 1941 it suffered a catastrophic reverse. By 1942, the output of civilian industry (Table 11) had fallen to less than half the prewar bench-mark; only the sternest measures held it back from outright collapse. After 1942 civilian output began to recover, and to make new resources available once more. But by 1945 it still fell far short of prewar levels.

The most threatening problems were found in heavy industry. In the first half of 1942 the supplies of electricity, steel and coal were respectively no more than one-half, two-fifths and one-third of the levels achieved a year previously. Daily shipments of railway freight had fallen to one-third of the prewar level. The main factor was loss of territory and the decommissioning of evacuated plant, but there was also a downward spiral at work as coordination was lost. Coal shortages meant a lower level of railway utilisation; since coal accounted for one-quarter of all prewar ton-kilometres shipped by rail, slower trains and more circuitous routes meant power stations and blast furnaces without fuel, power cuts and more loss of steel output. The need to extend railway track and replace rolling stock to avoid further degradation of the railway system meant another downward twist of the spiral.

During 1942 the natural tendency was for things to get worse, not better. With the German offensive in the south, more territory was lost. The Caucasian oilfields, until now protected by their remoteness, were directly threatened. Oil supplies had already begun to fall, because of equipment shortages and the difficulty of storing and transporting extracted oil; soon, yields would be down by one-half.

To reconcile such shortages with the rising needs of war production could be achieved only by ruthlessly cutting off supplies to inessential users, and by rigid economising. But to get this right demanded accurate calculation, tough leadership and hard choices. Accurate calculation – because coal could not be dug without steel and electricity, nor transported without more coal and steel; steel could not be smelted and forged without coal, transport services and electricity; in its turn, electric power required coal, steel and transport services, and so on. Tough leadership – because managerial and sectional interests had to be overridden; workers, managers and officials all had to live with increased demands for effort and reduced allocations of supplies. Hard choices – because more railway trucks for steel and coal meant, in the short run at least, a reduced capacity to supply the front with weapons or to distribute food in the interior; more steel for railways and more coal for blast furnaces meant less steel for firing at the enemy, and more civilian deaths from hypothermia in the freezing winters.

185

During 1942 the restoration of civilian industry and transport became just as important as making aircraft, guns, tanks and bullets. This restoration depended exclusively on the unaided efforts of the Soviet civilian work-force and economy within its shrunken territory, since for the time being there was neither improvement in the military situation nor significant Allied aid. And since the resources were quite inadequate for the task, the year 1942 was marked by continued desperation – emergency decrees, crash programmes, panic measures to try to break out of the vicious circle dragging industry down.[10] As each bottleneck was temporarily eased, new shortages would be felt; the strategic environment itself often changed more rapidly than plans and policies could be adapted. Coal, steel, the power industry, the railways and other forms of transportation were each in turn the object of attention; managerial shortcomings and wrong priorities criticised, new resources and cadres pumped in, along with exercises in boosting morale and tightening discipline (for example, the Kuzbass affair, above).

At this stage of the war self-reliance was forced on Soviet industry at every level. The economy as a whole was cut off from foreign trade and had to become a self-sufficient enclave; but this was not all. As central supplies ran out, every factory and locality was forced into greater self-sufficiency – better to produce one's own raw materials and components than have to rely on commitments from other factories and regions that might never be honoured. Prewar habits of self-reliance now helped wartime factory managers to weather the worst of the crisis.

For some branches of the economy, the scope for self-reliance was too limited to matter. This was especially true of consumer industry, where the collapse of output could not be avoided by turning to 'local resources'. When everything had been pre-empted by the need to boost war production and preserve the minimum required of heavy industry, there was not enough left to go on making cotton frocks or cups and saucers.

After 1942, things improved for all branches of civilian industry and transport (except food industry, see below). And it was this, more than the continued rise of war production, which signified that the Soviet war effort was becoming sustained and sustainable. While expanding defence output continued to be coupled with civilian economic collapse, the danger persisted that war production might at any moment grind to a halt. Munitions plants might simply run out of steel and

10 Harrison 1985: 175–82.

186

power, or munitions workers might starve. In 1941–2 these things were clear and present dangers, all of the time to some degree but especially in the winter months of 1941 and 1942. After the winter of 1942–3 they became less dangerous. During 1943–4, however, the menace of hunger continued to overhang the economy. This was because of the failure to turn around the situation in agriculture.

FOOD AND AGRICULTURE

As far as agriculture was concerned, 1941 was already terrible, and 1942 and 1943 were worse – awesomely so. In the autumn of 1941, as the Germans swept into the south and west, two-fifths of the grain harvest and two-thirds of the potato crop had been lost. The supply of livestock products had been held near to the 1940 level, but this was mainly because of heavy slaughtering of herds in face of the invading armies. In 1942 things got far, far worse. More rich farmlands fell under German occupation, and more livestock was lost. In that year total agricultural output would only reach two-fifths of the prewar level. In the mean time, the population under Soviet control had fallen by only one-third.

In wartime agricultural production was carried on only with great difficulty. There were three problems which compounded each other. First was the temporary loss of the Ukrainian and Volga black soil regions. The cultivation of field crops was therefore forced on to the inferior soils of the northern and eastern regions.

Second was the loss of draught power, for it is well established that shortage of draught power was a principal constraint on the expansion of sown area into marginal lands.[11] Horses were typically either handed over to Red Army units, or failed to survive civilian evacuation. (Cattle likewise died or were slaughtered.) It is true that by 1940 nearly half the draught power available to Soviet farmers was mechanised; but the production of tractors and combine harvesters had already fallen off because of the impact of prewar rearmament on Soviet industry. With the outbreak of war the supply of machinery and parts to agriculture ceased altogether. In wartime Soviet ploughs and carts were increasingly pulled by human beings.

11 Cf Hunter 1988: 206.

Third, the agricultural work-force also suffered sweeping change. As we saw in Chapters 5 and 8, young men disappeared from the countryside, recruited into war work in industry or the armed forces. The farm work-force collapsed, and became dominated by women, children, pensioners and evacuees. The evidence already put forward shows that this work-force struggled valiantly; men and women both worked harder than in peacetime, with more time worked on the collective, and with fewer breaches of discipline. The result, however, was that a reduced number of workers was multiplied by a lower index of productivity. Output per worker in agriculture was little more than two-thirds the prewar level in 1942, and failed to recover significantly thereafter. The outcome was the collapse of output, coupled with its striking failure to recover subsequently in line with population.

The recovery expected in 1943 was postponed. The growing season was relatively unfavourable;[12] in Central Russia there was too much rain, and it was too hot and dry in the south and east. In spite of an increase in the area sown, yields declined further, and the 1943 harvest was barely maintained at the 1942 level. There was perhaps a small improvement in total agricultural production, but the increase was very small and all of it went to restoring livestock herds, so that the supply of food for human consumption did not increase at all. At the same time, the demand for food was rising because in 1943 significant territory was being recovered, and on it lived hungry people who had themselves lost the means of cultivating the soil. Only in 1944 was significant recovery achieved, and prewar standards of output and productivity still represented an unreachable goal.

Closely tied to agricultural performance was the record of the food processing industry, which supplied bread and bakery products, preserved fruit and vegetables, canned and cooked meat, dairy products, sugar and confectionery to the urban population. Food industry output fell with that of agriculture; it recovered more slowly so that, presumably, as the war continued town dwellers became used to consuming more food in a less processed form. (The shortage of sugar and of other means of manufacturing alcohol was also significant for the Red Army because, in this war, most front-line infantrymen of most other countries were drunk most of the time.)[13]

---

12 That is, by the agrometeorological standards of 1886–1950, 1940–2 and 1944–5 were all good years; 1943 was merely average. See Wheatcroft 1989: graph 8.

13 Fussell 1989: 96–105.

MUTUAL AID

All the great powers which engaged in World War II, except one, relied heavily on foreign supply to augment their national resources. Only the United States was rich enough to supply resources freely to other nations. The others – the United Kingdom, the Soviet Union and Germany – all imported heavily, and used their net imports to pay for the war in various ways. Germany did this by looting and taxing her new colonies in France, Scandinavia and eastern Europe, and also by transferring millions of slaves to the Reich to work on Germany's account. The United Kingdom and the Soviet Union also had access to large net imports, made available to them primarily by the United States under Lend-Lease.

Aid arrived by three main routes. There were the Arctic convoys which ran the gauntlet of German air and U-boat attack up the coast of Scandinavia to the White Sea and the Soviet ports of Arkhangel'sk and Murmansk. Later, a land route was opened up through Iran (brought under Allied occupation in August–September 1941) over the mountains into Soviet Central Asia. And in the Far East there was the short voyage across the Bering Straits from Alaska.

For the Soviet Union, Lend-Lease meant thousands of aircraft, tanks, trucks and jeeps, 1.3 million tons of machinery and industrial equipment, 6 million tons of steel and non-ferrous metals, chemicals and petrochemicals, 4 million tons of foodstuffs and 15 million pairs of army boots. Nearly three-fifths of it arrived in the eighteen months from mid–1943 to the end of 1944. There was also a comparatively slight British contribution, the bulk of which arrived in 1942-3. The whole lot came to about $10 billions.

All this was supplied free of charge to the Soviet Union, but it was never an act of charity. Both the British and the Americans understood that the main thing was to encompass the defeat of Germany; while Germany controlled the continent of Europe from the Channel to Central Russia, the only people engaged in direct combat with the German ground forces were Russians, and it was in the western Allies' own interests to help them.

Nor did the Russians see it as charity. They saw themselves as carrying the brunt of the war in its most critical phase. They were glad to receive material aid from the west; they also saw the western Allies tying down and wearing away German forces in North Africa in 1942, and in Italy in 1943, and they understood too that the bombing of Germany drew off German forces from the eastern front. But what they really wanted was for the British and the Americans to join in the war on land in a decisive theatre, which could only mean France, and to take their share of the inevitably heavy human casualties when armies of millions vie for mastery. Consequently, they were not slow to criticise the scale and quality of the material aid actually supplied when it fell below expectation. Here, early shipments of British light tanks and American fighter airplanes set a bad precedent of low combat fitness.

Allied aid did not matter very much until after Stalingrad. There was too little of it at first, the tanks and aircraft unsuited for warfare in the east, and too much of it never arrived.

Eventually, however, Lend-Lease acquired a massive scale. Through the war as a whole, up to the beginning of 1945, one in six combat aircraft supplied to the Soviet front, and one in eight armoured fighting vehicles, came from the west. The Soviet Union supplied its own guns and ammunition, but its mobility and communications came to rely very much upon American trucks and jeeps, field telephones, tinned and concentrated foods. Thus, the Soviet ability to deny victory to the invader at Moscow, Leningrad and Stalingrad was home produced; but the rout of the invader was significantly aided from without, and the Soviet capacity to chase the retreating Germans thousands of kilometres from Stalingrad to Berlin was crucially dependent on imported means of mobility.

THE OVERALL BURDEN OF THE WAR

Soviet resources for war had to be found from within a rapidly diminishing total. This put the Soviet Union at a terrific disadvantage. In the case of Britain and the United States, war mobilisation was assisted by significant increase in the real national product, which greatly eased the problem of diverting resources to the war effort. Between the outbreak of war and the peak of the war effort, United States national income grew by about one-half in real terms. The United Kingdom was in an only slightly less favourable position; between 1939 and 1943 its national income grew by nearly one-third. The German economy expanded too, if less dramatically, 1943 national income reaching 116 per cent of the 1938 level.

Very different, and far worse, was the Soviet position, which is shown in Table 11. The USSR's real national income fell sharply when war broke out, bottoming out at less than two-thirds of the prewar level in 1942. By 1944, full recovery had not yet been accomplished, but the shortfall in comparison with 1940 had been cut to a little more than one-tenth.

How much of the USSR's depleted national income was used up by the war effort? This question is almost impossible to answer. If we value the national income at prices of prewar years, when munitions were expensive and food was at least relatively cheap, then the growth of munitions procurements and army costs was so great that by 1942 more than four-fifths of domestic output was earmarked for war outlays. This apparently huge share is in some sense an exaggeration, of course, because in 1942 munitions prices were falling sharply while food prices had quadrupled in comparison with 1940. Taking this into account sharply downgrades the share of the national income diverted to war purposes.

The least ambiguous and most meaningful indicator of wartime economic burdens may well be the share of the total work-force which was engaged in supplying and executing military operations. This means soldiers and munitions workers, and all those employed in supplying them with fuel and power, transport and other productive services, equipment, components and raw materials. Estimates contained in Table 12 show that their share in the total working population rose from one-seventh in 1940 to more than one-half, on a minimum reckoning, in 1942–3. Were it not for the relatively low productivity of agricultural workers, the difficulty of importing food, and the need to retain a relatively large number of workers in food production, this share would have risen even higher.

When the burdens of war are valued, 1942 was unquestionably the year of worst strain. By then the Soviet war effort had by no means reached its maximum in terms of the sheer quantities of soldiers and weapons deployed. These would expand significantly in 1943 before rising to the peak in 1944. But the domestic resources required, in proportion to national assets and capacities, were never greater than in 1942. No matter how bad the imbalances were in the second half of 1941, in 1942 they got worse.

The reasons why 1942 was so bad need careful disentangling. The most obvious reason is that for most of 1942 the Red Army continued to retreat eastward. Things were worse in 1942 than in 1941 simply by reason of the further loss of territory and assets. But there were other factors at work as well – the continued expansion of the Red Army and the munitions industries. These diverted huge stocks of labour, capital and material inputs away from the civilian economy; and at the same time they commanded a larger and larger share of the civilian economy's outputs of refined fuels, machinery and transport and building services. The civilian economy, not being infinitely elastic, came close to snapping.

After 1942, with the recovery of both territory and civilian output (in total and per worker), and with increasing access to foreign supply, things got better. In 1943, the Soviet authorities would commit far more of the total resources available, including net imports, to the war, but the domestic strains would be in some degree relaxed.

Just how important were net imports to Soviet economic stabilisation in 1943? According to Voznesenskii after the war, the industrial goods supplied in Lend-Lease totalled no more than 4 per cent of the gross value of output of Soviet public sector industry during the war as a whole.[14] Taking into account the low wartime rouble–dollar exchange rate, the wartime inflation of Soviet rouble prices, the double-counting inherent in the Soviet measurement of gross output value, and its inclusion of net indirect taxes, this figure is not out of the question and was probably not a lie.[15]

None the less Voznesenskii's 4 per cent clearly understated the importance of mutual aid for the Soviet economy in 1943–4. Revalued at Soviet factor costs of 1937, Lend-Lease may have amounted to one-fifth of the Soviet net national product in 1943, and only fractionally less in 1944 (Table 12). In 1943 it also freed up to one in seven of the Soviet work-force from war tasks. These figures suggest that without Lend-Lease the Soviet task in 1943 would have been far more difficult. To achieve the actual Soviet military effort of that year, as many as 7 million or 8 million additional workers might have had to be withdrawn from the civilian economy, and the pitch of overall mobilisation tightened further. This was quite probably infeasible. The result of attempting it would likely have been economic and military collapse – war factories without supplies, workers and soldiers without food or weapons. Without Allied aid, the authorities would have been compelled to withdraw major resources from fighting in 1943 in order to stabilise the economy.

This is not to downvalue the Soviet achievement in 1941–2. The rebuff administered to the Wehrmacht outside Leningrad and Moscow in late 1941 was of decisive strategic significance. Germany had lost the strategic initiative in the war as a whole, temporarily at least, and the German strategy was crucially dependent on holding it continuously. However, it had not yet changed hands, and Moscow was in no

14 Voznesensky 1948: 61.
15 Harrison 1991: 18.

condition to take the baton. More decisive here was the victory at Stalingrad. But these achievements were based on an unsustainable degree of economic mobilisation. In order to pursue the war at all, the authorities had to retreat and rationalise on the economic front in 1943. They were enabled to do so only by Allied aid. Without it, Germany's defeat would have taken many more months and years.

Speaking on 6 November 1943, Stalin declared:

> The past year marked a turn not only in the progress of hostilities, but also in the work of our rear. We were no longer confronted with such tasks as evacuating enterprises to the east and of switching industry to the production of armaments. The Soviet state now has an efficient and rapidly expanding war economy.[16]

Actually 'an efficient and rapidly expanding war economy' was an oversimplification. By peacetime standards everything was still awful. The economy was racked with crises and disproportions. Just a fortnight later, civilian food rations would be cut to their lowest level of the war. None the less it is quite true that the economy no longer stood on the knife edge of 1942. The moment of greatest danger was past.

This achievement was due in no small measure to the nerve, if not the skill, of the Soviet commanders on the economic front. We turn to them in Chapter 11.

16 Stalin 1945: 96–7.

CHAPTER ELEVEN
Planning: 'The Military-Economic Staff'[1]

PLANNING IN PREWAR PERSPECTIVE

In Soviet accounts of the war, the USSR state planning commission (Gosplan) is often described as 'the military-economic staff of the Soviet state'. But the wartime system of planning and management was actually created in peacetime, at the end of the 1920s, for tasks of peaceful industrialisation and economic transformation. How successfully did it measure up to the needs of warfare in 1941–5?

The prewar economic system was hierarchical and centralised. The main productive assets were owned by the state, and came under public sector management (except, in theory, for collective farms which were supposed to be managed cooperatively). *Hierarchy*, whether in the public or cooperative sectors, meant that production, distribution and investment were managed within narrow limits set by higher level plans and decisions reached by ministerial bureaucracies, very often in Moscow. The chain of command was organised on the production branch principle, so that steel mills were controlled by a People's Commissariat (ministry) of the Iron and Steel Industry, engineering plants by a People's Commissariat of the Engineering Industry, farms by a People's Commissariat of Agriculture, and so forth. Information

---

1 On the structure of ministerial and planning institutions before, during and after the war, see Harrison 1985: 267–86 and Crowfoot, Harrison 1990. On the formal and informal systems, see further Harrison 1990b. On the prewar and wartime evolution of the planning system see generally Harrison 1985.

and initiatives might flow from below, but the right to decide policies and appointments lay at the highest levels.

Centralisation was the other feature, This meant that ministerial plans and decisions were coordinated in Moscow. Commissariats were represented by their commissars in a collective executive body – the USSR Council of People's Commissars (Sovnarkom). (The Sovnarkom also included the usual complement of government leaders with non-production responsibilities – internal and external affairs, defence, finance, health, education and welfare.) In the Sovnarkom, groups of ministries tended to be supervised by a relatively small number of senior party leaders; usually appointed deputies of the Sovnarkom chairman (Prime Minister), they formed a kind of inner cabinet. These were people like Beriya, Kaganovich, Kosygin, Mikoyan, Malenkov and Voznesenskii. In addition, detailed coordination of ministerial plans was routed through Gosplan, the state planning commission. Gosplan had ministerial status and was headed for most of the time between 1938 and 1949 by Voznesenskii.

These, at least, were the formal institutions. They were bureaucratic and rule-bound. Bureaucracy and rules were not inconsistent with economic change; on the contrary, they comprised a dynamically expanding system, growing from year to year by regular and predictable increments. The rules of the formal management system were biased towards expansion because, right from the start, they gave priority to the increase in physical output over financial indicators of enterprise performance such as profit and loss.

As a result, managers and officials tended to encourage increased output, and increased capacity to produce output, rather than increased efficiency or an increased surplus of revenues over costs. If production fell below target, it was always easier to try to make up the shortfall by seeking to use more inputs for increased production in the old way than by going over to production in a new way that would increase output from the quantity of inputs already available. Indeed, innovators were often penalised; technical change often disrupted production in the short run, resulting in loss of rewards, and would also unsettle the work-force because of the need to renegotiate work norms and rates of pay.

The formal system also regulated the expansion process from the top down, through detailed, centralised and comprehensive plans on the 'railway timetable' model, and through quantity and price controls on supply and demand. In compiling plans, the planners started from two sets of data. One was the industrial policies and priorities set by the political leaders; the other was the economic results achieved in the most recent period. When they came to evaluate the latter the planners knew, of course, of the tendency of managers and ministerial officials to encourage increased output at the expense of additional inputs, without increased efficiency. In response, they tended to set factory targets to extract an arbitrary increase in the 'achieved level' of output relative to capacity. But, in the long run, planning 'from the achieved level' tended to have a perverse effect, encouraging technical conservatism, not forcing change. It focused attention on securing immediate percentage increases in output within the existing structure of production; it reinforced the factory managers' quest for additional current inputs, and it discouraged them from taking the risks of long-term innovation lest achievement of short-term targets be prejudiced.

These features contributed to an important paradox of the formal management system. It was dynamic, yet conservative. It encouraged the growth of output, but not the improvement of efficiency. Output grew, but radical structural and technological changes were inhibited. Instead, innovation was restricted to make-do-and-mend improvisation. Consequently, the formal system was bad at adaptive tasks. When the strategic, technical or cultural environment was changing rapidly, plans drawn up 'from the achieved level' tended to lag further and further behind reality.

The formal system started as a bureaucrat's dream which, as it became steadily more and more complicated, tended to become a nightmare. Rapid industrialisation was under way. The economy was expanding and becoming more diversified, with newly-specialised industries and plants growing up beside the old ones. As supply of the productive economy became more complicated, the multi-level administrative system of coordination and control became necessarily more elaborate.

It is not surprising, then, if we find beside the formal system an informal one. The formal system gave order and inevitability to the economic process, but the informal system gave life. It was the informal system which inspired the radical transformation of the entire economic and social structure in the prewar decade.

The informal management system was quite different from the formal one: simplified and direct, cutting across bureaucratic levels and departments with direct, personal relationships of unrestricted authority and subordination. It thrived on excitement and emergency, an atmosphere of unique and unrepeatable events – collectivisation, gigantic capital projects for industrialisation and urbanisation. The role of initiative lay with political leaders – Stalin, Molotov and their deputies. They ruled from above, by decree rather than on the basis of expertise and consent, but the power relationship required them to be able to mobilise masses of people down below, through the party and its 'transmission belts', and through the organised cult of their personalities. Impatient of rules and long-term perspectives, balances and cost-benefit evaluations, such leaders tended to rely instead upon key priorities and political campaigns of 'class warfare' aimed at achieving results regardless of cost. Rather than being centralised in a bureaucratic sense, the informal system focused economic management on a changing set of branch and regional priorities, each the responsibility of one or another personal leader, each developing on independent lines of maximum self-reliance.

The informal system was not more real than the formal one, which was also not just a paper creation. Both really existed, but each did not exist independently of the other. This is because the two systems complemented each other; movement without order tended to degenerate into directionless chaos, as periodic prewar economic crises demonstrated; but order without movement became stagnation, defeating the radical purposes of socialist construction.

The boundaries between the two systems and their relative importance were constantly shifting. Fluctuations in the state of the economy, the prestige of particular leaders and the morale of the people all contributed to this fluidity. The movement between them continued when war broke out.

THE EMERGENCY REGIME, 1941–2

Soviet accounts of wartime economic experience tend not to distinguish the attributes of the two systems, formal and informal. They stress the Soviet economy's exceptional manoeuvrability, its rapidity of structural change, its outstanding record of mobilising resources for the war effort, but they attribute these achievements to the formal system of planning and centralisation based on social ownership of productive means. In fact, the record of 1941–5 shows that, in the first and most dangerous period of the war, when the Soviet economic structure changed most rapidly, it was the informal system which ran things.

On the surface, it is true, there was an appearance of consolidation. The rapid multiplication of levels of hierarchy and chains of command which had characterised the formal system before the war came to an abrupt halt. Apart from a few sensible adjustments, Soviet government fought the war with the same ministerial structure which had existed on the day war broke out. The only exceptions were the creation of a war cabinet (the GKO), a handful of temporary commissions associated with wartime operational tasks, and new specialised commissariats for war supplies.

In reality, however, the formal system was entirely failing to coordinate the economy. Nothing showed this more starkly than the fate of the first wartime economic plan for July–September 1941, adopted on 30 June 1941. The plan called for a dramatic increase in munitions output, reallocation of new machinery to defence plant and of new investment to the eastern regions, and curtailment of non-essential investment and household consumption. These apparently sensible measures were, however, entirely irrelevant to the real situation. 'The turn made' (Voznesenskii wrote later) 'was still insufficient'.[2] On the one side, the planned increase in war production was far too small even to cover Red Army losses in the first weeks of the war; at the same time, the industrial capacities on which the plan relied were under immediate threat from the invading forces. The plan was too modest compared with military needs, but too ambitious compared with industrial capabilities.

Consequently, this plan was in reality replaced straight away by a series of *ad hoc* measures which collectively made up the real governmental response to emergency. These included the programmes to evacuate defence industry assets and bring in the harvest from frontline regions, to convert industrial capacity and redirect supplies to wartime needs, and to mobilise the working population into the armed forces and war work. All were managed by individual leaders on the basis of high-level personal initiatives and improvisations, their authority reinforced by decrees and dictatorial powers and supported by popular mobilisation. This was done entirely without the benefit of comprehensive plans, and with only the absolute minimum of effective coordination.

Informal principles of leadership dominated the system as a whole, right up to the highest level. The early *modus operandi* of the GKO itself reveals this. Its collective existence as a bureaucratic agency was tenuous. Instead, at least as far as the economy is concerned, every member had individual responsibility for some branch of war production – Molotov (the tank industry), Malenkov (aircraft and aeroengines), Voznesenskii, then Beriya (armament and ammunition), Kaganovich (railway transport). (The exceptions were Stalin, fully oc-

2 Voznesensky 1948: 34.

cupied with the tasks of Supreme CINC, and poor old Voroshilov.) The responsibilities and powers of each were effectively without limit. The special apparatus at the disposal of GKO members for the implementation of decisions comprised, on one hand, the pre-existing party and ministerial chains of command; on the other, a superimposed network of individual GKO trouble shooters (usually middle-ranking party and ministerial officials).

The decisions of the GKO were also reached informally (see Chapter 3), without agendas, secretaries or minutes. Procedures for consultation between Gosplan and the commissariats were 'simplified in the extreme', and boiled down to the presence of Voznesenskii, at first in his technical capacity as planning chief, later as a full GKO member.[3] And the lack of minutes often left considerable personal latitude to those charged with finalising details of an policy agreed after discussion.[4]

It was the informal system of high-level improvisation and individual initiative, coupled with mobilisation from below, which carried the Soviet Union through its greatest emergency. Without the informal management system, adaptation of the Soviet economy to the needs of World War II would have taken too long, or would never have been achieved. This adaptation could not have been managed on the basis of a 'railway timetable' type of conversion plan. The emergency situation of 1941 was simply not amenable to detailed foresight or the comprehensive planning of every nut and bolt.

The informal system also aided wartime mobilisation by weakening the perverse results of planning 'from the achieved level.' Detailed fulfilment of plan indicators was inevitably downgraded as a measure of enterprise performance. Since the plans were obviously unattainable, the important thing, the thing which brought recognition and medals and privileges, became simply to work as hard and produce as much as possible, not to secure mechanistic fulfilment of the plan.

At the same time, the positive role of the informal system in 1941–2 must be qualified in two respects. First, this was the very same system which, in prewar military–political management, had performed so desperately badly, failing to foresee German strategic designs and to prepare the Soviet military, economy and society for the true character of the coming war. The Stalinist leadership's failure of foresight went far beyond any lack of comprehensive, detailed plans, and was re-

3 Khrulev 1961: 66–7. Although Voznesenskii was technically not head of Gosplan during the first eighteen months of the war, he was still Stalin's first deputy as Prime Minister, with clear overall responsibility for national economic coordination.
4 Vannikov 1962: 78.

flected in excessive reliance on Hitler's guarantees, complacent faith in the ability to deter German aggression, susceptibility to German deception, arbitrary repression of alternative diplomatic forecasts and military plans for defence in depth, and failures of prewar industrial dispersal.

The second qualification to the role of the informal system is that in 1941–2 its managers did not know when they had gone too far, when to stop. In 1941 they had saved the country's munitions capacity and safeguarded the conditions of time and space for a sustained military–economic mobilisation. But to sustain the mobilisation was itself beyond them. Instead, they allowed the disproportions in the economy to rise to an unbearable degree of tension. We have seen that in the winter and spring of 1941–2, although munitions production was rising rapidly, the economic crisis actually worsened. And this was not just a result of military setbacks and territorial losses. Aside from munitions, the rest of the economy was in an utter shambles, and the production of steel, power, transport services and food (all of which were ultimately vital to maintenance of the country's fighting strength) was reduced to a small fraction of prewar norms. By 1942 the economy had been allowed to become overmobilised, with too great a volume of resources committed to combat and war production, compared to the resources remaining in civilian employment.

THE REVIVAL OF FORMAL PLANNING

The 'planned character' of the Soviet economy in wartime re-emerged out of the struggle to return from excessive mobilisation and stabilise the civilian economy. The process was worked out pragmatically and significant costs were evidently incurred.

During most of 1942 it was too early to talk about the revival of the formal system. The situation remained too changeable and crisis ridden, and the immediate priorities of adaptation too urgent. Lack of ready statistics meant that the planners were too often ignorant of what had really been achieved – or neglected – in evacuating industry and mobilising reserves. Plans continued to be compiled and launched, but were constantly overridden by unforeseen developments and new emergencies.

A positive achievement was that civilian industry and transport were brought back to an even keel. The means by which this was done reflect the contradictions of the time.

As we saw in Chapter 10, by the war's first winter these sectors had become locked in a self-reinforcing downward spiral. Coal and steel shortages were being translated into cancelled trains and power cuts, and further damage to the utilisation of what capacity remained. The economic situation was still one of emergency, but the emergency had become far more complicated than before. In 1941 the urgent need was simply for guns, shells, tanks and aircraft with which to resist the invader. By 1942 steel and coal, transport, fuel and bread had all acquired equal rank with munitions as war priorities.

To understand the problem required an understanding of the minimum requirements of the economic system for coordination and equilibrium, which relied in turn on comprehensive statistics and planning expertise. To solve the problem required, first, the designation of new priorities, the identification of new resources and non-essential claims on them, and their ruthless redirection. The new priority system had to be more comprehensive and finely graded than the old one (priority A-1 for munitions, 4-F for everything else) which had governed the first months of evacuation and conversion. There had to follow the design and implementation of urgent measures and crash programmes to revitalise the industrial infrastructure. All this had to be accompanied by the ceaseless pushing of tired, hungry citizens into sustained action on the home front – appealing, coaxing, encouraging, rewarding, shouting, threatening, compelling.

In achieving this the informal system played, as yet, an irreducible role. At the same time the framework for informal action was supplied, increasingly, by formal planning agencies. Gosplan, which had played little or no role in the first round of economic mobilisation, regained authority and moved back to the focus of effective policy. This became encapsulated not only in panic measures but also in regular monthly, then quarterly economic plans. Without this revival of formal institutions, informal management could not have sustained economic life.

The transition back to predominantly formal methods of resource allocation was sealed at the end of 1942. Three things made this so. First was the fact that the worsening of both military fortune and the resource balance was at an end. At Stalingrad the war had reached its strategic turning point. The relocation of industry was complete; moreover, the pooling of Allied resources would now work more and more in the Soviet favour. Second was the establishment of effective nation-wide control over the 'ultimate bottleneck': competition between rival claimants on the country's labour supplies had been eliminated, and a truly centralised system for coordinating the direction and allocation of the working population had been achieved. Third was the end of informal management at the highest level. This was the uncoordinated system of economic leadership by individual members of the GKO and Politburo. At the end of 1942 such personal responsibilities were devolved upon a new powerful cabinet subcommittee, the GKO Operations Bureau, set up in order to increase the centralisation of controls on industry and transport. Prominent among its members were Voznesenskii, the planning chief, and Mikoyan and Lyubimov (responsible for foreign and domestic trade respectively).

Thus, in economic management, personal dictatorship and rule by decree were being circumscribed by reassertion of formal management, and after the close of 1942 their role diminished sharply. As the national product began to recover from the post-invasion trough, newly available resources were directed more to expanding civilian production than to munitions output or resources for immediate combat. This transition was indispensable for the outstanding Soviet record of sustained resource mobilisation for war. Of course this does not mean that there were no more emergencies or panics, and in agriculture the crisis atmosphere persisted through 1944.

The revival of the formal system was also enhanced by the resumption of postwar perspectives involved in such issues as reconstruction of recaptured territories and reconversion of defence industries to peacetime needs. Draft perspective plans extending into the postwar era began to be compiled and discussed once more as early as 1943, and branch and regional plans with a post-wartime horizon actually began to be adopted in 1944. While the war continued, however, these plans were all strongly biased towards heavy industry and transport, although the needs of agriculture and textiles received some attention.

Different aspects of the Soviet economic system were therefore important at different stages of the war. Planning in the 'railway timetable' sense was not important in the initial battle for survival; everything depended upon improvised leadership and mobilisation. But improvisation could only stave off defeat, and could not secure victory. To restore coordination of the civilian and defence sectors, to revive the production of steel, electricity and foodstuffs, and to allocate resources intelligently for these purposes required something more which only detailed planning could secure.

The Stalinist economic system, even in peacetime, is sometimes described as of the general type of a 'war economy'. From the point of view of the experience of real fighting, this turned out to be a substantial simplification because in fact the economic system was not ready for war; it had to be significantly modified to fit it whether for immediate survival or for protracted fighting. The informal system over which Stalin exercised personal domination performed certain essential functions of mobilisation for war in the second half of 1941, but associated with it were also heavy penalties.

LIMITS TO CENTRALISATION

While centralisation was fundamental to achieving Stalin's 'efficient and rapidly expanding war economy', there was never any question that the whole war economy could be run from the centre. This had never been feasible in time of peace, and it would scarcely become more of a proposition when the planners were overwhelmed by new needs of war mobilisation.

Under the prewar Five Year Plans, important areas of economic life were still regulated from below. Wherever basic needs were left unfilled by the planning system, workers, managers and consumers created decentralised mechanisms to fill the gaps. These mechanisms were of two basic types. One was reflected in the trend to self-reliance – the factory develops its own sideline production of metals, components, fuels, tools or electric power; the family grows its own meat and vegetables. The other was the market – what the consumer, or the manager, cannot obtain from state supplies, is purchased for cash, legally or illegally. And although both these mechanisms contradicted the idea of an economy coordinated by means of comprehensive central plans, all attempts to eradicate them foundered.

The war brought change in the scope of centralised resource allocation, and the scope both of self-reliance and of the market altered correspondingly. The German invasion cut right back the total of resources available for producers and consumers. Huge shortfalls became general. One option for those trying to maintain normality was to buy needed goods and services *on the market*. Enterprises could seek to make up their labour shortfalls by offering cash in return for additional effort and extra recruits. Worker households with a significant cash income could resort to legal markets for peasant surpluses of foodstuffs (the kolkhoz market) or black markets for illegally resold state supplies of rationed goods. In Chapter 6 we saw the results of these efforts.

The most important obstacle was that at the same time the economy was becoming much more centralised. Everything available was being sucked into the centralised system of supply of industry, and drawn away from prewar uses into supply of the war effort. Regardless of people's readiness to resort to the market to meet their needs, the real scope for market transfers was therefore sharply reduced. As a result, the main phenomena to be observed were shrinking supplies and rising prices.

Given the impossibility of satisfying needs through increased resort to the market, *self-reliance* became more important than before. There were two main aspects to this. One was that supplies were immediately diverted away from existing industrial users towards new wartime priorities. This meant that producers of non-military goods were cut off from customary supplies of materials and components, fuel and power, and had to fend for themselves to a higher degree than in peacetime. Another reason was that, regardless of the diversion of supplies to military producers, the whole overloaded system of centralised distribution was brought to the point of breakdown by the shortage of transport and the decay of formal allocative routines; even supply of the most important defence factories could not be guaranteed. Everyone had to become more self-sufficient. Munitions and civilian engineering factories learnt to make their own instruments and machine tools, and developed their own construction brigades; the latter in turn learnt self-reliance in supply of building materials and tools. Sideline steel works became more widespread in heavy industry and railway engineering. Large specialised steel works expanded their own fuel bases and sideline engineering shops for making electrical and other equipment.

What was required to meet the needs of industry became even more essential for the consumer. In Chapter 6 we showed that big factories created their own sideline farm enterprises; in face of inadequate food rations, workers and consumers went heavily into allotment farming in order to achieve family self-sufficiency.

Without learning increased self-reliance, the industrial economy and its human agents could not have weathered the storms of 1941–2. At the same time, self-reliance was not a cheap strategy. Its price was paid in the lost benefits of specialisation and economies of scale, which raised the unit costs incurred by small auxiliary production units.

Neither self-reliance nor the market could act as a magic wand. They depended, ultimately, on the availability of local reserves of capacity – labour, land, materials – which could be mobilised to make good the shortages being registered in the official system of planned supply. But when the shortfalls continued to multiply and all reserves were exhausted, the scope for making them good whether through self-reliance or market exchange was at an end. When this point was reached, the lights went out, factories shut down and people retreated to their apartments and cottages to freeze and starve. This is what happened, most dramatically and tragically, in the Leningrad enclave in the winter of 1941–2. But it happened more typically in a small-scale, episodic, yet widespread fashion in towns and villages across the whole country through all the years of war. No factory complex can have worked entirely steadily, without interruption, from invasion through to victory, and no community can have completely escaped the pains of hunger and cold.

By a variety of measures the wartime economy was more centralised than before or after the war. There was a big increase in the number of centrally planned commodities and plan indicators. Planning of high-priority industrial goods became more comprehensive and detailed. Controls on big industrial producers were tightened by means of central compilation of their quarterly material supply plans. The share of national income claimed for government expenditure was clearly much higher than in the prewar years. At the same time, there were clearly limits to the centralisation process, and parallel to it could be observed a process of decentralisation. In some areas of life the centre interfered less, and left producers and consumers more to their own devices. Sometimes this meant a bigger role for the market, but more often it meant enforced self-reliance.

In this, as in many other ways, the war served to remind people that not everything could be decreed from Moscow. For purposes of waging a great war of national resources, centralised decision-making played an indispensable role. However, in wartime as in times of peace, the idea that the Kremlin could allocate every nut and bolt and direct the working life of every individual proved to be an impractical, utopian abstraction. The collective will and initiative of tens of thousands of local communities and working collectives, the preferences and creativity of a multimillion mass of individuals, ultimately decided the issue.

Epilogue

'Spending half of the night of VE day on a park bench, alone in the middle of a crowd gone wild with joy', K S Karol observed the end of the war in a provincial southern city, more than once the scene of fierce fighting and enemy occupation, now restored to peace:

> Here was Rostov, an early-to-bed town pulled from its slumber by a party, exuberant, though without alcohol.
>   . . . Stirred from sleep, I left the house in a hurry, without even pulling my trousers on. Halfway to Kola's place, we met, embraced, and began to weep. At the time of our reunion in 1944, we had been able to contain our emotion. Tonight, however, everything was different: we were intoxicated by this victory – no less of a miracle for having been expected and awaited. 'Now we really are going to be happy,' Kola repeated in between sobs. His voice was drowned by the cries of an agitated young girl: 'Wherever Stalin is, that's where victory is!' It was no exaggeration of the truth.
>   . . . Under the bright glare of the searchlights, half-destroyed Rostov resembled an abstract painting full of discordant forms, strange shadows and luminous stains. The people of Rostov gave themselves up to a display of genuine kindness.[1]

The euphoria, however, concealed an appalling bill of costs. Outstanding among these were the 27 million to 28 million premature deaths incurred by the Soviet population, which accounted for no fewer than one in seven of the prewar population, and up to half of global demographic losses attributable to World War II.

The bleeding wounds of victory were everywhere. The Soviet Army had lost nearly 9 million dead. No other army in history had

1 Karol 1986: 341–4.

achieved so much at such great cost. The civilian cost was still greater. Some 19 million civilians had perished before their time. One-third of the prewar capital stock had been destroyed, and twice that amount used up by wartime defence, economic conversion, and lost national income.

The Soviet costs incurred for the sake of victory outweighed the war losses of all other nations put together, but the fruits of victory had to be shared in a very different proportion. In Germany the Red Army now faced powerful Allied forces which had suffered only a small fraction of the battle losses, yet now occupied the richer half of Germany. In the Far East the United States had used its new nuclear monopoly to deny the USSR any significant part in the occupation of Japan. In contrast to shattered Europe and enfeebled Britain, the United States had emerged from the war with renewed prosperity and enlarged resources committed to an active foreign policy. Traditional hostility to Bolshevism was already re-emerging.

Of the effects of the war on Soviet society, most obvious and long lasting was the demographic impact. Virtually every family had suffered long separation from loved ones – husbands and fathers, wives and mothers, parents and children – and eventually the permanent loss of family members. Again, most families had experienced some forced change of residence or occupation; at the same time as almost all adults had become soldiers, war workers or farmers, huge multi-million flows had crossed the country, first eastward, then westward. The loss of young men seriously impaired postwar processes of marriage and child-bearing, to the extent that only two-thirds of women surviving in 1959 were married, who had reached the age of 20 during the decade from 1929 to 1938. In the Soviet population as a whole, the excess of women over men had increased by some 13 million; this was felt especially in the countryside where by 1945 there were also 13 million more women collective farm workers than men.

As for the personal deprivations and hardships endured by the survivors, these would continue for years afterwards. They were something to which Soviet citizens had already become habituated by prewar patterns of life. However, having just endured a terrible war, many now anticipated a more stable, peaceful world of Soviet partnership with their new (and economically much more affluent) allies; they hoped that peace would bring if not prosperity, then less strain and discipline, and more fairness and social justice. Later, Il'ya Ehrenburg wrote:

> When I recall conversations at the front and at the rear, when I re-read letters, it is clear that everybody expected that once victory had been

won, people would know real happiness. We realized, of course, that the country had been devastated, impoverished, that we would have to work hard, and we did not have fantasies about mountains of gold. But we believed that victory would bring justice, that human dignity would triumph.[2]

But realisation of these goals would be long postponed.

As for the Soviet political system, in the long run the war would have both conservative and liberating effects. On balance, and certainly for the first postwar generation, the conservative effects were stronger.

To begin with, Stalin's position was strengthened to the point of unassailability, and he would remain Soviet leader until his death in March 1953. Now portrayed as the architect of Soviet victory, he was seen everywhere as the great Soviet war leader, the Generalissimus who personally symbolised the military destruction of Nazi expansionism and confirmed the USSR as a great power. As a modernising statesman who changed both his own country and the world, Stalin invited comparison with Bismarck, Napoleon or Peter the Great. More than anything, the Soviet victory in 1945 was used to validate his rule on a popular basis. Support for the cult of Stalin's personality, which formerly had been limited to officialdom and the most privileged stratum of workers, became a mass phenomenon, and would persist long after his death.

Victory also entrenched the ministerial and party elite which had managed the war effort. For the next forty years the Soviet political system would be dominated by members of the same group which had led the USSR to victory under Stalin. Born in the years after the turn of the century, they came to prominence in the wake of the prewar purges. Having proved themselves in wartime, they would remain at the top long after Stalin's death, a few surviving briefly into the Gorbachev era. Some of these wartime chieftains of the Party, defence and heavy industry would later show themselves capable, at least, of a rational reform-mindedness, and would eventually distance themselves from Stalin's memory and the worst aspects of Stalin's personal despotism. But their reformism would never prevail over their conservative values and faith in the basic soundness of the authoritarian, centralised model which Stalin had presided over. For them the war had placed, if not Stalin himself, then the Stalinist system above criticism.

In the years just after the war, the reinforced legitimacy of Stalin and Stalinist institutions ran strongly against other, weaker currents welling up from below. The war experience would also supply a

2 Cited by Hough 1985: 255.

smothered impulse to reform. There was a widespread desire for liberalisation and relaxation, in politics as in culture and economic affairs. Veterans of military service and war work, whose loyalty to the Soviet system had passed the severest test, may have expected the system to reward them with greater trust and increased rights of participation, not just free bus passes. Some also believed that the war had revealed the weaknesses of Stalinist dictatorship, above all in 1941–2, and the necessity of limiting the arbitrary powers of individual leaders. The war had given many the opportunity to exercise their own personal initiative and responsibility on a wider scale than in peacetime, as military commanders, factory managers, farmers, war administrators, war writers and reporters, and had taught them that mere unthinking obedience to superior orders was not enough.

For the time being, however, such beliefs and values would remain implicit or, if voiced *en clair*, dangerous to the individuals who held them. Among the political leadership there were only confused ideological shadings, without sharp distinctions between overall political alternatives or coherent programmes.[3] In the absence of any clear challenge, Stalin would seek to restore everything as it was before the war to the rigid mould of personal dictatorship and rule from above by decree. And while he lived he would very largely succeed. Other nations – the two Germanies and Japan under Allied occupation, Britain under the Attlee government, France and Italy under new postwar constitutions – went through different postwar reforms. In the Soviet Union, in contrast, the prewar order of forced industrial accumulation, political dictatorship, and social mobilisation, would be restored.

As for the universal desire for peace, it was diverted into channels which ultimately led to increased militarism and great power nationalism. Peace was represented as so all-important that everything must be sacrificed to it, including the sovereign rights of the smaller nations of eastern Europe such as the Baltic republics, Poland and Czechoslovakia, seen from Moscow primarily as a new defensive buffer zone against aggression from the west. Peace at any price meant the continued priority of military spending and military-economic preparedness, entailing further sacrifices on the part of a tired, malnourished civilian population. Armed force, not paper treaties, had stopped Hitler. Military power was now seen, even more than before the war, as the sole means of Soviet security. The ability to wage war was now seen as the only guarantee against its renewed outbreak. The prevention of war was seen as sufficient justification for the continued militarisation of

3 Hough 1985: 255–66.

civilian life, and for the ruthless treatment of real or presumed enemies – collaborators, returning prisoners of war, minor national groups. As the United States tested out its new found confidence, prosperity and military power, war was presented in Moscow as increasingly inevitable, and became the justification for a new curtain of secrecy and repressive policies.

Under the surface of the Stalinist mould, changes were at work. New generations were rising, and the requirements of the Soviet economy and society would diverge steadily away from traditional models of secrecy, authority and dictatorial rule. These trends would have operated anyway, with or without the war; in a few respects the war fostered them, but the more dominant conservative effects of the war slowed down their effectiveness and delayed reform. De-Stalinisation would prove a protracted, tortuous process. Khrushchev's reforms of 1955–6 would be only the beginning. There would follow thirty years of complex political evolution away from the Stalinist model, with many standstills and even retreats under Brezhnev.

But even if actual progress wavered, one driving force behind it would be memories of World War II. This was already clear in 1956 when Khrushchev declared:

> Not Stalin but the party as a whole, the Soviet Government, our heroic
> Army, its talented leaders and brave soldiers, the whole Soviet nation –
> these are the ones who assured the victory of the Great Patriotic War.[4]

Over the years, a variety of revelations and reinterpretations has eroded the conservative, Stalinist lessons of the war. Modern historical writing tends to emphasise the price which the USSR paid for Stalin and Stalinism in World War II as well as before and after. All those who fell under the shadow which Stalin cast in the war years have now, at last, secured some public redress – the generals, the industrialists, the prisoners of war, the Leningraders, the rank and file of the Army and of civilian society.

Justice for Stalin is only part of what is at issue in this judgement. If not Stalin, then who can be credited with the great victory on the eastern front? Millions of ordinary people, infantrymen, officers, workers at the bench and in the field, managers, writers – even war administrators and Party secretaries: these shouldered the main burdens, whether they did it well or badly. For the most part they were not born great heroes, and they were not innately brave or noble, although many of them did very brave things. They were marked out

4 Khrushchev 1976: 57.

not by special personal qualities but by special circumstances, and an extraordinary history.

What enabled them to wage such a terrible war and emerge victorious? The answer to these questions is the same − everything in their history, their revolutionary and national traditions, their cultural ties and family roles, the social, economic and administrative webs which defined their place in Soviet life, the organs of state, the Party and its leaders, and Stalin too. All these are indispensable elements of the explanation of what made them fight, and why victory cost them so much.

Tables

Table 1 Consumer products available, per head of population, 1942–3
(1940 = 100)

	1942	1943
Light industry, total	72	73
sewn goods	109	117
leather, furs, footwear	70	73
silk weaves	61	68
cotton textiles	54	52
woollen textiles	48	47
Food industry, total	63	56
fish	101	117
dairy products	78	84
meat	78	65
sugar	7	8
Agriculture, total	57	50
wool	116	84
milk	70	66
potatoes	46	62
flax, hemp	90	61
meat, fats	58	52
raw cotton	88	43
grains	46	42
sunflowers	16	41
eggs	55	38
sugar beets	18	9

Source: Gross value of output indices are from IVOVSS vol 6 1965: 45, 63,
67. These are divided by population given by Narkhoz 1973: 9, as 194.1
million in 1940 and by IVMV vol 7 1976: 41, as 130 million in 1942 and
143 million in 1943.

213

Table 2 Official rations in 1944: some examples

	Child under 13 yrs	Adult dependant	White-collar employee	Manual worker[a]	Manual worker[b]
Bread and sugar category	2	2	2	1	1 (with supplement)
Non–bread ration	Basic	Basic	Basic	Special list	Special list (with special supplement)
GRAMS PER DAY:					
Bread, flour	400	300	400	700	1 200
GRAMS PER MONTH:					
Sugar, sweets	400	400	400	800	800
Cereals	800	600	800	1 500	3 000
Fats	300	200	300	600	1 000
Meat, fish	400	500	1 200	2 200	4 500
CALORIES PER DAY, TOTAL:					
State rations	1 067	780	1 074	1 913	3 460
Of which, from bread (% total)	81	80	81	79	80
F A O CALORY NORMS					
Emergency subsistence[c]	—	1 600	2 000	2 500	3 000
Temporary maintenance[d]	—	2 190	2 500	3 000	3 500
PROTEIN, GRAMS PER DAY, TOTAL:					
State rations	49	36	48	85	147
Of which, from bread (% total)	88	90	89	88	87

Sources: For ration tables see Lyubimov 1968: 28–30; for overall calorie equivalents see Chernyavskii 1964: 77, except for children under 13 years, estimated by the authors. Calorie equivalents from bread, overall protein equivalents, and protein equivalents from bread, are estimated by the authors. Davidson et al 1979: 171 state that the energy content of breads lie within the range 215–250 kcal/100 gm. The lower end of this range is consistent both with information about the quality of Soviet bread and flour in war time, and with the totals for calories available shown in the table, when combined with an estimate of calories available from non-bread rations. Similarly, the protein content of bread is assumed to lie in the range of 10–11 gm/100 gm (Davidson *et al* 1979: 168). For recommendations of the Food and Agriculture Organisation set out in 1946 (given in megajoules per day, converted at the rate of 4.2 mJ per 1,000 kcal) see Davidson *et al* 1979: 502.

Notes:
a   War workers in 'leading enterprises' of the defence and heavy industries, construction or transport.
b   War workers subject to unusual difficulty or hazard at work, for example underground face workers in the coal industry. Some underground face workers could obtain up to another 1,000 calories daily in the form of cold and hot meals at work.
c   The level 'needed to prevent the most serious undernutrition leading to disease and the danger of civil unrest.'
d   The level 'sufficiently high to maintain populations in fairly good health but not sufficient for rapid and complete recovery.'

Table 3 The composition of the Soviet working population, 1940–5 (millions, annual average)

	1940	1941	1942	1943	1944	1945
Military personnel[a]	4.2	7.5	10.9	11.1	11.2	11.6
Public sector employees[b]	31.2	28.0	18.4	19.4	23.6	27.3
western USSR[b]	19.6	—	5.6	6.1	10.5	14.1
eastern USSR[b]	11.6	—	12.8	13.3	13.1	13.2
Artels, industrial cooperatives, other[c]	2.7	2.3	1.4	1.4	1.6	2.1
Collective farmers[d]	47.0	34.9	22.7	23.8	28.9	33.6
Working population[e]	85.1	72.8	53.3	55.6	65.3	74.6
Forced labourers[f]	1.8	1.9	1.6	1.3	1.3	1.5

Notes and sources:
a   Cited or estimated by Harrison 1991: Table 4.
b   Mitrofanova 1971: 445 (pre–1965 definition).
c   Estimated public sector (including cooperative) employment (post–1965 definition) from Harrison 1991, less public sector employment (pre–1965 definition).
d   Estimated by Harrison 1991: Table 4.
e   This is strictly the working population at liberty, exclusive of forced labourers employed in prisons, labour camps and colonies, and internal exile.
f   Numbers reported in NKVD Gulag labour camps and colonies, according to Dugin 1990. These figures are of recent, untested provenance, and are left out of figures for the working population as a whole.

Table 4 The Soviet industrial work-force, 1940 and 1942–5 (millions, annual average)

	1940	1942	1943	1944	1945
Manual employees[a]	8.3	5.5	5.7	6.4	7.2
Non-manual employees[b]	2.7	1.7	1.8	1.8	2.3
Male employees[c]	6.5	3.5	3.5	3.9	4.7
Female employees[d]	4.5	3.7	4.0	4.3	4.8
All employees[a]	11.0	7.2	7.5	8.2	9.5

Notes and sources:
a   Mitrofanova 1971: 439. A figure of 7.8 million for 1941 is available from Mitrofanova 1984: 359–60.
b   All employees, less manual employees.
c   All employees, less female employees.
d   All employees, multiplied by the employment share of women, from Table 5.

Table 5 Women's share in employment, 1940–5 (per cent)

	1940	1941	1942	1943	1944	1945
Public sector[a]	38	—	53	57	57	55
industry	41	—	52	53	53	51
construction	23	—	24	29	—	32
transport	21	—	35	42	45	40
farming	34	—	54	61	—	61
Collective farming[b]	—	52	62	73	78	80

Notes and sources:
a   Women's share in annual average employment, from Mitrofanova 1971: 455.
b   Women's share in the able-bodied work-force, on 1 January, from Uchastie 1962: 26.

Table 6 The Soviet kolkhoz work-force, 1941–5 (millions, 1 January)

	1941	1942	1943	1944	1945
Able-bodied males	16.9	6.3	4.0	3.6	4.4
Able-bodied females	18.6	10.1	11.0	12.9	17.5
Youths	7.1	4.0	4.7	5.3	6.4
Retired, unfit	4.4	—	2.8	3.2	4.5

Source: Uchastie 1962: 26–7.

Table 7 The Gulag work-force, 1940–5

	1940	1941	1942	1943	1944	1945
THOUSANDS, 1 JANUARY:[a]						
Number in camps	1 344	1 501	1 416	984	664	716
of which, sentenced under Article 58[b]	445	420	408	345	269	289
Number in colonies	316	429	361	500	516	745
Gulag labourers, total	1 660	1 930	1 777	1 484	1 180	1 461
PER CENT OF ANNUAL AVERAGE CAMP POPULATION:[c]						
Net inflow into camps[d]	41	48	30	26	42	44
Releases from camps	22	43	43	41	22	51
Transit losses, escapes from camps[e]	5	4	1	4	3	6
Deaths in camps	3	7	21	20	9	7

Notes and sources:
a   As in annual reports, cited by Dugin 1990.
b   Numbers sentenced under Article 58 of the RSFSR Criminal Code ('Counterrevolutionary crimes').
c   Calculated from annual reports, cited by Zemskov 1989.
d   Inflow into Gulag camps from other places of confinement, less outflow.
e   Transit losses: the difference between camp outflows and inflows arising from transfers within the Gulag camp system (strictly, this also includes changes in the stock of prisoners in transit from one New Year's Eve to the next).

Table 8 The Soviet war economy, 1941–5: official indices (1940 = 100)

	1941	*1942*	*1943*	*1944*	*1945*
National income produced[a]	92	66	74	88	83
Productive fixed assets, excluding livestock[b]	72	68	76	84	88
Industrial production[c]	98	77	90	103	91
of which, MBMW[d]	111	119	142	158	129
Agricultural production[c]	62	38	37	54	60
Capital investment	84	52	57	79	92
Freight turnover of all modes of transport[e]	92	53	61	71	76
Employment in the public sector, annual average[f]	88	59	62	76	87
Retail turnover of state and cooperative trade[g]	84	34	32	37	43

Source: Narkhoz 1987: 43. Notes below are by the authors.
Notes:
a Net material product, valued at 'unchanged' prices of 1926/27.
b End–year figures at 'comparable' prices.
c Gross value of output, probably valued at 'unchanged' prices of 1926/27.
d MBMW: machine-building and metal-working – in wartime, mainly composed of munitions.
e Ton–kilometres.
f Excluding the collective farm work-force.
g Measured at 'comparable prices', excluding turnover in the unregulated collective farm markets.

Table 9 Soviet employment, by branch of output, 1940–5 (millions)

	1940	1941	1942	1943	1944	1945
Military services	4.2	7.5	10.9	11.1	11.2	11.6
Industry, of which:						
military MBMW[ab]	1.5	1.8	2.5	2.8	2.9	2.0
civilian industry[b]	11.6	10.1	5.7	5.8	6.5	9.1
all industry	13.1	11.9	8.3	8.6	9.4	11.2
Transport, trade						
and construction	9.5	10.3	5.9	6.2	8.5	—
Agriculture[c]	49.7	36.9	24.0	25.1	30.6	—
Civilian services	8.6	6.1	4.3	4.7	5.6	—
Working population[d]	85.1	72.8	53.3	55.6	65.3	74.6
of which, soldiers						
and war workers[e]	12.8	20.1	25.2	19.7	21.2	—
other workers[f]	72.3	52.7	28.1	35.9	44.1	—

Source: Cited or estimated in Harrison 1991: Table 4.
Notes:
a   MBMW: machine-building and metal-working
b   Estimated upper and lower bounds for employment in civilian industry
    and military MBMW respectively, reflecting limiting assumptions used to
    derive employment in military MBMW and (as a residual) in civilian bran-
    ches.
c   The kolkhoz working population (including workers participating in col-
    lective production despite youth, retirement or disability), plus estimated
    employment in public sector agriculture and MTS.
d   As in Table 3, this is the working population at liberty, exclusive of those
    employed in prisons, labour camps and colonies, and internal exile. The
    latter groups were also engaged in industry, agriculture, transport and con-
    struction, but are not distributed between these branches in the table.
e   Military personnel, plus estimated war workers employed in all branches
    in domestic supply of final and intermediate goods and services to the
    defence budget.
f   Working population, less soldiers and war workers.

Table 10 Net output per worker, 1940 and 1942–4 (1937 roubles)

	1940	1942	1943	1944
Military MBMW[a]	5 630	11 140	12 600	13 430
Civilian industry	5 630	5 020	5 500	5 820
Transport, trade construction	4 310	2 920	3 010	2 610
Agriculture	1 410	1 060	1 210	1 470

Source: Estimated in Harrison 1991: Table 5.
Note:
a   MBMW: machine-building and metal-working

Table 11 Net national product by branch of origin, 1940 and 1942–4 (billion 1937 roubles at factor cost)

	1940	1942	1943	1944
Military MBMW[a]	8.1	27.4	34.1	37.7
Civilian industry	65.6	29.1	32.2	38.3
Agriculture	69.9	25.3	30.4	45.0
Construction	10.6	3.2	3.4	4.4
Transport, communications	19.3	10.2	11.8	13.7
Trade, catering	11.1	3.8	3.5	4.1
Civilian services	33.8	16.9	18.3	22.1
Military services	6.8	17.6	17.9	18.1
Net national product	225.2	133.6	151.6	183.5

Source: Estimated in Harrison 1991: Table 2.
Note:
a   MBMW: machine-building and metal-working

Table 12 The burden of Soviet defence outlays, 1940 and 1942–4

	1940	1942	1943	1944
PER CENT OF NNP[a] (1937 roubles at factor cost)				
Total war outlays	20	83	89	79
– Receipts from mutual aid	–0	–7	–20	–19
= Supply from domestic output	20	76	68	60
PER CENT OF WORKING POPULATION				
Employed in supply of war	15	47	35	32
Freed by mutual aid[b]	0	4	14	11

Source: Estimated in Harrison 1991.
Note:
a NNP: net national product.
b This indicates the estimated proportion of the Soviet working population which would have been required to produce domestically the volume and assortment of goods supplied through Lend–Lease in each year, given average estimated output per worker in relevant branches of the Soviet economy.

Important dates

1941

22 Jun	'Barbarossa': German invasion of USSR
	Romania declares war on USSR
23 Jun	Sovnarkom–Central Committee order to implement mobilisation plan for ammunition production
24 Jun	Politburo decision to evacuate armour steel rolling mill from Mariupol'
	Sovnarkom–Central Committee decision to establish Council for evacuation under Kaganovich
25 Jun	Politburo resolution on increased output of medium and heavy tanks
26 Jun	Supreme Soviet decree on the extension of working hours in wartime
27 Jun	Hungary declares war on USSR
	Politburo approval of plan for relocation of evacuated aircraft factories
	Sovnarkom–Central Committee resolution on order of evacuation of people and assets
28 Jun	Fall of Minsk
	Finland declares war on USSR
29 Jun	Sovnarkom–Central Committee ('scorched earth') directive to party and Soviet organisations of frontline districts
30 Jun	Fall of L'vov
	Adoption of revised wartime economic plan for 1941 (3rd quarter)

	Formation of GKO (Stalin, Molotov, Voroshilov, Malenkov, Beriya)
	Formation of Sovnarkom Labour Committee
1 Jul	Fall of Riga
	Sovnarkom resolution on the extension of rights of people's commissars in wartime
3 Jul	Stalin's radio broadcast
4 Jul	GKO commission (Voznesenskii) to compile 1941 (4th quarter)–1942 plan for the interior regions
5 Jul	Sovnarkom decree on order of evacuation of population
7 Jul	Sovnarkom decree on increased use of 'local resources' for consumer supplies
8 Jul	Militarisation of construction labour (until Mar–Apr 1942)
12 Jul	Anglo-Soviet mutual assistance pact
16 Jul	Shvernik replaces Kaganovich at Council for evacuation
18 Jul	Food rationing in Moscow, Leningrad cities, oblasts
30 Jul	Harry Hopkins in Moscow
14 Aug	Bread rationing in towns and industrial settlements, Central Russia and Urals
16 Aug	Fall of Smolensk
	Sovnarkom-Central Committee approval of 1941 (fourth quarter)–1942 plan for the interior regions
	Stalin's Order No 270: Soldiers who allow themselves to fall into captivity are traitors to the Motherland
17 Aug	Fall of Dnepropetrovsk
25 Aug	Fall of Tallinn
30 Aug	Leningrad cut off by rail (fall of Mga)
8 Sep	Leningrad encircled on land (fall of Shlüsselberg)
17 Sep	Kiev encirclement completed
19 Sep	Stabilisation of the Leningrad front
	Fall of Kiev
28 Sep	Beaverbrook and Harriman in Moscow
29 Sep	German forces enter Donbass
30 Sep	'Typhoon', first stage: first German offensive against Moscow
3 Oct	Fall of Orel
7 Oct	Vyaz'ma encirclement completed
12 Oct	Fall of Kaluga
13 Oct	Fall of Kalinin
16 Oct	Evacuation of civil administration and foreign embassies to the interior
	The Moscow panic begins

	Fall of Odessa
19 Oct	Moscow: state of siege
24 Oct	Fall of Khar'kov
25 Oct	First German offensive against Moscow halted
	Formation of Committee for evacuation of stocks from Moscow under Mikoyan (wound up 19 Dec)
	Voznesenskii appointed to represent Sovnarkom in Kuibyshev (until end-Nov)
30 Oct	Sevastopol' cut off (falls 5 June 1942)
1 Nov	Food rationing in forty-three towns outside Moscow, Leningrad oblasts
3 Nov	Fall of Kursk
6 Nov	Stalin's eve of revolution speech
7 Nov	Stalin addresses Red Square parade
9 Nov	Fall of Tikhvin (cutting Leningrad's rail link to Lake Ladoga)
	Directive on schedule for relocation of evacuated plant in the interior
10 Nov	Bread, sugar rationing in all towns and industrial settlements
16 Nov	'Typhoon', second stage: second German offensive against Moscow
	Fall of Kerch
20 Nov	Leningrad food rations reach lowest point
19 Nov	Fall of Rostov-on-Don
29 Nov	Recapture of Rostov-on-Don
5 Dec	End of German offensive against Moscow
	Eden in Moscow
6 Dec	Soviet counteroffensive: Moscow sector
7 Dec	Pearl Harbor
8 Dec	First T-34s leave the Khar'kov tractor factory (now in the Urals)
	Britain and USA declare war on Japan
9 Dec	Recapture of Tikhvin
11 Dec	Italy and Germany declare war on USA
16 Dec	Recapture of Kalinin
23 Dec	First increase in Leningrad food rations
25 Dec	Committee for freight dispersal under Mikoyan replaces Council for evacuation
26 Dec	Militarisation of defence industry labour
29 Dec	Recapture of Kerch

1942

7 Jan	Soviet general counteroffensive (western, central, southern and south-western sectors)
28 Jan	Soviet forces re-enter Ukraine across upper Donets
3 Feb	Mikoyan, Voznesenskii join GKO
13 Feb	Decree on compulsory service liability of urban population
14 Feb	Formation of GKO transport committee under Stalin
20 Feb	Kaganovich joins GKO
13 Apr	GKO approval of crash programme for the iron and steel industry
8 May	German offensive in Crimea
12 May	Soviet offensive, Khar'kov sector
20 May	Fall of Kerch
23 May	Khar'kov encirclement completed
26 May	20-year Anglo-Soviet treaty
12 Jun	Central Committee resolution on improvement of political work in the Soviet Army
22 Jun	Formation of Commission for evacuation on the southern front under Shvernik
28 Jun	German offensive against Voronezh
4 Jul	Fall of Sevastopol'
6 Jul	Fall of Voronezh
19 Jul	Fall of Voroshilovgrad
24 Jul	Fall of Rostov-on-Don
28 Jul	Stalin's Order No 227: 'Not a step back!'
10 Aug	Fall of Maikop
11 Aug	Fall of Krasnodar
12 Aug	Churchill and Harriman in Moscow
23 Aug	German forces reach the Volga
	Area bombing of Stalingrad
25 Aug	Fall of Mozdok
3 Sep	German breakthrough south of Stalingrad
13 Sep	German offensive against Stalingrad
24 Sep	German occupation of most of central Stalingrad
	GKO resolutions on defects in party work in the Kuzbass and Karaganda coalfields
19 Nov	Soviet counteroffensive: Stalingrad sector
23 Nov	Stalingrad encirclement completed
8 Dec	Formation of GKO operations bureau
	Voznesenskii reappointed to head USSR Gosplan

1943

1 Jan	German retreat from Caucasus begins
18 Jan	Recapture of Shlüsselburg; the land encirclement of Leningrad broken
25 Jan	Recapture of Voronezh
29 Jan	Gosplan decision to draft reconstruction plans for recaptured territories plus the Donbass and Leningrad
31 Jan	German surrender at Stalingrad
8 Feb	Recapture of Kursk
14 Feb	Recapture of Rostov-on-Don
16 Feb	Recapture of Khar'kov
12 Mar	Recapture of Gzhatsk-Vyazma-Rzhev triangle
14 Mar	Fall of Khar'kov
15 Apr	Supreme Soviet decree on militarisation of railway labour
16 Apr	Soviet reply to German allegation of Soviet responsibility for murder of Polish officers at Katyn
26 Apr	Breach of relations with Polish government in exile (London)
22 May	Dissolution of Comintern
4 Jun	Area bombing of Gor'kii begins (two weeks) and destruction of Gor'kii motor factor (GAZ)
9 Jun	Area bombing of Yaroslavl' and destruction of SK-1 synthetic rubber factory (reconstruction completed mid-September)
5 Jul	German offensive against Kursk salient
10 Jul	Allied invasion of Sicily
15 Jul	Soviet offensive against Orel salient
26 Jul	Fall of Mussolini
5 Aug	Recapture of Orel
23 Aug	Recapture of Khar'kov
30 Aug	Recapture of Taganrog
3 Sep	Allied invasion of Italy
	Italian surrender
8 Sep	Recapture of Donbass completed
10 Sep	Recapture of Mariupol'
16 Sep	Recapture of Novorossiisk
25 Sep	Recapture of Smolensk
7 Oct	Soviet forces cross the Dnepr
13 Oct	Italy declares war on Germany
14 Oct	Recapture of Zaporozh'e

18 Oct	Allied foreign ministers in Moscow
25 Oct	Recapture of Dnepropetrovsk
28 Oct	Reconstruction of GAZ completed
6 Nov	Recapture of Kiev
	Stalin's 'fundamental turning point' speech
12 Nov	Recapture of Zhitomir
23 Nov	Nation-wide bread ration cut
28 Nov	Stalin, Churchill and Roosevelt in Tehran

1944

17 Jan	Leningrad blockade ends
4 Mar	Soviet offensive in the Ukraine
2 Apr	Soviet forces enter Romania
10 Apr	Recapture of Odessa
11 Apr	Soviet forces enter Crimea
9 May	Recapture of Sevastopol'
13 May	Recapture of Crimea completed
6 Jun	Allied invasion of France
10 Jun	Soviet offensive against Finland
23 Jun	Soviet offensive in Belorussia
28 Jun	Vitebsk-Bobruisk encirclement completed
3 Jul	Recapture of Minsk
18 Jul	Soviet forces enter Poland
20 Jul	German officers' attempt to assassinate Hitler
31 Jul	Soviet forces reach Praga (opposite Warsaw)
1 Aug	Warsaw uprising
15 Aug	Allied invasion of southern France
20 Aug	Soviet offensive in Bessarabia and Romania
23 Aug	Romanian surrender
4 Sep	Finnish surrender
5 Sep	USSR declares war on Bulgaria
9 Sep	Soviet forces enter Bulgaria
10 Sep	Fall of Praga (opposite Warsaw)
11 Sep	United States forces enter Germany
29 Sep	Soviet forces enter Yugoslavia
2 Oct	Surrender of Warsaw underground resistance
9 Oct	Churchill in Moscow
20 Oct	Soviet and Yugoslav partisan forces enter Belgrade

28 Oct	Bulgarian surrender
20 Nov	Bulganin replaces Voroshilov in GKO
16 Dec	German offensive in France (Ardennes)

1945

3 Jan	United States counteroffensive in France (Ardennes)
12 Jan	Soviet offensive in Poland
17 Jan	Fall of Warsaw
19 Jan	Soviet forces enter East Prussia
4 Feb	Stalin meets Churchill and Roosevelt in Yalta
13 Feb	Fall of Budapest
13 Mar	Allies reach Rhine
23 Mar	Allied crossing of Rhine
29 Mar	Soviet forces enter Austria
12 Apr	Death of Roosevelt
13 Apr	Fall of Vienna
16 Apr	Soviet offensive against Berlin
23 Apr	Soviet forces reach Berlin
27 Apr	Soviet and United States forces meet (Torgau)
28 Apr	Death of Mussolini
30 Apr	Death of Hitler
1 May	German surrender in Italy
2 May	Fall of Berlin
4 May	German surrender in Holland, Denmark and north-west Germany
7 May	German surrender (Jodl to Eisenhower)
8 May	German surrender (Keitel to Zhukov)
9 May	Fall of Prague
26 May	GKO directive on reconversion of defence plant
24 Jun	Victory parade in Red Square
17 Jul	Stalin, Churchill and Truman in Potsdam
6 Aug	Atom bombing of Hiroshima
8 Aug	USSR declares war on Japan
9 Aug	Atom bombing of Nagasaki
	Soviet forces enter Manchuria
14 Aug	Japanese declaration of intent to surrender
19 Aug	Surrender of Japanese forces in Manchuria begins

1 Sep   Surrender of Japanese forces in Manchuria, Sakhalin and Kuril islands completed

2 Sep   Japanese surrender to MacArthur

4 Sep   Dissolution of GKO

References

Places of publication are Moscow (for items in the Russian language) or London (for English-language items) unless otherwise specified.

IN ENGLISH

Alexiev A R 1985 Soviet nationalities under attack: the World War II experience. In Wimbush S E (ed) 1985 *Soviet nationalities in strategic perspective*

Anderson B A, Silver B D 1985 Demographic consequences of World War II on the non-Russian nationalities of the USSR. In Linz S J (ed) 1985 *The Impact of World War II on the Soviet Union*. Totowa, NJ

Barber J 1986 The development of Soviet employment and labour policy, 1930–41. In Lane D (ed) *Labour and employment in the USSR*. Brighton

Berghahn V R 1982 *Modern Germany: society, economy and politics in the twentieth century*. Cambridge

Bergson A 1961 *The real national income of Soviet Russia since 1928*. Cambridge, Massachusetts

Bialer S 1970 *Stalin and his generals: Soviet military memoirs of World War II*

Bidlack R 1987 Workers at war: factory workers and labor policy in the siege of Leningrad. Unpub PhD thesis. Indiana University

Brooke R 1926 *1914 and other poems*

Brown B D 1985 World War II in Soviet literature. In Linz S J (ed) 1985 *The Impact of World War II on the Soviet Union*. Totowa, NJ

231

Calder A 1969 *The people's war: Britain, 1939–1945*

Carr E H 1979 *The Russian revolution from Lenin to Stalin (1917–1929)*

Churchward L G 1973 *The Soviet intelligentsia: an essay on the social structure and roles of Soviet intellectuals during the 1960s*

Conquest R (ed) 1967 *Industrial workers in the USSR*

Cooper J M 1976 Defence production and the Soviet economy, 1929–1941. Soviet Industrialisation Project Series no 3. Centre for Russian and East European Studies, University of Birmingham

Crowfoot J, Harrison M 1990 The USSR Council of Ministers under late Stalinism, 1945–1954: its production branch composition and the requirements of national economy and policy. *Soviet Studies* 42(1)

Dallin A 1957 *German rule in Russia, 1941–1945: A study of occupation policies*

Dallin D J, Nicolaevsky B I 1947 *Forced labor in Soviet Russia.* New Haven, Connecticut

Davidson S, Passmore R, Brock J F, Truswell A S 1979 *Human nutrition and dietetics*, 7th edn. Edinburgh

Davies R W 1984 Capital investment and capital stock in the USSR, 1928–1940: Soviet and western estimates. In Davies R W (ed) *Soviet investment for planned industrialisation, 1929–1937: Policy and practice.* Berkeley, California

Davies R W 1989 *Soviet history in the Gorbachev revolution*

Davis C, Charemza W 1989 Introduction to Models of disequilibrium and shortage in centrally planned economies. In Davis C, Charemza W (eds) *Models of disequilibrium and shortage in centrally planned economies*

Denison E F 1967 *Why growth rates differ: postwar experience in nine western countries.* Washington, DC

Deutscher I 1966 *Stalin: a political biography*, 2nd edn

Dyker D 1987 Review of Harrison 1985. *Slavonic and East European Review* 75(3)

Ehrenburg I 1964 *The war, 1941–1945*

Erickson J 1962 *The Soviet high command: a military-political history, 1918–1941*

Erickson J 1975, 1982 *Stalin's war with Germany*, vol 1 *The road to Stalingrad.* Vol 2 *The road to Berlin*

Fussell P 1989 *Wartime: understanding and behaviour in the Second World War.* Oxford

Goldsmith R 1946 The power of victory: munitions output in World War II. *Military affairs* 10

Great Patriotic War 1974 *Great Patriotic war of the Soviet Union, 1941–1945: a general outline*. Moscow

Harrison M 1985 *Soviet planning in peace and war, 1938–1945*. Cambridge

Harrison M 1988 Resource mobilization for World War II: the USA, UK, USSR, and Germany, 1938–1945. *Economic History Review* 41 (2)

Harrison M 1990a The volume of Soviet munitions output, 1937–1945: a reevaluation. *Journal of Economic History* 50(3)

Harrison M 1990b Soviet industrialisation and the test of war. *History Workshop Journal* (29)

Harrison M 1991 New estimates of Soviet production and employment in World War II: a progress report. Soviet Industrialisation Project Series no 32. Centre for Russian and East European Studies, University of Birmingham

Hough J F 1985 Debates about the postwar world. In Linz S J (ed) 1985 *The Impact of World War II on the Soviet Union*. Totowa, NJ

Hunter H 1983 The new tasks of Soviet industry in the thirties. In Desai P (ed) 1983 *Marxism, central planning and the Soviet economy: Essays in honour of Abram Bergson*

Hunter H 1988 Soviet agriculture with and without collectivization, 1928–1940. *Slavic Review* 47

Kaldor N 1946 The German war economy. *Review of Economic Studies* 13

Karklins R 1989 The organisation of power in Soviet labour camps. *Soviet Studies* 41(2)

Karol K S 1986 *Solik: life in the Soviet Union, 1939–1946*

Khrushchev N S 1976 *The 'secret' speech delivered to the closed session of the Twentieth Congress of the Communist Party of the Soviet Union*. Nottingham

Kornai J 1980 *The economics of shortage* (2 vols). Amsterdam

Kravchenko V 1947 *I chose freedom: The personal and political life of a Soviet official*

Kuromiya H 1988 *Stalin's industrial revolution: Politics and workers, 1928–1932*. Cambridge

Lewin M 1985 *The making of the Soviet system: Essays in the social history of interwar Russia*

Lieberman S R 1983 The evacuation of industry in the Soviet Union during World War II. *Soviet Studies* 35(1)

Lieberman S R 1985 Crisis management in the USSR: the wartime system of administration and control. In Linz S J (ed) 1985 *The Impact of World War II on the Soviet Union*. Totowa, NJ

McNeal R H 1988 *Stalin: man and ruler*. Basingstoke

Medvedev R 1983 *All Stalin's men*. Oxford

Medvedev R 1989 *Let history judge: the origins and consequences of Stalinism* (2nd edn)

Millar J R, Linz S J 1978 The cost of World War II to the Soviet people: a research note. *Journal of Economic History* 38(4)

Mills G, Rockoff H 1987 Compliance with price controls in the United States and the United Kingdom during World War II. *Journal of Economic History* 47(1)

Milward A S 1977 *War, economy and society, 1939–1945*

Moorsteen R, Powell R P 1966 *The Soviet capital stock, 1928–1962*. Homewood, Illinois

Moskoff W 1990 *The bread of affliction: the food supply in the USSR during World War II*. Cambridge

Murray W 1988 *Luftwaffe: Strategy for defeat, 1933–1945*

Nove A 1982 *An economic history of the USSR*, 3rd edn. Harmondsworth

Nove A 1985 Soviet peasantry in World War II. In Linz S J (ed) 1985 *The Impact of World War II on the Soviet Union*. Totowa, NJ

Nuti D M 1989 Hidden and repressed inflation in Soviet-type economies: definitions, measurements and stabilization. In Davis C, Charemza W (eds) *Models of disequilibrium and shortage in centrally planned economies*

Nutter G W 1962 *The growth of industrial production in the Soviet Union*. Princeton, NJ

Olevsky M 1983 Contribution of the ordnance makers to the overall war effort. *Soviet Military Review* (11)

Pavlenko N 1989 Tragedy and triumph of the Red Army. *Moscow News* (19)

Pavlov D V 1965 *Leningrad 1941: the blockade*. Chicago

Piper D 1984 Soviet Union. In Klein H (ed) *The Second World War in fiction*

Salisbury H E 1971 *The 900 days: the siege of Leningrad*

Schulte T J 1989 *The German Army and Nazi policies in occupied Russia*. Oxford

Seaton A 1975 *Stalin as military commander*

Shlykov V 1988 On the history of tank assymetry in Europe. *International Affairs* (10)

Shtemenko S M 1970 *The Soviet General Staff at war*. Moscow

Siegelbaum L H 1988 *Stakhanovism and the politics of productivity in the USSR, 1935–1941*. Cambridge

Solzhenitsyn A 1973–8 *The Gulag archipelago, 1918–1956* (3 vols)

Stalin J 1940 *Leninism*
Stalin J 1945 *The Great Patriotic war of the Soviet Union.* New York
Trevor-Roper H R 1966 *Hitler's war directives, 1939–1945*
Tupper S M 1981 The mobilisation of Soviet industry for defence needs, 1937–1941. Unpub paper to West European conference on Soviet industry and the working class in the interwar years. University of Birmingham
Tupper S M 1982 The Red Army and Soviet defence industry, 1934–1941. Unpub PhD thesis. University of Birmingham
Urlanis B 1971 *Wars and population.* Moscow
Van Creveld M 1985 *Fighting power: German and U.S. Army performance, 1939–1945*
Voznesensky N A 1948 *War economy of the USSR in the period of the Patriotic War.* Moscow
War seen from Britain 1945 *The war seen from Britain, 1939–1945*
Werth A 1964 *Russia at war*
Whaley B 1973 *Codeword BARBAROSSA.* Cambridge, Massachusetts
Wheatcroft S G 1981 On assessing the size of forced concentration camp labour in the Soviet Union, 1929–56. *Soviet Studies* 33(2)
Wheatcroft S G 1989 Agriculture. In Davies R W (ed) The *Soviet economic transformation, 1914–1945* (in preparation)
White S 1988 *The Bolshevik poster*
Zaleski E 1980 *Stalinist planning for economic growth, 1933–1952*
Zhukov G K 1971 *The memoirs of Marshal Zhukov.* New York

IN RUSSIAN AND OTHER LANGUAGES

Alekseev V V, Isupov V A 1986 *Naselenie Sibiri v gody Velikoi Otechestvennoi voiny.* Novosibirsk
Aleshchenko N M 1980 *Moskovskii sovet v 1941–1945 gg.*
Aniskov V T 1966 *Kolkhoznoe krest'yanstvo Sibiri i Dal'nego Vostoka – frontu. 1941–1945 gg..* Barnaul
Arsen'ev V I 1972 *O nekotorykh izmeneniyakh v organizatsii upravleniya voennoi ekonomiki v pervyi period Velikoi Otechestvennoi voiny*
Arutyunyan Yu V 1970 *Sovetskoe krest'yanstvo v gody Velikoi Otechestvennoi voiny,* 2nd edn
Belonosov I I 1970 *Sovetskie profsoyuzy v gody voiny,* 2nd edn
Bukin S S 1985 Byt rabochikh Sibiri v gody Velikoi Otechestvennoi voiny. *Izvestiya sibirskogo otdeleniya akademii nauk SSSR* (3(1))
Chalmaev V 1981 *Malyshev,* 2nd edn

Chernyavskii U G 1964 *Voina i prodovol'stvie. Snabzhenie gorodskogo naseleniya v Velikuyu Otechestvennuyu voinu (1941–1945 gg.)*

Dokuchaev G A 1973 *Rabochii klass Sibiri i Dal'nego Vostoka v gody Velikoi Otechestvennoi voiny*

Dugin A 1990 GULAG glazami istorika. *Soyuz* (9 February)

D'yakov Yu L 1978 Promyshlennoe i transportnoe stroitel'stvo v tylu v gody Velikoi Otechestvennoi voiny. In *Istoricheskie zapiski* (101)

Eshelony 1966 *Eshelony idut na vostok*

Ginzburg S Z 1983 *O proshlom – dlya budushchego*

Granin D 1988 Zapretnaya glava. *Znamya* (2)

ISE vol 5 1978 *Istoriya sotsialisticheskoi ekonomiki SSSR* vol 5

Istoriki 1988 *Istoriki sporyat. Trinadtsat' besed*

Istoriya KPSS vol 5(i) 1970 *Istoriya Kommunisticheskoi partii Sovetskogo Soyuza* vol 5(i)

IVMV 1973–82 *Istoriya Vtoroi Mirovoi voiny 1939–1945* (12 vols)

IVOVSS 1961–5 *Istoriya Velikoi Otechestvennoi voiny Sovetskogo Soyuza 1941–5* (6 vols)

Kapital'noe 1961 *Kapital'noe stroitel'stvo SSSR*

Khrulev A V 1961 Stanovlenie strategicheskogo tyla v Velikoi Otechestvennoi voine. *Voenno-istoricheskii zhurnal* (6)

Kir'yan M M 1988 *Velikaya Otechestvennaya voina 1941–1945. Slovar'-spravochnik*

Kolesnik A D 1988 *Opolchenskie formirovaniya Rossiiskoi Federatsii v gody Velikoi Otechestvennoi voiny*

Kosyachenko G 1944 Voennoe khozyaistvo SSSR. *Planovoe khozyaistvo* (1)

Kozlov V A, Bordyugov G A, Zubkova E Y, Khlevnyuk O V 1989 *Istoricheskii opyt i perestroika. Chelovecheskii faktor v sotsial'nom-ekonomicheskom razvitii SSSR*

Kozlov V I 1989 O lyudskikh poteryakh Sovetskogo Soyuza v Velikoi Otechestvennoi voiny 1941–1945 godov. *Istoriya SSSR* (2)

Kravchenko G S 1970 *Ekonomika SSSR v gody Velikoi Otechestvennoi voiny*, 2nd edn

Kulagin G 1978 *Dnevnik i pamyat'. O perezhitom v gody blokady*. Leningrad

Kumanev G A 1966 Podvig zheleznedorozhnikov. In *Eshelony idut na vostok*

Kumanev G A 1976 *Na sluzhbe fronta i tyla. Zheleznedorozhnyi transport SSSR nakanune i v gody Velikoi Otechestvennoi voiny. 1938–1945*

Kumanev G A 1988 *Voina i zheleznedorozhnyi transport SSSR. 1941–1945*

Kumanev G A (ed) 1988 *Sovetskii tyl v pervyi period Velikoi Otechestvennoi voiny*

Kurskii A 1975 Planirovanie v gody Velikoi Otechestvennoi voiny. *Ekonomicheskie nauki* (4)

Lerskii I A 1943 *Kapital'noe stroitel'stvo v usloviyakh Otechestvennoi voiny*

Lerskii I A 1945 *Vosproizvodstvo osnovnykh fondov promyshlennosti SSSR v usloviyakh voiny*

Likhomanov M I, Pozina L T, Finogenov E I 1985 *Partiinoe rukovodstvo evakuatsiei v pervyi period Velikoi Otechestvnnoi voiny 1941–1942 gg.*. Leningrad

Lipatov N P 1966 Stranitsy pobedy (kratkii obzor literatury o perebazirovanii promyshlennosti SSSR v 1941–1942 gg.. In *Eshelony idut na vostok*

Litovkin V 1990 'Zeki' na altare pobedy. *Soyuz* (38), February

Lyubimov A V 1968 *Torgovlya i snabzhenie v gody Velikoi Otechestvennoi voiny*

Maksimova E (ed) 1988 *Deti voinnoi pory*

Michalka W (ed) 1985 *Das Dritte Reich: Dokumente zur Innen- und Aussenpolitik*, vol 2 *Weltmachtanspruch und nationaler Zusammenbruch, 1939–1945*. Munich

Mitrofanova A V 1971 *Rabochii klass SSSR v gody Velikoi Otechestvennoi voiny*

Mitrofanova A V 1984 *Rabochii klass SSSR nakanune i v gody Velikoi Otechestvennoi voiny*

Mitrofanova A V (ed) 1989 *Sovetskii tyl v period korennogo pereloma v Velikoi Otechestvennoi voiny. Noyabr' 1942–1943*

Moiseev M A 1990 Tsena pobedy. *Voenno-istoricheskii zhurnal* (3)

Morekhina G 1974 *Velikaya bitva za metall*

Nachalo voiny 1990 Nachalo voiny (22–30 iyunya 1941 g.). *Izvestiya TsK KPSS* (6)

Narkhoz 1960 *Narodnoe khozyaistvo SSSR v 1959 godu*

Narkhoz 1973 *Narodnoe khozyaistvo SSSR 1922–1972*

Narkhoz 1987 *Narodnoe khozyaistvo SSSR za 70 let*

Nekrasov V F 1989 Desyat' 'zheleznykh' narkomov, *Komsol'skaya Pravda*, 29 September

Novikov N V 1989 *Vospominaniya diplomata. Zapiski. 1938–1947*

Pavlenko N 1989 Tragediya i triumf Krasnoi Armii, *Moskovskie novosti* (19)

Pogrebnoi L I 1966 O deyatel'nosti Soveta po evakuatsii. In *Eshelony idut na vostok*

Prikhod'ko Yu A 1968 Vosstanovlenie promyshlennosti v osvobozhdennykh ot nemetsko-fashistskoi okkupatsii raionakh SSSR (1942–1945 gg.). *Istoriya SSSR* (6)

Resheniya vol 3 1968 *Resheniya partii i pravitel'stva po khozyaistvennym voprosam* vol 3

Rogachevskaya L S 1977 *Sotsialisticheskoe sorevnovanie v SSSR. Istoricheskie ocherki. 1917–1970 gg.*

Rybakovskii L 1989 Dvatsat' millionov ili bol'she? *Politicheskoe obozrenie* (10)

Samsonov A M 1988 *Znat' i pomnit'. Dialog istorika s chitatelem*

Savel'ev V M, Savvin V P 1974 *Sovetskaya intelligentsiya v Velikoi Otechestvennoi voiny*

Selyunin V, Khanin G 1987 Lukavaya tsifra. *Novyi mir* (2)

Shakhurin A I 1975 Aviatsionnaya promyshlennost' nakanune i v gody Velikoi Otechestvennoi voiny (Iz vospominanii narkoma). *Voprosy istorii* (3)

Simonov K 1990 *Glazami cheloveka moego pokoleniya. Razmyshleniya o I.V. Staline*

Sokolov B V 1988 O sootnoshenii poter' v lyudyakh i voenoi tekhniki na Sovetsko–Germanskom fronte v khode Velikoi Otechestvennoi voiny. *Voprosy istorii* (9)

Sokolov P V 1968 *Voenno-ekonomicheskie voprosy v kurse politekonomii*

Sokolov V 1946 *Promyshlennoe stroitel'stvo v gody Otechestvennoi voiny*

Sovetskaya ekonomika 1970 *Sovetskaya ekonomika v period Velikoi Otechestvennoi voiny 1941–1945 gg.*

Sovetskii Soyuz 1988 Sovetskii Soyuz v mirovoi ekonomike (1917–1987). *Mirovaya ekonomika i mezhdunarodnye otnosheniya* (11)

Tamarchenko M L 1967 *Sovetskie finansy v period Velikoi Otechestvennoi voiny*

Tel'pukhovskii V B 1958 Obespechenie promyshlennosti rabochimi kadrami v pervyi period Velikoi Otechestvennoi voiny. *Voprosy istorii* (11)

Tel'pukhovskii V B 1968 O vosstanovlenii promyshlennosti, razrushennoi vragom. In *Stroiteli – frontu*

Tyl SVS 1977 *Tyl Sovetskikh Vooruzhennykh Sil v Velikoi Otechestvennoi voine 1941–1945 gg.*

Uchastie 1962 Uchastie kolkhoznikov v obshchestvennom khozyaistve kolkhozov za gody Otechestvennoi voiny (po godovym otchetam kolkhozov za 1940–1944 gg.). *Istoricheskii arkhiv* (6)

Vannikov B L 1962 Iz zapisok narkoma vooruzheniya. *Voenno-istoricheskii zhurnal* (2)

Vinogradov I I 1976 *Politotdely MTS i sovkhozov v gody Velikoi Otechestvennoi voiny (1941–1943 gg.)*

VO voina 1970 *Velikaya Otechestvennaya voina Sovetskogo Soyuza 1941–1945. Kratkaya istoriya* 2nd edn

VO voina 1984 *Velikaya Otechestvennaya voina Sovetskogo Soyuza 1941– 1945. Kratkaya istoriya* 3rd edn

Volkogonov D M 1989 *Triumf i tragediya. Politicheskii portret I.V. Stalina* (2 vols)

Yaroslavskii E 1941 Velikaya Otechestvennaya voina Sovetskogo naroda. In *Pravda* (23 June)

Zelkin I I 1969 *Kuznetskii ugol'nyi bassein v gody Velikoi Otechestvennoi voiny*

Zemskov V 1989 'Arkhipelag GULAG': glazami pisatelya i statistika, *Argumenty i fakty* (45)

Zemskov V 1990 Na rabote sorokovye, "trudovye". *Soyuz* (18 May)

Zinich M S 1971 Iz istorii stankostroeniya i tyazhelogo mashinostroeniya v pervyi period Velikoi Otechestvennoi voiny. *Istoriya SSSR* (6)

Maps

1. The republics, major cities and other towns of the USSR, 1938–45

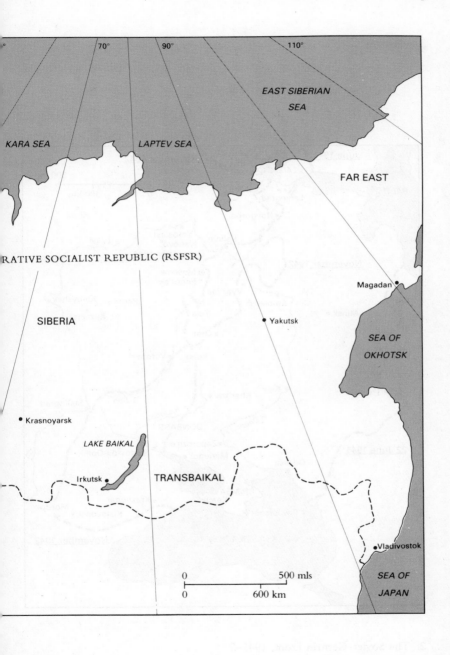

2. The Soviet–German Front, 1941–2

3. The Soviet–German Front, 1942–4

Index

agriculture
  collectivisation of, 4, 6, 96, 99
  emergency measures in, 134, 168
  food procurements from, 85, 102,
    173
  impact of war on, 104, 127, 134,
    187, 202
  livestock in, 127–8, 163, 187
  machinery in, 100–1, 187
  private plots in, 102
  production of, 78, 101, 187, 213,
    218, 220
  productivity of, 85, 100, 162–3,
    168–9, 178, 188, 220
  work-force in, 99–100, 148–9,
    151, 157, 188, 215, 217, 219
  workpoints, xiii, 101, 168–9, 178
  see also evacuation; kolkhoz;
    kolkhoz market; machine
    tractor stations; political
    departments; peasants
aircraft industry, 130, 149, 176,
  183, 198
Aliger, Margarita, 107
All-Union Communist Party
  (Bolsheviks), xii, 10–11, 46,
  48–9, 74–5, 109
  Central Committee of, xii, 47–8,
    56, 59; decisions of, 61, 226
  Politburo of, xiii, 46–8, 51, 53,
    56, 202; decisions of, 128, 223

Alliance (of UK, USA and USSR),
  26, 33–6, 39
Allied aid to the USSR, 26, 33–4,
  37, 70, 189–90, 192, 221 see also
  United Kingdom; United States
  of America
allotments, 83–4, 204
Andreev, A.A., 56
Antonov, Marshal A.I., 51
Armament, People's Commissariat
  of, 110
armament industry, 5, 17, 95,
  124–5, 149, 164, 175, 177, 198
Armed Forces of the USSR, 18, 23,
  28, 32, 64, 67, 75, 101, 131, 226
  and German invasion, 23, 45, 50
  combat losses of, 38, 40–2, 65,
    147, 182, 206
  effect of Lend-Lease on, 190
  force levels of, 17, 145, 147–8,
    191, 215, 219
  high command, 50–1
  mobilisation for, 60–1, 90, 93,
    100, 145, 148, 151
  quality of, 17, 183
  servicemen, 65, 79, 91, 188
  see also losses, Soviet; mobilisation;
    penal battalions; Stavka
Austria, 227

Bakh, A.N., 107

ball-bearings industry, 103
Baltic republics, 20, 21, 27, 28, 54,
    114, 152, 209
Bardin, I.P., 107
Beaverbrook, Lord W.M., 224
Belorussia, 20, 27, 42, 54, 62, 113,
    141, 228
Berggolts, Olga, 107
Beriya, L.P., 25, 47, 52 n12, 53,
    55n, 56, 117, 195, 198, 224
Bessarabia, 20, 228
birth-rate, 92–4
Bosyi, D.F., 174–6
Brooke, General Sir Alan, 55
Bukin, F., 174, 176
Bulganin, General N.A., 56
Bulgaria, 228
Budennyi, Marshal S.M., 55

capital construction, 137–42
Caucasus, 26, 31–2, 113, 115, 185,
    227
censorship, 65–7
Central Asia, 74, 113, 130, 132, 140
Chelyabinsk, 139
chemical industry, 133
children, 79, 82, 97, 147
Chuikov, General V.I., 32
Church, Orthodox, 70
Churchill, Winston S., 24–5, 33,
    34, 35, 72, 226, 228, 229
civilian industry, 5, 136, 147, 177,
    184–6, 192, 200, 220
Coal, Commissariat of, 47
coal industry, 97, 133, 166–7, 173,
    177–8, 183, 185–6, 201
collaboration, 113–5
Comintern (Communist
    International), 35, 227
Commissars, People's, xiii, 47–8,
    194–5
commissars, political, xii, 31, 51, 109
Communications, People's
    Commissariat of, 52
Communist Party, *see* All-Union
    Communist Party (Bolsheviks)

construction industry, 6, 131, 133,
    137, 139, 149, 151, 170, 178, 200
Construction, Commissariat of, 131
consumer industry, 134, 186
consumption, civilian personal,
    125, 213
cotton industry, 168–9
crime, 89–90
Crimea, 31, 37, 226, 228

Defence Committee, 135
defence fortifications, 62
Defence, People's Commissariat of,
    23, 50, 53, 71, 73, 96, 147, 156,
    170
disease, 86–8
divorce, 91
Dnepr river, 227
Dneprpetrovsk, 224
Dneprstroi hydroelectric station,
    127, 228
Donets basin (Donbass), 22, 27, 98,
    129, 151, 224, 227

Ehrenburg, Il'ya, 72, 107, 207
electricity, 142, 183, 185–6
employment, 145–6, 149, 157,
    218–9
engineering industry, 134, 147, 175,
    183
Estonia, 20, 113, *see also* Baltic
    republics
evacuation
  of agricultural assets, 127–9
  of government and Party
    apparatus, 27, 47, 55, 64, 224
  of industry, 123n, 128–32, 136,
    139
  of labour, 113, 139
  of population, 94, 224
Evacuation, Committee for, 47, 225
Evacuation Commission, 226
Evacuation Council, 128–9, 224

family, 90–3
Far East, Soviet, 74, 95, 96, 140

ferrous metallurgy, 133, 139, 142, 172, 176, 183, 185–6, 201, 226
Ferrous Metallurgy, People's Commissariat of, 47
Fersman, A.F., 107
Finance, People's Commissariat of, 47
Finland, 20, 22, 223, 228
food industry, 186, 188, 213
food supplies, 49, 78–83, 85, 100, 213 *see also* rationing
Foreign Affairs, People's Commissariat of, 47, 55
France, 19, 21, 22, 228, 229

German-Soviet Pact, 19–20, 68, 113
Germany
  decision to invade USSR, 21–5, 126
  defeat of, 38, 229
  economic mobilisation of, 144
  munitions production of, 180–1
  Operation 'Barbarossa', 3, 22–7, 40, 45, 223
  Operation 'Typhoon', 27, 29, 224, 225
  Operation 'Citadel', 36
  1941 offensive, 22–30, 192
  1942 offensive, 26, 30–2, 185
  1943–5 campaigns, 26, 36–8
  policy towards Soviet population, 104, 113
  pre-war relations with USSR, 13–15, 17
  support from Soviet population, 104, 108, 113–5
  war aims of, 21, 39
  see also losses
Ginzburg, S.Z., 131, 139
GKO, xii, 46–9, 53–5, 87, 90, 107, 225
  composition of, 47, 225, 227
  decisions of, 151, 199, 224, 226, 229
  dissolution of, 230
  formation of, 46, 198, 229
  individual responsibilities in, 47, 198–9, 202

Operations Bureau of, 202, 226
  role of, 46–8, 156, 199
  Transport Committee of, 226
Gor'kii, 74, 174, 176, 185, 227, 228
Gosplan of the USSR, 47–8, 55, 107, 195, 201
Greece, 22
Grossman, Vasilii, 107
Gulag, *see* labour, forced; NKVD

Harriman, W.A., 224, 226
health care, 87–8
Health, People's Commissar for, 87
heavy industry, 98, 124, 140–1, 149, 185
Hitler, Adolf, 3, 14, 21–3, 30–1, 32, 39, 46, 54, 228
Hopkins, Harry, 33, 224
Hungary, 223, 229

industry, Soviet
  conversion to war production, 100, 123n, 133–6, 138, 148
  pre-war policies concerning, 5–8, 124–6, 132
  official production indices, 218
  reconversion for peacetime, 202
  vulnerability to invasion, 125–7
  see also evacuation; heavy industry; light industry
intelligentsia, 104–8
Internal Affairs, People's Commissariat of, *see* NKVD
investment, Soviet
  in pre-war period, 123–6, 141
  in wartime, 100, 123n, 137, 140–2, 218
Ioffe, A.F., 107
iron and steel, *see* ferrous metallurgy
Italy, 226, 227, 229

Japan, 13, 26, 38–9, 225, 229–30

Kabalevskii, D., 106
Kaganovich, L.M., 56, 110, 128, 195, 198, 224, 226
Kalinin, 87, 225

Kalinin, M.I., 64, 151
Kaluga, 224
Kapitsa, P.L., 107
Karaganda, 97, 166, 226
Karol, K.S., 85, 206
Kazakhstan, 74, 115, 130, 140
Kerch peninsular, 54, 225, 226
Khar'kov, 36, 54, 139, 225, 226, 227
Khrulev, General A.V., 110
Khrushchev, N.S., 55, 75, 210
Kiev, 27, 54, 62, 76, 151, 224, 227
Kislovodsk, 66
kolkhoz, xii, 4, 6; *see also* agriculture; peasants
kolkhoz market, 83–6, 172, 203
Komsomol, xii, 46, 68, 74, 99, 175–6
Konev, Marshal I.S., 51
Kornai, Janos, 159n
Kosygin, A.N., 56, 64, 195
Kovalev, General I.V., 110
Krasnodar, 226
Krasnoyarsk, 60
Kravchenko, Victor, 87, 111, 112, 118
Kuibyshev, 55, 111, 225
Kulik, Marshal G.I., 55
Kursk, 225
  battle of, 36, 40, 93, 227
Kutuzov, M., 70
Kuznetsk basin (Kuzbass), 97, 166, 176, 186, 226

labour
  as the 'ultimate bottleneck', 143–5
  controls, 153, 201
  discipline, 62, 158–61, 161–71
  forced, 12, 116–9, 156, 165, 169–71, 177, 215, 217
  mechanisms of motivation of, 158n, 161–2, 171–4
  militarisation of, 63, 110, 164–5, 176, 224, 225, 227
  mobilisation of, 145, 147–8, 151–7, 163–5, 177; for

  agriculture, 63; for construction, 60–2, 151; for industry, 60–3, 145, 147–52
  morale of, 174–7
  productivity of, 158–62, 166–7, 174–89, 220
  recruitment of, 96, 148, 153–4
  reserves, 145–7, 151, 160, 177
  shortage of, 143–4, 147, 149, 150–1, 159, 170
  vocational training of, 150, 153
  working time of, 61, 163–4
  see also women; workers
Labour Committee (Sovnarkom Committee for the Registration and Allocation of Labour), 96, 148, 154–6, 224
Latvia, 20, 113; *see also* Baltic republics
Lend-Lease, *see* Allied aid to the USSR; United States of America
Lenin, V.I., 46, 51, 54, 67
Leningrad, 3, 30, 62, 89, 92, 109, 111, 135, 151, 192
  evacuation of, 66, 128–9
  food supply in, 78, 80, 82, 87, 89
  people's militia of, 73–6
  reconstruction of, 227
  siege of, 27, 54, 65, 67, 87, 205, 225, 226, 228
  wartime deaths in, 38, 42, 87
  workers in, 74, 97–9, 148
light industry, 78, 98, 134, 148, 213
Lithuania, 20, 113; *see also* Baltic republics
living standards, 77–90
local government, 48–50, 109
losses in World War II
  American, 38–40; British, 38–40; German, 28, 30, 40, 65; Japanese, 39; Polish, 38; Soviet, 27–9, 38, 40–3, 65, 147, 181–2, 206–7; total, 40, 206
Lunin, N.A., 175
L'vov, 113, 118, 223
Lyubimov, A.V., 202

machine tractor stations, xii, 85, 101
Magnitogorsk, 109
Malenkov, G.M., 25, 47, 56, 195, 198, 224
Manchuria, 38–9, 229
Mariupol', 128, 129, 139, 223, 227
marriage, 91–3, 207
Mekhlis, General L.Z., 55
metalworking industry, 175, 219, 220
Mikoyan, A.I., 56, 195, 202, 225, 226
Military Soviets, 51, 55
Minsk, 46, 223, 228
Moldavia, 20
Molotov, V.M., 20, 46, 47, 54, 55, 56, 60, 198, 224
mortality rates, 88–9
  infant, 89
  by nationality, 112–3
Moscow, 62, 135
  battle of, 27, 29, 54, 76, 109, 111, 176, 192, 224, 225
  evacuation of, 64, 66, 67, 111, 128–9
  panic in, 27, 64, 66, 107, 224
  people's militia of, 74, 76, 151
  rationing in, 80, 82
Moskatov, General P.G., 154, 156
Mozdok, 226
munitions industry, 123–4, 134, 147, 149, 164, 177
munitions, production of, 5, 17, 126, 180, 183–4, 186–7, 191, 201

narodnoe opolchenie, xii; *see also* people's militia
national income, 191–2
national product, 220–1
nationalism, Russian, 115–6
nationalities, Soviet, 112–6;
  Armenians, 113–5; Baltic, 114–5, 127; Belorussions, 112; Crimean Tartars, 52, 114; Georgians, 113–5; Germans, 52, 115; Jews, 42; North Caucasian, 52, 114; Russians, 113, 115;

Tartars, 112; Ukrainians, 112–5, 127
Nazi ideology, 21, 113
Nizhnii Tagil, 174
NKVD, xii, 11, 12, 51–3, 56, 66, 73, 115, 116, 118, 154, 156
nomenklatura, xiii; *see also* officials
nonferrous metallurgy, 183
Novikov, N., 111
Novorossiisk, 227
Novosibirsk, 92

Odessa, 151, 228
officials, 108–12, 208
oil industry, 133, 185
Omsk, 92
Orel, 224, 227

panic, 27, 59, 64, 66, 107, 109, 224
partisans, 52, 61, 113
Pasternak, Boris, 105
patriotism, 43, 68–70, 112, 176
Pavlov, General D.G., 53
peasants, 4, 12, 85–6, 99–104; *see also* agriculture
penal battalions, 117
people's militia, xii, 29, 64, 73–6, 151–2
Perm', 109
planning, economic
  pre-war system, 194–7
  in wartime, 197–205
plans, economic, 6
  Five Year, First (1928–32), 7, 138, 160, 162; Second (1933–7), 7, 138, 161; Third (1938–41), 7, 138, 141
  for 3rd qtr 1941, 136, 198, 223
  perspective post-war, 202
plenipotentiaries, xiii, 47–9, 87, 110
Poland, 19, 20, 21, 38, 152, 209, 227, 228, 229
political departments, 101
population, Soviet
  reactions to German invasion, 37, 59–60, 64, 136
  see also losses, Soviet

prices, 80, 84, 171–2, 191
prisoners, *see* labour, forced
prisoners of war, 31, 41, 53, 114
Prokoviev, Sergei, 106
propaganda, 68–73
purges, 12, 52
   of Armed Forces, 18, 53, 129, 182

rationing system, 79–82, 89, 172–3,
   193, 224–6, 228
rations, 78–9, 81–4, 98, 214
rearmament, Soviet, 16–17, 77,
   123–6, 134
Red Army, *see* Armed Forces of the
   USSR
Riga, 224
Romania, 21, 22, 223, 224
Roosevelt, Franklin D., 24–5, 34,
   36, 38, 228, 229
Rostov on Don, 29, 31, 54, 64, 85,
   206, 225, 226, 227
RSFSR, xiii, 42, 113, 141
rubber industry, 184
rumours, 66

scorched earth policy, 61, 127, 223
Sergei, Metropolitan, 70
Sevastopol', 31, 225, 226, 228
Shakhurin, A.I., 129
Shaposhnikov, Marshal B.M., 51
Shostakovich, Dmitrii, 106
Shvernik, 128, 156, 224, 226
Siberia, 21, 88–9, 91–2, 96, 130,
   132, 149
Simonov, Konstantin, 72, 107
Smolensk, 74, 224, 227
socialist emulation, 174–6, 178
Solzhenitsyn, Alexander, 117, 119,
   170
Sorge, R., 24
Soviet economic system, 158–163
   adaptation to war of, 123, 133–8,
      148, 199, 203
   costs of war for, 42–3, 190–1, 221
   crisis of 1942, 132, 136–7, 144,
      152, 157, 181–7, 191, 193, 200

degree of centralisation of, 195,
      203–5
   formal and informal systems,
      194–202
   mobilisation of, 126, 135, 140,
      144–5, 151–2
   preparation for war of, 124–6,
      135–6
   role of market in, 203–5
   and self-reliance, 186, 203–5
Soviet political system, 9–13, 24,
   208–9
soviets, xiii, 48–9, 109
Sovinformburo, 65
sovkhoz, xiii; *see also* agriculture
Sovnarkom of the USSR, xiii, 48,
   53, 55, 64, 107, 195
   decisions of, 61, 80
Stakhanov, A.G., 161, 174
Stakhanovism, 81, 160–1, 174–6;
   see also socialist emulation
Stalin, I.V., 27, 66, 209, 210
   and appeal to patriotism, 71–2
   attitude to masses, 182
   broadcast of 3 July 1941, 46, 55,
      61, 66, 71–4, 224
   and evacuation of industry, 128
   'fundamental turning point'
      speech, 228
   image of, 55, 70–3, 208
   and military strategy, 30–2, 50–1,
      53–6
   and NKVD, 53
   Orders to Red Army, 28, 31–2,
      55, 63, 67, 72, 224, 226
   peace offer to Germany, 54
   posts held in wartime, 47, 50, 53,
      56, 71–2
   and preparations for war, 3–15,
      18–20, 24–5
   pre-war policies, 3–13
   reaction to German invasion,
      45–6, 60
   role in decision-making, 5, 9, 11,
      25, 51, 53–6, 196, 198
   and Russian nationalism, 115–6
   and Soviet war economy, 193

speeches of 6–7 Nov. 1941, 55, 105, 225
and year of 'ten great victories', 38, 71
Stalingrad, 22, 27, 31–2, 201, 226, 227
battle of, 40, 65, 93, 193
State Defence Committee, *see* GKO
State Security, People's Commissariat of, 52 n12; *see also* NKVD
Stavka, xiii, 50–1, 53–5, 65; decision of, 91
steel, *see* ferrous metallurgy
Supreme Societ of the USSR, 48
decisions of, 93, 223, 227

Taganrog, 227
Tallinn, 224
tank industry, 125, 134, 149, 198
Tarle, E.V., 106
territory of the USSR
occupied, 42, 100, 127, 141, 147
liberated, 37, 101, 138, 141–2, 227
Timoshenko, Marshal S.K., 50
Toidze, I.M., 69
trade, 178, 218
Trade, People's Commissariat of, 90
trade unions, 90
transport, 63, 110, 133, 149, 151, 157, 178, 200–1, 218–20
for evacuation, 128–31
railway, 63, 135, 142, 172, 175, 177, 185–6, 198, 227
Transport Committee, *see* GKO
Truman, Harry S., 38, 229
Tula, 151
Tupolev, A.N., 105
Tvardovsky, Alexander, 70, 107

Ukraine, 20, 21, 27, 28, 31, 41, 54, 114, 131, 141, 226, 228
United Kingdom, 19, 43 n26
aid to the USSR from, 189–90

alliance with the USSR, 224, 226
economic mobilisation of, 144, 190
United States of America, 26, 225
economic mobilisation of, 144
entry into war, 26
Lend-Lease to the USSR from, 189–90, 192
Ural region, 130, 132, 140, 149, 176

Vasilevsky, Marshal A.I., 32, 51
Vavilov, S.I., 107
Vedenev, B.E., 107
Vipper, R., 106
Vlasov, General A.A., 109, 114
Volga region, 130, 132
Volga river, 22, 31, 226
Voronezh, 31, 226, 227
Voronov, Marshal, N.N., 32
Voroshilov, Marshal K.E., 47, 55–6, 73, 155, 198, 224
Voroshilovgrad, 226
Voznesenskii, N.A., 55–6, 110, 195, 198–9, 202, 224, 225, 226
Vyazma, 22, 54, 224, 227

wages, 80
women, 41, 92, 146
in agriculture, 100, 149, 216–7; in construction, 216; in industry, 96–8, 146, 150, 166, 216; in transport, 216
workers, 74–7, 79, 81, 85, 94–9, 147–8, 155
working population, 215–6, 221

Yaroslavl', 184, 227
Yaroslavskii, E., 69
Yugoslavia, 22, 228, 229

Zaporozh'e, 139, 228
Zhdanov, A.A., 25, 55
Zhitomir, 228
Zhukov, Marshal G.K., 29, 32, 51, 131